# Sharing the Burden

SUNY series in Contemporary Jewish Thought

*Richard A. Cohen, editor*

# Sharing the Burden

*Rabbi Simḥah Zissel Ziv and the Path of Musar*

Geoffrey D. Claussen

SUNY PRESS

Cover: Charcoal drawing, Reb Simcha Zissel Ziv's Talmud Torah in Kelm by Loren Hodes. Used by permission.

Published by State University of New York Press, Albany



Printed in the United States of America



For information, contact State University of New York Press, Albany, NY
www.sunypress.edu

Production, Ryan Morris
Marketing, Anne M. Valentine

**Library of Congress Cataloging-in-Publication Data**

Claussen, Geoffrey D., 1979- author.
Sharing the burden : Rabbi Simḥah Zissel Ziv and the path of musar / Geoffrey D. Claussen.
pages cm. – (SUNY series in contemporary Jewish thought)
Includes bibliographical references and index.
ISBN 978-1-4384-5835-9 (hc : alk. paper)—978-1-4384-5834-2 (pb : alk. paper)
ISBN 978-1-4384-5836-6 (e-book)
1. Broida, Simḥah Zissel ben Israel, 1824–1898–Philosophy. 2. Rabbis—Lithuania–Philosophy. 3. Ethicists–Lithuania–Philosophy. 4. Jewish ethics. 5. Musar movement–History. I. Title.

BM755.B755C53 2015
296.3'6–dc23 2014045866

10 9 8 7 6 5 4 3 2 1

In memory

*Elsie Young Lerner*

(August 30, 1912–February 7, 2006)

*Martin Paul Claussen, Jr.*

(April 12, 1942–April 21, 2007)

# Contents

# Acknowledgments

I have worked on this project for many years, and I am grateful to the many individuals and institutions that have helped with its development. I began to think about the questions that have inspired this book when I was an undergraduate student at Carleton College, studying with Professor Louis Newman, and I owe particular gratitude to him. My first serious intellectual engagement with the Jewish tradition took place in Louis's classroom, and over the years Louis introduced me to the field of Jewish ethics and to the questions that brought me to write this book. He has continued to offer his time, his wisdom, and his friendship throughout the years, serving on my PhD dissertation committee and guiding me through the completion of this project.

I was first introduced to the writings of Rabbi Simḥah Zissel Ziv in classes with Rabbi Ira Stone at the Jewish Theological Seminary (JTS) in New York. Ira introduced me to the study of the Musar movement and pointed me to the great value of the literature produced by that movement and especially by Simḥah Zissel. He encouraged me to take Simḥah Zissel seriously and to embark on this project, and I have been deeply grateful for his inspiration, guidance, and friendship as I have worked on it.

Professor Alan Mittleman served as my dissertation advisor at JTS, and I am fortunate to have worked closely with such an outstanding Jewish philosopher as this book first took shape in the form of a dissertation. I am incredibly grateful to Alan for all of his time, support, and good judgment. He has provided constant mentorship, kindness, and friendship. He has taught me much about how to approach Jewish thought charitably, critically, and with philosophical rigor. I thank him for all the knowledge that he has shared with me, for his clear-sighted wisdom, and for helping me to transform my dissertation into this book.

While I was studying at JTS, Professor Neil Gillman also provided much advice and encouragement to pursue this project. Professor

David Fishman taught me a great deal about the history of Lithuanian Judaism and the Musar movement, and he answered my regular questions about the historical material I discovered. Professor Tamar Ross, Professor Benjamin Brown, and Professor Shaul Stampfer offered their encouragement and guidance as I began to immerse myself in the literature of the Musar movement. Professor Eitan Fishbane carefully read my writing on Simḥah Zissel Ziv, helped me situate his thought within the history of Jewish thought, provided many valuable references, and engaged in many conversations about Jewish virtue ethics over the course of many years. Professor Carol Ingall helped me think carefully about my language and the relevance of my work for Jewish educators. Professor Jonathan Jacobs closely read my manuscript and offered outstanding philosophical insight. Professor Leonard Levin graciously helped me to work through some of the most difficult texts written by Simḥah Zissel, and I benefited immensely from his deep knowledge of Jewish and Western philosophy and from his skills as an accomplished translator of Hebrew texts. Rabbi Meir Goldstein also spent many hours reading Simḥah Zissel's writings with me, offering much depth, insight, and friendship. And I owe particular thanks to my *hevruta* Rabbi Michael T. Cohen, who regularly studied Simḥah Zissel's writings with me over the course of three years. I gained much from Michael's perceptiveness, his commitment to take Simḥah Zissel's teachings seriously, and his unfailing encouragement and friendship.

While I began this project in New York, much of my research for this volume took place in Charlottesville, Virginia. I was privileged to spend the 2009–2010 academic year as a doctoral fellow at the University of Virginia's Institute for Advanced Studies in Culture, a wonderful interdisciplinary center directed by Professor James Hunter. I am deeply grateful for the Institute's support, and I thank all those who helped arrange my fellowship there. I am especially grateful to Professor James Hunter and Dr. Ashley Rogers Berner, and also to Professors Josh Yates, Stephen Garfinkel, and Bruce Nielsen; and I am grateful for additional funding provided by the Jewish Theological Seminary Graduate School. During my time in Charlottesville, I was able to participate in the Institute's Love and Justice working group and to share my work on Simḥah Zissel with that group, as well as with the broader Institute community. I benefited from feedback from, among others, Professors Nicholas Wolterstorff, Jennifer Geddes, Regina Schwartz, Talbot Brewer, Daniel Philpott, Charles Mathewes, Murray Milner, Joseph Davis, Karen Guth, and Rev. Greg Thompson. When I presented chapter 1 of this book at the Institute, Professor James Loeffler responded to my paper and offered a good deal of insightful and stimulating feedback. I was able to also share some of my research at a University of Virginia Jewish Studies Department colloquium, and I thank Professors Vanessa Ochs, Peter Ochs, Asher Biemann, Gregory Goering, James Loeffler, and Emily Filler for helpful feedback and questions there. Lew Purifoy and the Interlibrary Services staff at the University of Virginia's Alderman Library also played a key role in my research, delivering obscure Hebrew books and articles to me with incredible speed and skill, and Regina Kopilevich provided access to the Kaunus achives.

Significant work on this project took place after I moved from Charlottesville to Cleveland Heights, Ohio, and to a new position at Oberlin College. I am especially grateful to Eric Cohen of the Tikvah Fund, to Professors Abraham Socher, David Kamitsuka, and Shulamit Magnus, and to Dean Joyce Babyak (as well as Peter and Vanessa Ochs, Emily Filler, and Daniel H. Weiss) for their help in making it possible to dedicate the fall 2010 semester to writing. Friends at Beth El—The Heights Synagogue provided incredible support, and David Hanlon and Lindsay Wise provided a good deal of inspiration and joy at a pivotal moment in my writing. My work on this project in Ohio was also made possible thanks to grants from the Tikvah Fund, the Memorial Foundation for Jewish Culture, and Targum Shlishi (a Raquel and Aryeh Rubin Foundation), as well as continued support from the Institute for Advanced Studies in Culture.

I presented material from this book at meetings of the Association for Jewish Studies and the Society of Jewish Ethics. At the SJE meeting, I was especially grateful for a response to my paper offered by Professor Diana Fritz Cates of the Society of Christian Ethics, a response that brought Simḥah Zissel into dialogue with Thomas Aquinas. Professors Jonathan Schofer, Jonathan Crane, Laurie Zoloth, and Louis Newman also offered helpful questions and comments, and Mary Jo Iozzio edited the paper. That paper was printed as "Sharing the Burden: Rabbi Simḥah Zissel Ziv on Love and Empathy," in the *Journal of the Society of Christian Ethics* 30, no. 2 (2010), pp. 151–169, published by Georgetown University Press. Portions of that paper are included in this book, reprinted by permission of the *JSCE*.

I have completed this book after moving from Ohio to Greensboro, North Carolina, and to my position at Elon University. I am grateful to many friends in Greensboro who have supported my family's move here, and especially to our communities at Beth David Synagogue and B'nai Shalom Day School. I owe special thanks to Rabbi Harry Sky for reading Simḥah Zissel's writings with me; to Beth Socol, Lia Sater, Rabbi Eli Havivi, and Muriel and George Hoff, for providing wonderful opportunities to teach some of the material in this book; and to members of the Beth David Synagogue Musar Group, who have helped me reflect on many of the virtues and vices discussed in this book.

I have been grateful to complete my work on this book at Elon University. The university has provided outstanding institutional support, and many colleagues at Elon have provided tremendous encouragement and support for this project. I owe particular thanks to Professors Amy Allocco, Evan Gatti, Lynn Huber, Brian Pennington, Rebecca Todd Peters, Michael Pregill, Jeffrey Pugh, L. D. Russell, Jeff Stein, and Pamela Winfield; to Rabbi Becky Joseph, Nancy Luberoff, and Ginny Vellani; to the Belk Library staff, especially Patrick Rudd and Lynn Melchor; to Dean Alison Morrison-Shetlar, Dean Gabie Smith, Associate Provost Tim Peeples, Provost Steven House, Vice President Jim Piatt, and President Leo Lambert. I am especially indebted to Lori and Eric Sklut for their incredible generosity and commitment to Jewish Studies scholarship, and for establishing the Lori and Eric Sklut Emerging Scholar in Jewish Studies endowment, which has made it possible for me to complete my work on this book.

I have also been fortunate to work with SUNY Press on this project. I am grateful to my editor James Peltz and series editor Professor Richard Cohen for their interest in and commitment to this project, and to Rafael Chaiken, Ryan Morris, and Anne Valentine for all of their assistance. And I am grateful to the talented artist Loren Hodes for permission to reproduce her charcoal drawing, *Reb Simcha Zissel Ziv's Talmud Torah in Kelm*, on the cover of this book.

Most of all, I owe tremendous gratitude to my family. My sister, Hillary Zaken, has offered much love and support, and cheered for me at every step along my path toward completion of the book, along with my nephews Lahav and Abir. I have received much support from my brother-in-law and sister-in-law, Kevin Jones and Laura Joukovski, and their families. My mother-in-law and father-in-law, Jo Ann and Bruce Jones, have generously cared for us all, and I thank them for their constant support, encouragement, and love, as well as for their careful reading of this manuscript.

My mother, Eileen Claussen, has supported and loved me at every step along the way. She taught me to love learning, literature, and language, and she provided me with the best educational opportunities imaginable. Her generosity, her integrity, her thoughtfulness, and her deep concern for justice have consistently inspired me and have shaped this book in many respects. My debt to her is incalculable.

Among the other family members who helped guide me on the path to writing this book, two are no longer living, and I dedicate this work to their memories. My grandmother, Elsie Lerner, provided me with a strong connection to the Jewish tradition, and especially with a connection to the world of Eastern European Jewry in which I have come to immerse myself. Above all, both through her stories and her actions, my grandmother taught me about the Jewish ideal of *menschlichkeit*, an ideal which I treasured deeply in my childhood. This was the very ideal that many in the Musar movement sought to cultivate, and in some of my final conversations with my grandmother before her death, we discussed my aspirations to study and learn from their vision of what it might mean to be a *mensch*. I treasured her excitement about my work, and I know that she would have been so proud to see this book come to fruition. Her spirit fills its pages.

My father, Paul Claussen, also died just as I was developing my vision for this project. It reflects his influence in many ways. He was a historian who very much encouraged my study of history, and he was thrilled that I was following in his footsteps in pursuing a PhD. His love of researching, taking copious notes, and writing late at night also rubbed off on me. My father aspired to engage in writing that might help to make the world a better place, and I seek to do the same with this project. I wish that he, too, could have lived to see me complete this project.

My beloved daughters, Eliana and Talya, entered the world as I worked on this project, adding new joy and wonder to my life, cheering me on while I wrote, and teaching me much about the meaning of love and care. And so has their mother, my dear wife, Katy. Katy's love, kindness, and intelligence have sustained me over the past sixteen years in ways that words cannot begin to describe. She has been my partner in the work of *musar*, and she has taught me to be more aware, more compassionate, and more loving. She has been an incredible teacher, full of creativity and curiosity, and she has supported me in countless ways. Katy discussed the Musar movement with me daily, and she read this manuscript with great care and thoughtfulness, offering insightful comments and questions throughout. I am grateful beyond words for her partnership, for her support, for her friendship, and for her love.

# Introduction

The Jewish moral tradition is sometimes depicted as a tradition of rules governing outward behavior that cares little about the inner life. Baruch Spinoza, the modern thinker who most forcefully advanced this view, argued that Judaism is simply a tradition of law. Moses legislated as he did, Spinoza argued, to coerce people to act in ways that would establish order and security in Israel. Moses did not care whether, deep down, the Jews were virtuous people. Having little expectation that they could develop inner virtues, Moses instead designed a tradition focused on external compliance with the law.[1]

Yet many of the injunctions found in the Torah and rabbinic literature appear to concern not only external behavior but also thoughts, feelings, and virtues. As Rabbi Baḥya Ibn Pakuda put it in his eleventh-century *Book of Direction to the Duties of the Heart,* the Torah ordains both "duties of the limbs" and "duties of the heart." The duties of the heart that Baḥya cataloged included the obligation to love God and to love one's neighbor, to meditate on the wonders of creation and on one's own deeds and inner life, and to rid one's heart of covetousness, indifference, and hatred. For one's outward behavior to be truly good, Baḥya argued, it must reflect the virtues called forth by these sorts of obligations. Nonetheless, he observed, Jews have often accepted the rightful importance of "the duties of the limbs" while paying less attention to "the duties of the heart."[2]

Baḥya's work was among the earliest of many books published in the Middle Ages that responded to this perceived lapse and, drawing on classical Jewish literature, stressed the importance of cultivating inner virtue. Offering a path for disciplining the often-wayward human soul, these books came to be referred to as the literature of *musar*—the literature of "moral discipline" (or, alternatively, "moral correction" or "moral instruction"). Jews throughout the Middle Ages, ranging from philosophers such as Maimonides to Kabbalists such as Moses Cordovero, continued to add to this literature, protesting the neglect of the inner life and continuing to reframe the ways in which virtue should be understood and cultivated. Indeed, musar literature was highly popular, and the conviction that the Torah aims at inculcating virtue was central to medieval Jewish thought.[3]

The stress on musar, on moral discipline that could transform the inner life, continued with the emergence of modernity in eighteenth-century and early nineteenth-century Europe. Each of the major movements that emerged in that era offered its own sort of focus on musar. The Haskalah, the Jewish "Enlightenment" movement, produced its own musar literature, focusing on the moral virtues and urging that the direct study of such virtues—rather than the study of Talmudic law—should lie at the heart of Jewish education. The mystically focused Hasidic movement offered its own emphasis on the musar tradition, urging greater attention to inner qualities and, like the Haskalah, suggesting that Talmud scholarship is not the best path to a good life. The passionate enemies of the Hasidic movement, the Mitnagdim, the traditionalist rabbinic elite based in Lithuania, also upheld the importance of cultivating inner virtue, but they emphasized that the highly intellectual study of Talmudic law offered the best form of "musar" for the soul. They scorned those in the Hasidic movement who immersed themselves in the study of medieval musar literature, and they argued that other forms of Jewish piety were inferior to Talmudic scholarship. Such study was seen as nearly sufficient for guaranteeing proper moral character and reverence for God, both because of the supernatural powers ascribed to it and because of a conviction that knowledge of morality is the essence of moral education. While the Haskalah became highly influential among nineteenth-century German Jewry, and Hasidism came to dominate most of traditionalist Jewish culture in Eastern Europe, it was the study-focused approach of the Mitnagdim that dominated Lithuanian Judaism.[4]

## The Musar Movement

It was in this Lithuanian atmosphere that a charismatic rabbi known as Israel (Lipkin) Salanter (1810–1883) sought to develop a mass movement that would be unprecedented in its dedication to the task of cultivating virtue. Salanter sought a transformation of human nature, urging an all-out war against the "evil inclination" (*yetzer ha-ra*) that reigns in human hearts. Breaking with the central message of the Lithuanian rabbinic elite, he suggested that the intellectual study of Talmud is important but insufficient to effect real moral transformation.

Salanter indicated that, despite their impressive dedication to Talmud study, the Mitnagdim of Lithuania were lacking in moral virtue: even the greatest Torah scholars were guilty of grave moral transgressions, especially when it came to attending to the needs of the poor and downtrodden. Despite their knowledge of moral ideals, Salanter suggested, they failed to take the necessary steps to bring their knowledge into their hearts. The human intellect is weak, he taught, and its insights will not prevail unless it can bring discipline to the irrational emotions and desires and divert them to rational ends.

To engage the irrational forces in the human soul, Salanter championed "musar" exercises such as the contemplative chanting of passages from medieval musar literature. He also urged allotting time for serious moral introspection, and for soliciting critical feedback on one's moral situation from one's teachers and friends. Moreover, Salanter urged Jews to take the time to devise individually tailored strategies that could help to improve their particular moral situations. And he emphasized the moral value not only of the commandment to study, but also of the wide range of commandments pertaining to one's relationship with God and one's relationships with other people. He did in fact see his contemporaries as insufficiently attentive to traditional Talmud study—but he saw them as especially neglectful of a range of moral duties, particularly in their business dealings and in their speech. And when his fellow Jews did take their obligations to study seriously, Salanter noted, they did not make time for the work of musar, for the difficult work of cultivating moral discipline.[5]

It was in response to this situation that Salanter laid the foundations for an organized movement of traditionalists, which came to be called the "Musar movement." The Musar movement was an Orthodox movement that sought to strengthen the traditional Jewish virtues that Salanter saw as threatened by adherents of the Haskalah who promoted acculturation. At the same time, it was a reformist movement, critiquing the scholarship-centered program of the Mitnagdim that dominated traditionally observant Lithuanian culture.[6]

Salanter's activities to establish the Musar movement began in Vilna (Vilnius), the central address in Lithuania both for supporters of the Haskalah, known as "Maskilim," and for supporters of the Mitnagdim. Beginning in 1840, Salanter served as a teacher of Talmud there; by the mid-1840s, he began to give lectures on the subject of musar to the small group of men who frequented the study house (*beit midrash*) where he taught. He also established what he called a "musar house" (*beit musar*)—a separate space where men from a variety of social backgrounds could come to study, contemplate, and chant phrases from books of musar. During the same period, he republished works of Musar literature that were not widely available: two classic works by the medieval philosopher Shlomo Ibn Gabirol, as well as one musar text written by an eighteenth-century leader of the Haskalah, Menaḥem Mendel Lefin.[7]

His interest in the writings of Lefin notwithstanding, Salanter positioned himself as a firm opponent of the Haskalah and a firm defender of Lithuanian Orthodoxy.[8] The Haskalah movement in Lithuania was characterized in part by its rationalism and its respect for modern science, its focus on interpersonal ethics, and its emphasis on other Jewish literature beyond Talmudic legal texts. It also promoted greater acculturation to Russian society, both through adopting European styles of dress and manners and also, most significantly, through studying Russian language and other "secular" subjects. Although Maskilim in Lithuania in the 1840s were typically committed to traditional Jewish law, avowed traditionalists such as Salanter were disturbed by their hopes for increased integration into Russian society, and especially disturbed by their efforts to create Jewish schools that would require knowledge of Russian language and general studies along with specifically Jewish studies. The Maskilim urged the Russian government to support such institutions, which it did. The government-supported school that aroused the ire of traditionalists more than any other was a modern rabbinical seminary opened in Vilna in 1848.

Some traditionalists were horrified by the fact that the seminary was directed by non-Jewish authorities and that Christians taught the general studies courses there; some were concerned over the growing influence of the Maskilim, who threatened traditional religious and cultural norms; some were dismayed by the very inclusion of non-Jewish subjects in the seminary curriculum. To stave off the opposition of traditionalists, the seminary leadership sought to bring a sympathetic traditionalist rabbi onto its faculty, and they invited Israel Salanter to become an instructor of Talmud. Salanter, however, rejected the offer, indicating his opposition to the Haskalah movement and the sort of curriculum that it endorsed. He seems to have concluded that rabbis trained in the spirit of the Haskalah would lack proper reverence for God, dedication to tradition, and moral fortitude. Rejecting the pressure of government authorities and the opportunity for personal advancement, Salanter departed from Vilna, settling in the Lithuanian town of Kovno (Kaunas).[9]

In Kovno, which was itself a center of Haskalah activity, Salanter continued to advocate the practice of musar as the best way to stave off the threats to traditional Jewish morality that he saw emanating from the Haskalah and the wider world. He was appointed as a preacher in Kovno, and he regularly delivered sermons to the general public focused on musar. Not all of the traditionalists in Kovno were content with this approach, however, and he resigned from his communal post in approximately 1851. He took up a new job, teaching and supervising a group of students who met in a private study hall, a *kloiz*, at the house of Rabbi Tzevi Hirsch Nevyozer, a wealthy and staunchly Orthodox opponent of the Haskalah.

Salanter's several dozen students included younger teenagers, who attended regular classes with Salanter, as well as married students in their late teens and early twenties, who learned more independently. Talmud stood at the heart of the curriculum, but Salanter also required his students to study and practice musar, and he would preach to them on themes of musar on a weekly basis. His sermons were filled with emotion and would sometimes last for hours, punctuated by tears and the impassioned group chanting of biblical verses. These sermons focused on the means for conquering the evil inclination, the virtues required for serving God wholeheartedly, the promises of divine reward and punishment, and the ways in which both he and others stood guilty before God.[10]

As part of their musar work, Salanter's students at the Nevyozer *kloiz* were also encouraged to seek out personal moral guidance from both their teacher and fellow students. They spent an inordinate amount of time together and seem to have developed a special closeness. According to one report, Salanter established a private dormitory for his students and ensured that their meals were provided at the *kloiz*, rather than following the customary practice of having them eat at homes in the neighborhood. Among other things, this sort of arrangement allowed for a more insular environment—Salanter's students seldom needed to leave the *kloiz*. Seemingly, one of Salanter's innovations was creating an environment that allowed for a particularly tight-knit community and that allowed for total concentration on learning and moral transformation.[11]

A good number of these students went on to become well-known rabbis.[12] They included Eliezer Gordon (1840–1910), later the chief rabbi of Kelm (Kelmė) and Telz (Telšiai), Lithuania; and Jacob Joseph (Yaakov Yosef, 1840–1902), later appointed as the chief rabbi of New York City. The three students who were especially close to Salanter went on to succeed him as the leaders of the Musar movement: Naftali Amsterdam (1832–1916), who later became the rabbi of Helsinki; Isaac Blazer (1837–1907), who later became the rabbi of St. Petersburg and a director of an educational institution in Kovno; and his senior student, Simḥah Zissel (Broida) Ziv (1824–1898), an educator who became known as "the Elder of Kelm" (in Yiddish, *Der Alter fun Kelm*), widely regarded as Salanter's closest disciple.[13]

## Rabbi Simḥah Zissel Ziv

Rabbi Simḥah Zissel Ziv was born in 1824 as Simḥah Mordekhai Ziskind Broida in Kelm, a small Lithuanian town in the region of Zamet (Samogitia) on the western edge of the Russian Empire.[14] His family was one of the more distinguished Jewish families in Kelm, as both his parents were descended from renowned rabbis. His father, Rabbi Israel Broida, was a merchant, a teacher of Talmud, and a rabbinic judge, whom Simḥah Zissel described as an exemplar of lovingkindness. His mother, born as Ḥayyah Ziv, was herself regarded as an expert in Jewish law, and she was also legendary in Kelm for her compassion and kindness toward those in need. Simḥah Zissel studied Talmud with his father throughout his youth, and his father reportedly also hired tutors who taught him "modern" subjects that were not part of the traditional Talmudic curriculum—Bible, Hebrew grammar, and German. Insofar as they supplemented their son's traditional Talmudic education with the sorts of subjects that were championed by the Haskalah, Simḥah Zissel's parents seem to have been at least somewhat supportive of efforts to build an "enlightened Orthodoxy" (what would elsewhere be called "neo-Orthodoxy" or "modern Orthodoxy"), which combined a traditionalist outlook with some of the values promoted by the Haskalah.[15]

After his marriage to Sarah Leah, the daughter of a rabbi in a neighboring town, Simḥah Zissel traveled to Kovno, apparently expecting to investigate and critique the approach that Salanter was promulgating there. Instead, Simḥah Zissel was enthralled by Salanter's musar sermons and, according to the stories recounted by his students, he spent his first year in Kovno studying nothing but musar, focusing on discerning and critiquing his own moral character.[16] Simḥah Zissel's dedication to Salanter's model of musar work continued through successive years, and he became not only Salanter's closest disciple but also one of his more influential disciples. While many of Simḥah Zissel's friends took up appointments as community rabbis, Simḥah Zissel focused on shaping an elite group of younger students into future teachers of musar. His students formed the core of the leadership of the Musar movement in the following generation.

Simḥah Zissel served as the director of yeshivas in Kelm and Grobin (Grobiņa). His yeshivas are of particular historical significance, because they broke with established precedents in a number of respects: they isolated themselves from their surrounding communities in a variety of ways; they devoted comparatively little time to the study of Talmud; they devoted significant time to the study of musar; and they were the first traditionalist yeshivas in Eastern Europe to teach general, non-Jewish studies. Simḥah Zissel, however, struggled in his attempts to build and sustain institutions. He preferred to spend much of his time engaged in private study and meditation and in crafting the discourses that he shared with his students. His legacy lives on above all in his writings, a large corpus of discourses and letters that reveal his attempts to work out a philosophy of musar.

Simḥah Zissel was the only one of Salanter's students to leave behind a substantial body of writings focused on musar, and his writings often explore questions of moral virtue more deeply than Salanter's writings. Indeed, many of Salanter's admirers have found that Salanter's writings do not seem to befit his legendary stature. Salanter was revered for his deep concern for others, and one might expect his writings to be full of profound meditations on the practices of lovingkindness. His writings are, instead, often unclear and without depth. They say little about the nature of central moral virtues such as lovingkindness, and they are instead dominated by exhortations to fear God's punishments in the world to come. Salanter's literary corpus is also quite slim, as might befit a figure who was more of an activist rabbi than an author. Understandably, subsequent Jewish ethicists have often turned to legendary tales about Salanter's ethical qualities, but they have seldom turned to his ethical writings.

Simḥah Zissel's writings are, like Salanter's, unsystematic and sometimes unclear. They were often written with a small group of elite students in mind, and Simḥah Zissel's failing health during the latter part of his life led him to abbreviate his writings in ways that can make it difficult to decipher their meaning.[17] But his writings also contain a treasure-trove of meditations on the nature of virtue and happiness, reason and revelation, the purpose of human life, the difficulties of moral improvement, and the virtue of love. While they contain some fire-and-brimstone preaching, they also reveal a figure who was attracted to many of the aspects of the Haskalah. Among other things, Simḥah Zissel's writings are distinguished by their interest in classical philosophy and philosophers—for example, in Aristotle, whose *Nicomachean Ethics* Simḥah Zissel read in Hebrew translation.

Simḥah Zissel often rejected the positions of the classical philosophers, and he sometimes caricatured them in crude and simplistic terms, but he also urged his students to learn from their wisdom. At times he urged his students to follow their examples—to seek to be like philosophers. He seems to have aspired to be a sort of philosopher himself, and while his writings do not qualify as philosophy by any conventional definition of the term—especially because they are totally unsystematic—they do contain reflections of philosophical significance.[18] Simḥah Zissel offers serious answers to perennial human questions about the nature of virtue and human flourishing, answers that should be studied not only out of historical interest but so that they can be evaluated on their merits. In this book, I seek to offer a philosophical exposition of those writings, considering Simḥah Zissel as a thoughtful exponent of a Jewish "virtue ethics"—an ethics focused on the character and inner lives of moral agents.

In the pages that follow, after exploring the nature of Simḥah Zissel's yeshivas and further considering his biography (chapter 1), I analyze his general theory of virtue (chapter 2), his vision of human reason and its relationship to divine revelation (chapter 3), and his contention that moral development requires exceedingly great effort and discipline (chapter 4). This book culminates with an exploration of Simḥah Zissel's vision of moral perfection, which is characterized above all by "loving one's fellow as oneself"—with responsive, compassionate love motivated by a powerful sense of empathy (chapter 5). I explore how Simḥah Zissel sees such love as achieved through overcoming self-centeredness, seeing people's needs from an objective point of view—from "God's perspective"—and acting in accordance with practical wisdom. I also consider how Simḥah Zissel sees proper love as potentially developed through disciplined contemplation as well as through involvement in activities such as commerce and politics.

Throughout these pages, I consider the strengths and weaknesses of Simḥah Zissel's moral vision. I argue that there is much to admire in Simḥah Zissel's ethically focused rationalism, in his virtue-centered approach, in his appreciation of the moral significance of the emotions, appetites, and imagination, and in his vision of how human beings might be more empathic, more loving, and less self-centered. The contemporary Jewish revival of interest in the Musar movement can learn much from this nineteenth-century Musar master.

Nonetheless, I also see real weaknesses in Simḥah Zissel's approach. Simḥah Zissel's attempts at empathy often seem misguided, insofar as he failed to fully appreciate the perspectives of those who lived beyond the walls of the insular yeshiva environment in which he spent most of his life. His unwillingness to challenge the accepted teachings of the Torah also limits his efforts to think critically about morality. Contemporary Jewish ethics, I hope, can improve on such flaws. At the same time, it would do well to heed aspects of Simḥah Zissel's wisdom. I hope that this book will help to show both the merits and the faults of this Musar master, especially so that his thought can serve as a resource for the ongoing development of the Jewish moral tradition.

1

# Rabbi Simḥah Zissel Ziv and the Talmud Torah

In 1857, Israel Salanter left the Nevyozer *kloiz* and moved to Germany, and Simḥah Zissel began a period of wandering. He spent some time back in his hometown of Kelm, where he reportedly withdrew to a private room to immerse himself in musar study and meditation. He spent some time in Ruzhany, studying with his cousin Rabbi Mordekhai Gimpel Yaffe, a prominent exponent of "enlightened Orthodoxy." He spent a short time serving as a bathhouse attendant in Palanga (Polangen) and as a teacher in nearby Kretinga. At one point, he was dispatched by Israel Salanter to the town of Zagare, to strengthen the "musar house" that had been founded there by another student of Salanter's, the tea merchant Kalonymus Ze'ev Wissotzky. And when Wissotzky moved to Moscow at the end of the 1850s to pursue business interests, Simḥah Zissel is said to have joined him there on Salanter's instruction to help ensure that Wissotzky would maintain his commitment to traditional Judaism.[1]

By the mid-1860s Simḥah Zissel returned to Kelm, where his wife Sarah Leah and, now, his three children (Naḥum Ze'ev, Raḥel Gittel, and Neḥama Liba) had remained during the course of his travels. Sarah Leah worked full time at a grocery store, supporting her family as best she could. While Simḥah Zissel made some efforts to learn a profitable trade, occasionally engaging in bookbinding work, he was unwilling to take a well-paying position as a community rabbi. Simḥah Zissel may have viewed himself as unfit for such a job, perhaps believing that he could not withstand the moral dangers that accompany a position of great prestige and power, and perhaps also because of his more reticent personality.[2] Despite her difficulties in supporting the family, Sarah Leah is said to have supported her husband's choice, following a widespread pattern among pious women in Lithuania who agreed to support their scholarly husbands.[3]

While mostly dedicating himself to private study, Simḥah Zissel did take on one public task upon his return to Kelm: he began to give regular Sabbath sermons at the major synagogue there. His sermons were in the spirit of musar, critiquing the moral deficiencies of the town's public institutions and its inhabitants, especially the wealthier among them; unsurprisingly, such preaching was not readily welcomed, and Simḥah Zissel (like Israel Salanter in Kovno) was barred from the pulpit. Some community members, no doubt, did not appreciate the emphasis on their flaws and the failures of established conventions. Some did not appreciate Simḥah Zissel's unfamiliar style of preaching, which, according to one testimony, was overly philosophical. Some—perhaps many—were opposed to giving a platform to the proponent of a new sect of Judaism, which seemed to resemble "a modern sort of Hasidism," as the biographer Ya'akov Mark put it.[4]

Hasidism, which had spread rapidly throughout the rest of Eastern Europe during the eighteenth and early nineteenth centuries, had been widely opposed by Lithuanian Jewry. The Mitnagdim, Lithuanian rabbis who opposed Hasidism, were especially offended by the movement's failure to embrace Talmud study as the supreme religious activity, its ecstatic, movement-filled mystical prayer practices, and its attempts to set up its own communal structures under the direction of charismatic leaders rather than joining with the wider Jewish community. Despite its many differences with Hasidism, the Musar movement seemed to present some of the same features. It encouraged other religious practices at the expense of Talmud study, including ecstatic chanting sometimes accompanied by movement. It also challenged established conventions, setting up institutions such as "musar houses" outside of accepted communal frameworks. The appearance of Salanter's Musar movement revived memories of the struggle against Hasidism, and Salanter's disciples were labeled scornfully as the "Hasidim of Zamet." Like the Hasidim, they were condemned for their sectarianism and for their pretensions to higher levels of piety than other Jews.[5]

Some residents of Kelm were particularly concerned that the Musar movement's pietism disrespected the town's culture of Talmudic scholarship. One Kelm native named Eliezer Eliyahu Friedman, in his memoirs, accused Simḥah Zissel of setting himself up as a charismatic leader, a Hasidic-style "rebbe" who taught that "even if a person has learned little of Torah and hair-splitting dialectics . . . he will stand on a level above the level of the scholars"—if only he purifies his heart through musar. Such a perspective was anathema to Friedman, who took the conventional view that status should be determined by scholarship, and who saw Kelm as a town where, historically, men of all social classes had devoted themselves to the study of Talmud and legal codes.[6]

Who, then, supported Simḥah Zissel's efforts in Kelm? Friedman describes a group of recent migrants to Kelm—merchants with a less scholarly bent who had come to Kelm to explore commercial opportunities there. These merchants were apparently not readily welcomed by the established community, but they found that Simḥah Zissel respected them. After Simḥah Zissel stopped preaching at the central synagogue, they formed the core of a group that began to meet at his house on Sabbath afternoons to study musar.[7]

Faced with the difficulties of changing the moral habits of adults, however, Simḥah Zissel came to focus on the education of youth. He followed the lead of Salanter, who had himself turned toward focusing on younger students (in their teens and twenties) while in Kovno. Simḥah Zissel, however, aimed to teach even younger students, and he developed plans for a primary school dedicated to cultivating moral discipline.[8]

## The History of the Talmud Torah

Sometime in the course of the 1860s, Simḥah Zissel established a school for boys in Kelm known as the Talmud Torah.[9] A school called a "Talmud Torah" was usually a tuition-free school funded by the local Jewish community for orphans and impoverished children. A standard Talmud Torah taught the same subjects taught in ḥeders, the widespread private one-teacher schools that offered a basic Jewish education to all boys whose families could afford it, providing some familiarity with the prayer book, the Pentateuch, and Talmudic literature. Under the influence of the Haskalah, however, a number of Talmud Torah schools in nineteenth-century Russia also began to teach general studies of the sort taught in Russian elementary schools, particularly practical subjects such as Russian language and mathematics. These institutions became the only Jewish primary schools to combine traditional Jewish studies with general studies—a deeply attractive educational model for many parents, including some with greater financial resources. While some Talmud Torah schools, committed to their charitable mission, refused to accept students who were not poor or orphaned, others began to accept boys from wealthier families so long as these families paid full tuition. This arrangement improved the reputation of the schools while offering them greater funding, and so a new model of Talmud Torah schools developed: schools that offered a "modern" education to students from a range of socioeconomic backgrounds.[10]

Simḥah Zissel's Talmud Torah was of this reformed variety, as it taught general studies and accepted tuition-paying students. During the time that Simḥah Zissel directed it, however, the school does not seem to have received any public funding from the town of Kelm. It instead came to depend on private donations—among its most prominent supporters was Kalman Ze'ev Wissotzky—and on tuition dues.[11] Simḥah Zissel seems to have made substantial efforts to draw in students from wealthy families from throughout Zamet and the region to its north, Courland. Indeed, while it continued to teach poorer boys as well, the Talmud Torah's student body came to be largely made up of the sons of successful businessmen.[12] This arrangement not only provided income for the Talmud Torah but allowed Simḥah Zissel to reach children who would be more likely to grow up to have substantial influence in their communities. Though Simḥah Zissel was seemingly committed to aiding the poor and other marginalized Jews, he was also interested in transforming Jewish culture as a whole, and so he sought to reach the children of an elite—not the scholarly elite, who disdained Simḥah Zissel's vision, but the ranks of businessmen whose status was rising and whose children might grow up to change the nature of Jewish culture. Rather than focusing on influencing the parents, who were already set in their ways, Simḥah Zissel focused on their young children, who could be more easily persuaded to dedicate their lives to the work of musar.[13]

Within a number of years, however, the Talmud Torah expanded to accommodate older students as well, eventually constituting itself as a yeshiva—a more advanced academy dedicated to the study of Talmud—which served sixty or seventy students primarily between the ages of ten and seventeen.[14] Like other Lithuanian yeshivas, the Talmud Torah devoted time to the Talmud and its commentaries, but it also set aside time for two untraditional areas of study. First, time was devoted to musar—to efforts at improving moral character—to an unprecedented degree. Second, the Talmud Torah was the first traditionalist yeshiva in Eastern Europe to set aside time for general studies—mathematics, geography, and Russian language, literature, and history. Both of these additions to the curriculum came at the expense of Talmud study, and most traditionalists saw Simḥah Zissel as impugning the honor of the Talmud.[15]

Simḥah Zissel's efforts to reform traditional education and his continued criticism of established conventions seem to have made him an unpopular figure in Kelm. Already by 1873, a newspaper article about the Talmud Torah referred to efforts by its opponents to close the school.[16] The Talmud Torah did successfully gather the signatures of eight residents of Kelm who supported a petition for the school to be officially licensed by the Russian government, and in 1878, the school finally received its official license.[17] Its opponents, however—perhaps in response to this recognition—apparently employed an old trick that had been used in many instances in the struggle against the Hasidic movement, informing governmental authorities that the Talmud Torah was in fact a center for fomenting rebellion against the czar. After government investigators arrived at the Talmud Torah, confiscating its books and records, Simḥah Zissel seems to have concluded that it was not possible to run his school in Kelm.[18] He saw a more hospitable environment to the north in Courland (in modern-day Latvia), a region on the border of Germany where Jews imbibed both Lithuanian Jewish culture and German Jewish culture. Courland was an area where other Musar movement leaders had found little opposition, and it was at the same time a region that offered a greater openness to general studies.[19] Moreover, Simḥah Zissel seems to have admired aspects of non-Jewish culture in Courland, which he described as reflecting the "moral decency" of German culture; in one later letter, for example, he declared that Jews should aspire to be like "the non-Jewish craftsmen in Courland who adopt the German ways of loving order and who understand the importance of honoring one's promises."[20]

The Dessler family, Courland residents whose sons had been students at the Talmud Torah in Kelm, offered to fund the reestablishment of the school in the quiet Courland town of Grobin, and by 1880, Simḥah Zissel had reopened the Talmud Torah there.[21] Presumably to change his fortune, he changed his name, adopting his mother's family name, Ziv, in place of his father's family name, Broida.[22] He was found innocent of the charges brought against him in Kelm, and his efforts in Grobin had the full support of the Russian government.[23] The general structure of the curriculum in Grobin seems to have remained the same as in Kelm. As an 1882 newspaper article put it, the Talmud Torah "was established by the government to teach the children of Israel Torah, Wisdom, and Moral Decency [*Derekh Eretz*]." "Torah" here refers to the traditional study of the Talmud and its commentaries; "wisdom" refers to general studies; and the teaching of "moral decency" refers to the teaching of musar, to Simḥah Zissel's efforts to cultivate the virtues among his students.[24]

## Talmud Study and Musar Study

The school day at the Talmud Torah began with a lengthy prayer service, followed by breakfast. Students then spent approximately three hours immersed in the study of Talmud, until it was time for afternoon prayers (preceded by five minutes of musar study) and lunch.[25] Spending three hours a day studying the Talmud is not insubstantial, but other yeshivas dedicated considerably more time to the study of Talmudic law. As a result, the Talmud Torah developed a reputation as an institution where—in the words of Ya'akov Mark, a keen observer of the era's yeshiva culture—"they did not learn much Talmud" because "the essence of the learning was musar and character traits."[26]

Rabbi Dov Katz—whose father had studied with Simḥah Zissel, and who became the first chronicler of the Musar movement's history—notes that, to the yeshiva's credit, skills in understanding the dialectics of the Talmud mattered little in the assessments of students given by Simḥah Zissel and his fellow administrators: "At the Kelm Talmud Torah, they did not judge everyone based on their skills, as was customary at other yeshivas, but rather they first and foremost evaluated their character traits and the virtues of their souls."[27] While the Talmud was viewed as the repository of God's law and a source of great moral wisdom, focusing on the study of Talmudic law was seen as insufficient for the task of moral improvement. Musar literature, which generally expanded on the nonlegal portions of the Talmud, was seen as a necessary supplement. The Talmud Torah encouraged its students to give particular attention to the study of that literature and to various other practices of musar—various practices intended to build moral discipline.

The Talmud Torah schedule devoted time each evening to musar, generally beginning with a sermon from Simḥah Zissel. Sermons focused on the nature of moral excellence, the work of overcoming moral vice, the rewards and punishments associated with virtue and vice, and other musar themes—and they were sometimes sparked by particular moral failings within the Talmud Torah community. The sermons were intended, Simḥah Zissel said, "to renew the spirit" of each student, "and to place a new heart in him, that he might use reason, and do good, and love Torah and reverence and the words of the sages."[28]

Simḥah Zissel's sermons seem to have had much in common with the musar sermons that he heard from Israel Salanter at the Nevyozer Kloiz in Kovno. But whereas Salanter allegedly preached on themes of musar on a weekly basis, Simḥah Zissel generally preached daily, taking more time away from the study of Talmud. And whereas Salanter's students described their teacher's sermons as filled with fervent emotional outbursts, Simḥah Zissel reportedly did not adopt his teacher's style. According to Dov Katz, other Musar movement rabbis spoke "with overpowering words, causing excitement and enthusiasm," but Simḥah Zissel maintained a strikingly calm spirit and spoke with "words of logic and thoughtfulness." Even when he sometimes shook with excitement and awe, Katz reports, "this did not stem from emotional excitement, but from serious, reflective deliberation and penetrating moral accounting." Equanimity and self-control were virtues that Simḥah Zissel prized greatly, and he apparently did his best to harness the power of the emotions while remaining in control of them.[29]

Even so, it seems that the sermons did create a highly emotionally charged atmosphere. After each sermon, there was a time for continued musar study, and while some reports describe a period of silent, reflective meditation, others speak of students and teachers sitting in the study hall chanting passages from musar literature to evocative melodies, seeking to move themselves toward repentance. One student recalled how, as the sun went down, the room was filled with sighs and quiet sobbing, gesticulating, fists beating on hearts, and the passionate chanting of Biblical and rabbinic passages.[30]

Periods of extended musar meditation would also take place at other times during the day, especially during the morning, afternoon, and evening prayer services, which were considered not only times for supplication but times for cultivating virtues such as humility, reverence, equanimity, and lovingkindness. Simḥah Zissel urged his students to take their time with their prayers—for instance, to move very slowly through descriptions of God's moral goodness so that they could meditate on these ideals and consider their own personal potential for improvement. Prayer services were, consequently, quite lengthy; the standard morning service, for example, which might have lasted for half an hour in standard Lithuanian yeshivas, is said to have lasted an hour, or sometimes even two hours or longer, cutting further into the limited time for Talmud study. Talmud classes were occasionally canceled altogether, to allow for an extra chanting session following prayer, an extra musar lecture from Simḥah Zissel, or other sorts of musar activities.[31]

One additional practice was a sort of group therapy practice. Students would divide into "musar groups" (*kittot* or *va'adim*), often referred to as "reinforcement groups" or "encouragement groups" (groups for *ḥizzuk*), designed to provide mutual criticism and support. These groups met at least once a week, generally on Saturday nights after the conclusion of the Sabbath. Some groups dedicated each week to focusing on a particular character trait, and spent the week engaging in exercises designed to strengthen that trait; when these groups met, a student appointed to lead each group would begin the group session by offering a sermon on the character trait in question, and students would then discuss their experiences with that trait. Other musar groups dedicated themselves to one particular issue or practice—one group focused on love for others, one focused on the observance of the Sabbath, and one committed to Simḥah Zissel's personal practice of setting aside every tenth day as a special day for contemplation.[32] Beyond these group sessions with their peers, students also received individual counseling from Simḥah Zissel and the staff of "spiritual supervisors" (*mashgiḥim*), former students who were in their twenties.[33]

The various sorts of musar activities occurred on Sabbaths and holidays as well as during the week. Simḥah Zissel apparently gave three musar sermons over the course of the Sabbath, and there was little time set aside for recreation or relaxation. Students and teachers alike felt compelled to actively focus themselves on the never-ending work of healing their souls—just as, during the week, students apparently chose to use much of their free time for musar study, meditation, chanting, and group work.[34] And they appear to have been, on the whole, proud of their school's unprecedented commitment to the work of improving moral character. Other yeshivas may have studied more pages of Talmud, they thought, but they did not do the work necessary to impress the virtues on their souls. Even more so, they thought, supporters of the Haskalah missed the mark by encouraging Jews to attend Western universities, which surely did not attend to the work of musar. Indeed, the legend circled among Simḥah Zissel's students that, during a conference of German university presidents, one admitted that there was one important subject that was not taught by professors in German universities. That subject, he said, was "the repair of human character traits" (*tikkun middot ha-adam*)—and in fact, the university president noted, the repair of human character traits was taught seriously in only one place in the world: at a Jewish school in the small Russian town of Kelm.[35]

## The Talmud Torah as a Total Institution

Shaul Stampfer, one of the only academic historians to have discussed Simḥah Zissel's Talmud Torah, has astutely observed that the yeshiva had some of the characteristics of what sociologists call a "total institution."[36] Indeed, the Talmud Torah was a "total institution" in many respects.

Sociologist Erving Goffman coined the term "total institution" to describe an institution where "a large number of like-situated individuals, cut off from the wider society for an appreciable period of time together, lead an enclosed, formally administered round of life." In such an institution, individuals live together in a highly scheduled, supervised, and regulated environment, cut off from social intercourse with the outside world. They participate in the same activities together, all of which fit into a "single rational plan" imposed from above by an authority figure. Commonly, the "encompassing or total character" of such institutions "is symbolized by the barrier to social intercourse with the outside and to departure that is often built right into the physical plant, such as locked doors, high walls," and the like. Among the many examples of total institutions that Goffman cites are boarding schools and "those establishments designed as retreats from the world even while serving also as training stations for the religious; examples are abbeys, monasteries, convents, and other cloisters."[37]

Simḥah Zissel's Talmud Torah fits Goffman's description to a significant degree in ways that other Jewish institutions in nineteenth-century Eastern Europe did not. For one thing, as Stampfer points out, it was a boarding school with a dormitory, an arrangement common in Christian communities but highly innovative for a traditionalist Jewish academy. The common model for advanced Jewish learning in Eastern Europe was that learning took place in a communal study hall, sponsored by the Jews of a given town. Students were integrated with the town in many respects, taking their meals with townspeople and sleeping in the communal hall; they were, at the same time, largely free to study independently, pursuing whatever Talmudic studies interested them. The nineteenth-century introduced an alternative arrangement, the model of the private yeshiva (pioneered in Volozhin) where studies were far more directed in accordance with a fixed schedule, and where the institution was funded by donors rather than being supported by the local community; but in this model, students continued to be integrated into the community, sharing their meals with local householders and renting rooms from them, which also gave students a fair amount of privacy.[38]

At the Talmud Torah, by contrast, food and sleeping quarters were provided by the institution. This sort of arrangement seems to have been pioneered by Israel Salanter at the Nevyozer Kloiz, discussed above; building on this model, Simḥah Zissel made particular efforts to isolate his students from the broader Jewish community, to regulate their lives, and to grant them little privacy. Though it was a "traditionalist" institution—ostensibly seeking to preserve past customs in the face of modernity—the Talmud Torah broke with traditional customs in a number of respects, including in its efforts to create such an insular total institution. With his efforts to shield students from the outside world and transform them through musar activities and through constant supervision, Simḥah Zissel created a distinctly modern school.

Like others in the Musar movement, Simḥah Zissel sought to defend Orthodox values in the face of liberalism and to defend his focus on musar in the face of widespread hostility to it. He bemoaned increasing laxity in traditional religious observance, increasing acceptance of a range of theological heresies, and increasing treatment of self-indulgence as a positive virtue. He bemoaned decreased faith in divine providence in this world and the next, decreased attention to those in need, and decreased interest in the work of musar, which, in his view, was once widely valued in the Jewish community. Simḥah Zissel seems to have envisioned creating a total institution that would shield his students from these sorts of influences and allow them to focus on the work of musar. His attempt to create an insular environment in Kelm had not succeeded, because the Kelm Talmud Torah was in the midst of a bustling town filled with those who condemned the school's approach. Not only did Grobin provide a less hostile environment, but Simḥah Zissel was able to build an institution there surrounded by a tall fence, an insular yeshiva that was described by Dov Katz as "a world unto itself."[39]

Israel Isidore Elyashev, who later became the founder of Yiddish literary criticism, spent some years as a student at the Talmud Torah in Grobin—before he was expelled for his heretical tendencies—and he later recalled just how insular the yeshiva was. As Elyashev saw it, the Talmud Torah was an institution much like a Christian monastery, in which students renounced contact with the rest of the world and dedicated themselves to their spiritual work. They spent little time outside the walls of the institution, and they were discouraged from having too much contact with their families; instead, Elyashev noted, they came to regard Simḥah Zissel as a father figure. In general, Elyashev recalled how those who dedicated themselves to musar at the Talmud Torah saw themselves as spiritually superior to those beyond its walls. The Talmud Torah may have aimed at instilling the virtue of humility—one of the central virtues in Simḥah Zissel's thought—but, in Elyashev's account, it cultivated a sense of arrogance among its students. Elyashev's account is colored by his eagerness to criticize the Talmud Torah, which he despised, but as is characteristic for students living in a "total institution," it would not be surprising if students at the Talmud Torah developed a strong sense of their own superiority. Simḥah Zissel himself seems to have thought that he was conveying essential moral teachings that were readily ignored by much of the Jewish community.[40]

If he thought that he possessed such teachings, though, why would Simḥah Zissel build a highly insular academy? Would he not want to spread his teachings to the broader world? Indeed, Simḥah Zissel's writings do reflect a strong sense of public-spiritedness that may be difficult to square with his yeshiva's insularity. He warned his students not to be recluses, exhorted them to care for the physical and spiritual needs of their broader communities (of non-Jews as well as Jews), and encouraged them to be involved in public life and commerce (activities made possible by the general studies curriculum). It seems likely that he viewed an insular environment as important to the training of such students, though. Elyashev suggested as much in one comment: Simḥah Zissel was interested in developing a spiritual elite, raised in an environment where they were shielded from negative influences; these students could effect change in the wider world only after having completed a substantial period of training under close supervision.[41]

Students at the Talmud Torah were certainly supervised, especially thanks to the "spiritual supervisors" who kept close watch on their moral development. Meritorious behavior was recorded in a white book, and demerits were recorded in a black book. These books would seem to resemble the sorts of ledgers in which, according to a classical mishnaic image offered by Rabbi Akiva, God records merits and demerits; Simḥah Zissel and the supervisors surely saw themselves as doing God's work in keeping such records and in calling students to task. On a monthly basis, they asked students to account for their behavior; this was the central monthly examination, an examination of a very different sort from the monthly test of Talmudic skills that was offered at the rival yeshiva in Kelm, led by Eliezer Gordon. The Talmud Torah seems to have created a culture in which moral excellence was indeed valued highly; students reportedly felt a good deal of shame to have their vices exposed, and the threat of shame had a positive effect on their behavior.[42] Notably, contemporary newspaper articles on the Talmud Torah remarked that corporal punishment was never used there, a fact which might be taken as a sign of the Talmud Torah's modernity; whereas the value of the rod was upheld throughout medieval musar literature, Haskalah reformers sought to do away with its use and to encourage educators to create school environments more along the lines of what Simḥah Zissel created.[43]

The Talmud Torah proclaimed that it would only enroll "students of virtue, who possessed fine character traits and manners" and who were fully prepared to engage in the work of musar.[44] Students who might become negative influences on their peers were asked to leave the institution. Elyashev reported that he was expelled from the Talmud Torah on account of his strong doubts about divine providence.[45] For all that Simḥah Zissel encouraged introspective questioning of oneself, he did not support questioning of the dogmas which he saw as undoubtedly true and as necessary to proper moral formation. The Talmud Torah was a deeply orthodox institution which did not tolerate deviance; it mandated, like Goffman's "total institution," a significant degree of uniformity among its students.

## Models of Authority

Elyashev described the students at the Talmud Torah as "hypnotized" by Simḥah Zissel's personality, and the various reports gathered by Dov Katz indicate that he was certainly deeply revered by his students. Katz cites many testimonies of how Simḥah Zissel's students viewed him as a saint—an exemplar of lovingkindness, thoughtfulness, and reverence. They were awed by the way he weighed each action he made, the way he saw God's greatness everywhere, the way he kept his sleep to a minimum and dedicated himself with great concentration to the study of Torah and the work of musar.[46] They were also inspired by the way he expressed his gratitude: they told stories, for instance, of how he would come home on the eve of the Sabbath—after spending the week away at the Talmud Torah—and stop at the entrance of his home in joyous appreciation of his wife's preparations for the holy day.[47] So too, they told stories of his empathy—for example how, while on the main road in Kelm, which was built by prison laborers, he would focus himself on the cruelty that such workers experienced. "How is it possible for people to walk with serenity in this place," he asked, "when people suffered through such great hardships here, leaving behind their blood and sweat?"[48]

But while Simḥah Zissel's revered personality loomed large at the Talmud Torah, he was not always present there. Both in Kelm and Grobin, his office was located in the Talmud Torah's attic, and he spent much of his time locked in the room, engaging in private study and meditation.[49] As his health declined during the Grobin period, moreover, he began to spend increasing time in Kelm, though his absence did not seem to diminish his authority among his students in Grobin.[50] Strikingly, though, he did his best to downplay that authority. He refused to let his students rise when he entered the room, a traditional display of respect for teachers, and he refused to use the title of "rabbi," even in formal contexts such as when called to the Torah in the synagogue. Seeking to cultivate the virtue of humility, he refused all titles and honorifics other than the title "Reb," which was used by all Jewish men. Seeking another acceptable title that could convey their respect for him, his students eventually began to call him "Der Alter"—"the elder."[51]

In another uncharacteristic move for a school director with a good deal of authority, Simḥah Zissel is said to have delighted in hearing criticism directed against him. His writings consistently stress the importance of accepting criticism, and while his delight doubtlessly had its limits, it seems to have been an ideal that he took seriously. According to student reports, for instance, Simḥah Zissel once fired a teacher at the Talmud Torah, and the teacher publicly decried his former employer as a wicked man, guilty of a variety of sins, who would have "no share in the world to come"; Simḥah Zissel calmly responded that all of the insults and accusations were true, welcoming the opportunity to embrace a posture of humility and equanimity and to focus on his faults.[52] This sort of posture may not have been good for the reputation of the Talmud Torah or for Simḥah Zissel's authority, but it did offer a model of how to value humility and self-improvement over power and prestige. Simḥah Zissel remained the powerful authority in his total institution, to be sure, but his authority was often not expressed in an authoritarian way.

His authority was, however, institutionalized in the many rules that governed life at the Talmud Torah. Rules were often designed to build a sense of unity, love, and respect. The regulations governing musar group meetings, for example, included the following:

- [Students] are obligated to act with moral decency [*derekh eretz*] and in [a spirit of] unity, so that there can be consensus among everyone.
- One should not interrupt the words of his fellow, and there is double value in this: first, as this is part of the laws of proper moral decency; and, second, so that each may hear the words of his fellow and move toward consensus with them, and so the intended goal of the session can be achieved well.

- One who is late to three sessions will no longer participate in the sessions, as it will be apparent that he is not seeking the good of the community and that he is not habituating himself to negating his will in deference to the will of others.
- No one has permission to say to his fellow: "accept my opinion." Rather, the matter should be decided according to the majority opinion.
- They are obligated to hold sessions each week.
- One should not seek to justify oneself during the session.
- Before the session, everyone needs to think about the significance and value of the session.
- One should not say something during the session unless one has weighed it on the scales of one's reason.
- When they need to offer reproof to someone who is in the session, one should not offer reproof unless it is done with respect.
- One should not speak words that will not have value for supporting the group's ordinances.[53]

These rules were designed to support the introspection and criticism that these musar group sessions encouraged, and to create an atmosphere of care, respect, and solidarity. The stress on overcoming divisiveness and fostering like-mindedness within the group is rather pronounced, revealing a hope for a group united by bonds of love. Love, in this vision, required respectful criticism of one's fellows, and so required a willingness to disagree with them. But love also required seeking common ground with one's fellow—accepting another's criticism or withdrawing one's critique—and respecting the consensus of the group. Similar regulations regarding respect also governed other activities at the Talmud Torah—and certain Jewish customs could even be abrogated for the sake of respect, as when, out of respect for the Russian teacher who taught general studies at the Talmud Torah, students were required to take off the hats that they otherwise wore.[54]

Other rules aimed to establish order and cleanliness at the Talmud Torah. Students had to keep their possessions in their rooms and throughout the building in orderly fashion, and they were required to keep their clothes and their bodies clean. They were prohibited from extinguishing the flame lit at the end of the Sabbath inside the building, lest it leave a bad odor. They were required to be careful when using the samovar at the Talmud Torah, ensuring that it not drip on the floor. Simḥah Zissel was sometimes mocked by outsiders for taking matters of external order a bit too seriously—one visitor reportedly mistook a talk that he gave about disordered student boots for a eulogy, as it was delivered in a tone of such solemnity. But Simḥah Zissel insisted that developing habits of order was a serious matter, essential for the moral growth of his students. How his students took care of their boots, he insisted, affected their souls. Those who developed habits of keeping their surroundings and possessions clean were better equipped to keep their souls clean as well.[55]

Dov Katz recounts that the Talmud Torah did not hire a custodian. Instead, selected students were honored with the opportunity to carry out cleaning and maintenance work, which was seen as an honor—seemingly a prime opportunity to serve the community and to cultivate virtues of beneficence, humility, alacrity, and order within one's soul. Legend has it that one wealthy student's mother was horrified when she discovered that her son was in charge of sweeping floors at the Talmud Torah in Grobin, and she complained to Simḥah Zissel: "Are you turning my son into a housecleaner?" Simḥah Zissel responded that he was, playing with the Yiddish verb *kern*, which can mean both "to sweep" and "to transform." "One who sweeps [*kert*] here," he explained, "transforms [*kert*] the world." Sweeping the floors in Grobin was seen as a practice of musar, a form of discipline for the soul that could help to transform human character and, ultimately, transform the world.[56]

## Simḥah Zissel and the Haskalah

Creating a "total institution" was a distinctively modern enterprise; there is little precedent for Simḥah Zissel's efforts to build a school that would be a bastion of virtue, separated from the wider world and even from the local townspeople. Like many of the institutions designed by those who came to be known as Orthodox Jews, the Talmud Torah was a traditionalist institution, but its fierce defense of "tradition" required breaking with tradition and introducing new reforms into Jewish schooling. With its musar groups and its chanting sessions and its dormitory and its system of supervision, the Talmud Torah was offering a distinctly modern vision of how to preserve classical Jewish virtues. In an era in which rabbinic authority was waning and the vision of the Haskalah was seen as encroaching on more traditional values, Simḥah Zissel introduced a series of reforms designed to strengthen those values.

But the story of Simḥah Zissel's modernism is considerably more complicated than this. Simḥah Zissel adopted a traditionalist posture, but at the same time he subscribed to many of the values of the Haskalah. He built an institution which closed itself off from the wider world, but the ethical vision that he nurtured there engaged with untraditional subjects and sources. He sought to isolate his students from liberalizing trends in Judaism and in the wider world, but he also sought to isolate them from the narrow-minded Talmudism that dominated Lithuanian Orthodoxy. Indeed, the Haskalah had critiqued traditional educational institutions for being too focused on Talmudic law and for their insufficient focus on general studies, ethical values, rational thinking, and decorum, and Simḥah Zissel echoed precisely these critiques in building his Talmud Torah. Unsurprisingly, a number of his contemporaries viewed him as an "Orthodox *Maskil*," an "enlightened" Orthodox Jew, a rabbi who combined his commitment to tradition with the values of the Haskalah in developing a new model for Jewish education.

Some of the contemporary accounts that describe the Talmud Torah as a Haskalah-influenced institution focus on the outward signs of acculturation that Simḥah Zissel promoted. Simḥah Zissel admired European notions of decorum, dress, and hairstyling; following the lead of the Haskalah, and the example of Israel Salanter as well, he advocated that men cut their sidelocks and wear short, modern jackets rather than long coats. He appears to have felt that European styles were neat and orderly, such that adopting them could help to inculcate traits of order, modesty, and moderation. Simḥah Zissel himself was strikingly Western in his own appearance; Israel Elyashev describes him, with his trimmed beard, shiny shoes, German-style clothes, and white collar, as looking "like a Protestant minister"—a style that had also been adapted by leaders of the Haskalah-influenced "neo-Orthodox" movement in Germany.[57] As Eliezer Eliyahu Friedman recalls, the Talmud Torah in Kelm was also strikingly Western in appearance, with its spacious rooms, high windows, and general cleanliness. Friedman suggests that Simḥah Zissel's interest in the Haskalah was mostly superficial—like many nineteenth-century Russian Jews, he admired the "gleam, sparkle, and beauty" associated with European culture, but had little of the Haskalah's intellectual engagement with modern European ideas.[58]

On the other hand, many of the ideas of the Haskalah are also present in Simḥah Zissel's writings. Like Israel Salanter, and in keeping with the ideals of the Haskalah, Simḥah Zissel favored a naturalistic accounting of human psychology, giving little attention to metaphysical and Kabbalistic speculation. He adopted a generally rationalist tone, keeping with the spirit of the medieval rationalist philosophy that the Haskalah sought to revive while also, in line with Haskalah ideals, keeping his thought focused on morality and the social good. His effort to revive the study of virtue-centered medieval musar literature, while cautioning against extreme asceticism, was also in line with the efforts of many *Maskilim*, as was his limited interest in the complex legal dialectics of the Talmud. And many of the themes of Simḥah Zissel's writings that will be explored in the following chapters also echo major themes of Haskalah writings—themes such as the gradual nature of moral change, the importance of integrity and trustworthiness, the value of productive labor, a relatively benevolent view of political authority, and an interest in improving Jewish attitudes toward the non-Jewish world.

Simḥah Zissel's most pronounced adoption of Haskalah values came with his decision to teach general studies alongside Jewish studies at the Talmud Torah. As noted above, one of the central goals of the Russian Haskalah in the mid-nineteenth century was to introduce subjects such as mathematics and Russian into Jewish schools, a goal opposed by a wide range of traditionalists, including most figures associated with the emerging Musar movement. Salanter was among those who opposed the teaching of general studies in yeshivas, which he saw as detracting from the honor of the Talmud. His disciple Simḥah Zissel, by contrast, took a very different path, building an institution which saw general education as an important part of its mission.

Just as the Talmud Torah dedicated three hours in the morning to Talmud study, it typically dedicated three hours in the afternoon to general studies—or, as Israel Elyashev described it, "Haskalah studies."[59] The teachers were Christians, who seem to have also taught in Russian government schools.[60] At the Talmud Torah in Kelm, they taught mathematics and Russian language, and the study of Russian exposed students to geography and to Russian and world history and literature. When the Talmud Torah moved to Grobin, the general studies curriculum expanded to also include bookkeeping, physical education, science, and an additional language that was common in Courland—German.[61] All of these subjects challenged the norms of what should be taught in an Orthodox institution in Eastern Europe. German instruction was particularly frowned on by Eastern European Jewish traditionalists, who noted that German provided easy access to the heretical views of German-speaking Jews.[62]

From one perspective, there was nothing revolutionary about Simḥah Zissel's efforts to teach general studies. Throughout the course of Jewish history, deeply traditional Jews often learned fluency in the vernacular, pursued vocational studies of all sorts, and studied mathematics, science, history, and geography at a much higher level than what was taught at the Talmud Torah. In Simḥah Zissel's own day, neo-Orthodox institutions on the other side of the German border encouraged a deep knowledge of general German culture with far more enthusiasm than Simḥah Zissel himself mustered.

The Orthodoxy which emerged in Russia during the same period, however, was of a very different sort. An overwhelming majority of traditionalist Jews within the Russian Empire opposed any efforts to encourage these sorts of studies. They saw a commitment to non-Jewish learning as implying that there was truth to be found beyond the Jewish tradition, an idea that they feared would lead to the abandonment of that tradition, and they saw the Russian government's encouragement to study Russian as a tool to encourage assimilation and apostasy. Among Eastern European traditionalists, Hasidic Jews were especially vehement in their opposition to general studies, but Lithuanian traditionalists maintained a fierce opposition as well, convinced that the study of Talmud needed no supplement.[63]

With newly emerging commercial opportunities, however, interest in general studies grew steadily. Liberal reforms introduced by Czar Alexander II in the 1860s, seeking to integrate Jews into Russian society, opened up new professional possibilities and educational opportunities. In response, Jews flocked to Russian-language schools of all sorts during the 1860s and 1870s. The study of Russian itself opened up new economic possibilities, technical schools emerged that would train Jews for newly opened fields, and gymnasia would prepare them for universities and prestigious professional careers. The Jewish passion for gymnasia and universities was also nurtured by the emerging sense that higher education would, as one student put it, "raise a person to a higher moral level."[64]

Educational institutions run by traditionalists—the ḥeder for elementary school students, the *beit midrash* or yeshiva for more advanced students—responded to the growing enthusiasm for general studies by affirming the dangers of such studies.[65] The only older institutions that did experience some change were a number of communal Talmud Torah schools designed for poor children, which, as discussed above, began to include general studies in their curriculum. Simḥah Zissel's original Talmud Torah in Kelm was built on this model. When it developed into a yeshiva focused on secondary education, it became the first yeshiva in the Russian Empire to teach general studies. Simḥah Zissel's decision to innovate in this way was probably spurred along by economic and political factors, by the desire to gain new applicants for the Talmud Torah, and by his sense that general studies could contribute to the moral formation of his students.

It would seem likely, first of all, that Simḥah Zissel viewed Russian, mathematics, and related subjects as valuable because of the economic and professional opportunities that they made possible. The subjects taught at the Talmud Torah were subjects that had clear economic utility. And unlike other yeshiva directors who only praised the life of scholarship, Simḥah Zissel considered commerce to be a worthy endeavor. In fact, he saw commercial activity as an arena in which lovingkindness could thrive, as I will discuss further in chapter 5. He seems to have encouraged his students to pursue commercial careers with sufficient force that some of his closest disciples—including his own son, Naḥum Ze'ev Ziv—spent much of their lives engaged in commerce.

Introducing a general studies program would have also had political benefits. Traditionalist Jewish leaders in the Russian Empire—including Israel Salanter—had been criticized throughout the nineteenth century for not studying the language necessary for communicating with Russian government officials.[66] As Mordekhai Gimpel Yaffe noted in one 1873 newspaper article, Simḥah Zissel's decision to teach Russian at the Talmud Torah was creating a group of traditionally minded Jews who would be able to communicate with their political leaders.[67] Simḥah Zissel's move would have also created a favorable impression with the Russian government, and it may have come to serve his students particularly well after an 1874 government reform reduced military service obligations for Jewish students who had studied Russian. But, along with being politically expedient, teaching general studies might also have reflected a heartfelt concern, visible in Simḥah Zissel's writings, for engagement with political life and respect toward the government, themes that I will also discuss further in chapter 5.

Supporting general studies—and designing an institution marked by European notions of decorum—may have also been an effective means of outreach to the growing number of traditionally inclined Jews who supported various ideals of the Haskalah, whether those ideals were intellectual or more superficial. Numerous sources suggest that the Talmud Torah was perceived as providing a unique and attractive way to combine the world of the yeshiva and the world of the gymnasium—"to unite Haskalah with the fear of heaven," as Israel Elyashev put it. In an era when Jewish parents were increasingly sending their children to schools that taught general studies but no Jewish studies, Simḥah Zissel may well have been appealing to those parents who wanted their sons to study Russian and mathematics, and to dress like modern Europeans—but in a traditionalist Jewish institution where Talmud and Jewish moral values would also be taught.[68]

The potential for general studies to entice such families into a Musar-movement institution might explain Israel Salanter's cautious support of the Talmud Torah's general studies program. Salanter generally opposed general education—even publically condemning his son, at one point, for his pursuit of secular studies. He was deeply troubled by the efforts in Germany, under the guidance of Rabbi Samson Raphael Hirsch, to develop neo-Orthodox institutions that taught general studies. But he conceded that a general studies curriculum could be acceptable insofar as it might appeal to modernizing German Jews—and thereby draw them into Orthodox institutions that they would otherwise avoid. Salanter also cautiously endorsed Simḥah Zissel's program, so long as Simḥah Zissel was in charge of it, and it seems likely that he viewed it as he viewed Hirsch's program—as a sort of concession that could be part of an effective outreach strategy. And he would have presumably admired how Simḥah Zissel was enticing assimilating families to affiliate with an institution that was not only "Orthodox" but that was committed to the Musar movement.[69]

But Simḥah Zissel, while he doubtlessly saw himself as doing outreach work, seems to have viewed general studies as more than just attractive bait for unsuspecting parents. When he outlined the mission of the Talmud Torah in the 1870's, for example, he described the general studies program in strikingly positive terms, as one of the three foundational pillars of the yeshiva alongside Talmud study and musar study. In this passage—parts of which have been excised from later Haredi editions of his writings—he describes general studies as entailing the study of

> the laws of the way of moral decency [*derekh eretz*] in accordance with the spirit of the age, that one may behave [well] with people in speech and behavior, and understand the subtleties of language. But know, and let it be known, that *all these studies are grounded in the path of reverence, the fulfillment of the Torah*—and this is done very wisely and carefully.
>
> The way of moral decency is not only what is all over scripture, but that one should "keep *the way* of the tree of life" (Gen. 3:24)—as the midrash teaches, *the way* is "the way of moral decency" that precedes Torah. It also includes the art of writing, studying the language of the state, studying mathematics and knowing geography, as is taught in this

> school under our supervision. We have implanted in their hearts a fixed understanding that *students should grasp these things as part of the fulfillment of the Torah*, not just on account of their desire, so that they not turn their steps away from the way of God.
>
> We have set up many righteous courses for this, to direct their education to the goal of Torah [i.e., Talmud study], reverence [i.e., musar study], and the way of moral decency [i.e., general studies] all together. For he who understands, these are truly all one.[70]

Simḥah Zissel refers to general studies as the study of *derekh eretz*, here translated as "the way of moral decency," a term that we have also seen used to refer to the study of musar. In the above context, the concept—which literally means "the way of the land"—also refers to knowledge about the world in which one lives.[71] Using the term *derekh eretz* to speak of general studies was popularized a generation before Simḥah Zissel by Orthodoxy's most prominent advocate of general education, Samson Raphael Hirsch in Germany. In the above passage, Simḥah Zissel appears to follow Hirsch in interpreting the traditional Jewish requirement to "study *derekh eretz*" as requiring Jews to study and appreciate their surrounding cultures and "the spirit of the age," with the goal of developing moral uprightness. Like Hirsch, Simḥah Zissel by no means endorses all prevailing social conventions, and he cautions that one should be "careful" when considering them, but there is nonetheless a requirement to study them as part of one's efforts to serve and revere God. General education appears to be more than merely utilitarian, but as something that can be done as part of "the fulfillment of the Torah."

While Simḥah Zissel did not advocate for general education and the values of the Haskalah with the passion that Samson Raphael Hirsch did, he shared Hirsch's vision of seeing Jewish and general education as part of a seamless whole directed at moral excellence.[72] It should not be surprising that a number of Simḥah Zissel's contemporaries described him, then, as an ally of Hirsch's German neo-Orthodoxy.[73] Simḥah Zissel himself, moreover, praised German Orthodoxy under Hirsch's leadership for reaching a level of moral excellence that far surpassed the moral level of Russian Jews. Noting the heartfelt empathy that Hirsch and his community displayed for the suffering of Jews beyond their own community, Simḥah Zissel argued that such empathy stemmed from their model of education. Not only were German Jews taught to "fear heaven," he wrote, but their general education (again, "the way of moral decency") focused them on the importance of building a "civilized" society:

> Do they fear God more than our brothers do here? No! . . . Rather, our sages of blessed memory put it well in teaching that one should "keep *the way* of the tree of life" (Gen. 3:24)—teaching you that "*the way* of moral decency" precedes the Torah.[74] The matter is as our sages of blessed memory said, that "anyone who does not have moral decency is not part of civilization" (BT Kiddushin 40a), and a person should habituate himself to sacrifice his will on the altar of bringing civilization to the world. . . . When one habituates himself to considering moral decency and the civilizing of the world, the consideration of justice will emerge from this—and this will be the fulfillment of the Torah, for the Torah aims at civilizing the world as well as going beyond reason. . . . Indeed, in our countries, they do not study and habituate themselves to considering the civilizing of the world, as we have said a number of times. . . . It is not the case in the other countries where, as I have seen myself, they study the wisdom of bringing civilization to the world, and so it is easy for them to arrive at this sentiment. . . . And so we can see with our eyes that he who is wiser regarding the human work of musar [*musar enoshi*], such musar being part of moral decency as is known among the philosophers, is closer to knowing the Torah. He who understands will understand the greatness of this meditation, and will be astonished and aroused in realizing that applying one's reason well to the wisdom of moral decency is part of musar.[75]

General studies, in this model, may teach "the wisdom of bringing civilization to the world"; such wisdom is not just Jewish wisdom, but a concept that "precedes the Torah" and with which (non-Jewish) "philosophers" are familiar. As we will see in chapter 3, Simḥah Zissel had much to say about gaining wisdom from non-Jewish philosophy, and as I noted above, Simḥah Zissel seems to have admired aspects of non-Jewish German culture. Here, focusing on the question of school curricula, he describes non-Jewish wisdom as "part of musar"—as wisdom that can help to bring moral discipline to human souls, building habits of concern for others. It seems, based on passages such as this, that Simḥah Zissel viewed general studies as contributing to the formation of his students—"civilizing" them, making them fit to be citizens of the communities in which they lived, and even helping to build the habits of concern for others that Simḥah Zissel saw as present in German Jewry but lacking among his brethren in Russia.

With Simḥah Zissel's sympathy for Germany's Haskalah-informed Orthodoxy, his embrace of general studies, and the various other themes of his writing mentioned above, Simḥah Zissel can be characterized as the most Haskalah-friendly leader in the nineteenth-century Musar movement. But Simḥah Zissel only endorsed certain values conventionally associated with the Haskalah, and he clearly rejected a number of other Haskalah values. Most significantly, Simḥah Zissel continued to stress the centrality of the Talmud and other traditional rabbinic literature. Though he downplayed the study of Talmud in his curriculum, so that the Talmud Torah allotted essentially equal time to the study of Talmud and to general studies, his writings make it clear that he did not see these two areas of study as having equal value. Though he appreciated the insights of other philosophers, he generally saw their insights as inferior to the insights of the Torah as interpreted by Talmudic tradition. Simḥah Zissel viewed Talmudic law as divinely given and other literature as humanly created; the latter deserved attention, but its value paled by comparison.[76]

Simḥah Zissel also lacked the optimism often associated with the Haskalah. Haskalah leaders—especially in Western Europe—tended to see modernity as promising great moral and spiritual improvement, overcoming the darkness that had characterized the Middle Ages.[77] Simḥah Zissel, by contrast, saw modernity as an era of lost faith, immorality, and lax observance, and he sought to protect his students from its temptations. He may have hoped that a renewed dedication to the work of musar could take hold across the Jewish world, but he does not seem to have had much hope that the increasingly popular universities could do much to promote moral discipline in the same way; in fact, as mentioned above, his students imagined that presidents of the most prominent of universities envied Kelm for its focus on the work of shaping virtue.

Nor did Simḥah Zissel have much hope that the light of reason could easily take hold across the world, as many supporters of the Haskalah hoped. In fact, as will be explored in chapter 2, Simḥah Zissel felt that the best way to get people to do the right thing was, often, to urge them to contemplate the punishments in store for their souls after their deaths. This sort of emphasis was common in medieval musar literature, but adherents of the Haskalah avoided it in the musar literature that they produced, preferring to focus on more pure motivations for right action.[78] Simḥah Zissel shared the Haskalah interest in pure motivation, but he simultaneously acknowledged that people would not embrace reason and keep away from sin without a strong focus on otherworldly rewards and, especially, otherworldly punishments. While Haskalah leaders aimed at overcoming the sense of fear and dread that dominated medieval musar literature, Simḥah Zissel sought to keep that fear and dread front and center.

Simḥah Zissel's own ideal of "purifying the heart" might at times have sounded less informed by the Haskalah and more informed by pietism—by earlier Jewish pietistic movements such as Hasidism, or perhaps by the Christian pietistic spirit that had swept Germany in the eighteenth century. Simḥah Zissel not only had the appearance of a modern Lutheran preacher, but he may have sometimes sounded like a modern Lutheran preacher of a pietistic bent, given his preference for purity of the heart and performance of good deeds over academic erudition, his reliance on emotion to effect repentance and moral change, his sense of modernity's moral decline, and his stress on God's punishment for wayward souls. At the same time, though, Simḥah Zissel did not share the German pietistic focus on a personal, intimate friendship with God, and neither did he share Hasidism's pietistic antirationalism or its rejection of general education. Simḥah Zissel's pietism was of a deeply rational sort, informed by the legacy of medieval Jewish philosophy and the values of the Haskalah, deeply appreciative of the intellect even if it saw the intellect as insufficient, by itself, for effecting moral transformation.

## The Closing of the Talmud Torah of Grobin and the Return to Kelm

When the Talmud Torah moved to Grobin, the space it left behind in Kelm continued to function as a "musar house," a space where former students and others came to pray, meditate, study, and chant. Simḥah Zissel would regularly return to Kelm to visit his family, who remained there while he was in Grobin, and he would also give sermons at the old Talmud Torah building. In 1881 he reported in a letter to Israel Salanter that ten men studied full time in that building, studying Talmud and engaging in the work of musar. Central to their musar work, Simḥah Zissel wrote, was that they met in groups each evening to discuss the virtues on which they were focusing, providing mutual support and devising strategies for inculcating those virtues.[79]

Simḥah Zissel began to spend increasing amounts of time in Kelm while he continued to direct the Talmud Torah in Grobin. He had developed a heart condition, and the stress of directing and fundraising for an institution seemed to be making his illness worse.

In 1881, Simḥah Zissel had apparently written to Salanter, wondering whether he might close the school on account of his troubled health, but Salanter had insisted that the school should remain open and that Simḥah Zissel was the only person fit to run such an institution. And so Simḥah Zissel continued to run the Talmud Torah, though he spent increasing amounts of time in Kelm and sometimes had to send his sermons on paper to the students in Grobin.[80]

Simḥah Zissel's struggles in maintaining the Talmud Torah in Grobin were not just on account of his health, though. His published letters also contain cryptic hints about those who criticized, maligned, and sought to close the institution. In one letter to his son, Simḥah Zissel speaks of an anonymous former student of the Talmud Torah, "one known to us," who was asked to no longer visit and "join us in prayer."[81] Though this individual's name is left out of the only version of this letter that I have seen, Shlomo Tikochinski has pointed to other testimonies indicating that this student was Rabbi Natan Tzevi Finkel, a close student of Simḥah Zissel's who went on to found his own yeshiva, the Slobodka yeshiva.[82]

As Finkel sought to create his own Musar movement yeshiva that would be more within the mainstream of elite Lithuanian traditionalism —fully dedicated to the study of Talmud, with less time dedicated to special "musar study" and without any general studies curriculum— he appears to have criticized Simḥah Zissel for denigrating Talmudic scholarship and for promoting non-Jewish wisdom. Finkel's student Rabbi Yeḥiel Ya'akov Weinberg, for example, suggests that Finkel was seeking to develop a model of a yeshiva that would correct the failures of Simḥah Zissel:

> In recent generations prior to the period of Slobodka, [Talmudic] scholarship and musar were made into two exclusive domains . . . [but Finkel] forcefully erased this division of domains between scholarship and musar. . . . He was the first to integrate scholarship and musar and to bind them together. . . . Musar, [Finkel] would say, is not freely available [*hefker*] and is not handed over for the freedom of the imagination or for the arousal of emotions. Musar must be built upon a strong foundation of strong, healthy consideration of *halakhic* thought. . . . As is known, he opened up a new window for Jewish thought that was original, from the sources, with no mixing with non-Jewish wisdom, and with no inquiring into what is beyond the domain of our Torah.[83]

As Tikochinski has argued, reports like these from Finkel's students indicate that Finkel saw himself as the first Musar movement leader to successfully combine "musar study" and scholarship, succeeding where Simḥah Zissel had not, as Simḥah Zissel instead indulged his students' emotions, neglected foundational studies in Talmud, and sought out non-Jewish wisdom.[84]

For all that Simḥah Zissel may have sought to welcome criticism, he does not appear to have welcomed this critique from Natan Tzevi Finkel. Weinberg's letters report that Simḥah Zissel saw Finkel "ruining musar for future generations." Among Simḥah Zissel's complaints were that Finkel was "drawing in students through flattery and by offering money and honor," and using musar as a tool to defend traditionalism but failing to acknowledge that "it is actually the purpose of life."[85] Finkel's approach to musar was, indeed, less radical and less single-minded than his teacher's, and this helped the Slobodka yeshiva to attract more students than the Talmud Torah ever could. Though Finkel seems to have been careful not to express criticism of his teacher in an overt, public manner, he seems to have privately indicated his concerns about the Talmud Torah to a number of colleagues and students, such as Weinberg. Another confidant, Rabbi Yosef Dinkels, testified that he heard Finkel overtly express his hope to see the Talmud Torah in Grobin close.[86]

The Talmud Torah in Grobin did close in 1886, three years after Israel Salanter's death. Simḥah Zissel decided that he could not succeed in running the institution and, in accordance with Salanter's will, he closed the school rather than finding someone else to direct it. He returned to Kelm full time and began to attend to the small group of students who had continued to gather at the Talmud Torah in Kelm. The students were generally married, over the age of seventeen, and able to study independently without a set curriculum in place. Simḥah Zissel organized them into a new yeshiva, which continued to be called the "Talmud Torah." But this was a postsecondary yeshiva for independently directed students, very different from the highly scheduled junior yeshivas that had previously existed in Kelm and in Grobin. It accepted a limited number of students, which kept expenses down, and it was generously financed by a small number of donors—foremost among whom was a German banker, Samuel Strauss, a German neo-Orthodox Jew who funded Simḥah Zissel's efforts while also supporting Finkel's yeshiva in Slobodka.[87]

Simḥah Zissel envisioned his new yeshiva in Kelm as having a narrow and explicit purpose: it would train an elite group of rabbinic leaders and teachers who could dedicate themselves to musar and spread their practices to some of the yeshivas where interested students might be found. "Most of the world finds this wisdom [of musar] to be strange," he wrote in one letter, "and I have learned only a little of it—but now I am like a guardian for musar, [seeking to] spread it."[88] Whereas institutions like the Slobodka yeshiva were seeking to increase their enrollments by appealing to what Simḥah Zissel saw as base impulses, Simḥah Zissel seems to have envisioned that he could counteract those tendencies by training a few elite students who would be missionaries for the Kelm approach at institutions such as these. As he wrote in an article on the subject, perhaps directly contrasting his own approach with what he saw as Finkel's approach in Slobodka,[89] he wanted his students to be few in quantity and excellent in quality: "I only want to draw in men whom I can examine and find that they 'share the burden of their fellows,' without taking pleasure for themselves at all, neither from wealth nor from prestige." People with the disposition to "share the burden of their fellows," as he went on to explain, were people who were not focused on their own needs but were instead disposed to see the needs of others and to respond to them with compassionate love.[90]

To find students of such character, Simḥah Zissel contacted his colleagues in the Musar movement, urging them to send him their most promising students. They did so; the student who sent him the most students was in fact Natan Tzevi Finkel. Even though Finkel may have thought that Simḥah Zissel's model for the education of youth was a flawed model, he seems to have concluded that this approach was ideal for advanced students who had already developed "a strong foundation of strong, healthy consideration of *halakhic* thought," as Weinberg put it. Finkel sent a number of his best students to spend significant time with his former teacher at the new Talmud Torah in Kelm, including rabbis such as Isser Zalman Meltzer, Moshe Mordekhai Epstein, Naftali Trop, and Leib Ḥasman, all of whom went on to become influential yeshiva directors or spiritual supervisors themselves.[91]

The number of students who spent substantial time in Kelm remained small, but the Talmud Torah also functioned as a sort of retreat center that was visited by others seeking a taste of Simḥah Zissel's teachings and his model of musar practice. Other figures who emerged as prominent figures in the next generation of the Musar movement, such as Rabbi Yosef Yoizel Horowitz of Novaredok, Rabbi Yosef Bloch of Telz, and Rabbi Yeruḥam Levovitz of Mir, were among those who spent time with Simḥah Zissel at the Talmud Torah of Kelm.[92] The Talmud Torah was most often visited during the month of Elul, the month dedicated to introspection and repentance before the holy days of Rosh Hashanah and Yom Kippur. The yeshiva opened its doors to all during this month, and students with an interest in musar streamed into Kelm from all over Lithuania and beyond, seeking to engage in the work of musar under Simḥah Zissel's direction.[93]

Among those who returned to Kelm during the month of Elul each year was a group of ten or so of Simḥah Zissel's closest students, a group known as "Devek Tov"—the "well-attached" group. The group was made up of disciples who had spread out across Europe, but who vowed to maintain a connection with each other and a dedication to the work of musar throughout their lives. The group included Simḥah Zissel's son Naḥum Ze'ev Ziv, his son-in-law Tzevi Hirsch Broida, and his close disciple Reuven Dov Dessler.[94]

The members of Devek Tov attempted to form a model community, dedicated to caring for each other with mutual love, committed to staying in touch with one another and to helping each other along their spiritual paths. The compact that they signed committed them to a range of musar practices: they agreed to engage in the study of Torah for the sake of heaven, rather than for selfish reasons; they agreed to spend at least half an hour each day (and more on Sabbaths and festivals) engaging in focused musar study; they agreed that their daily prayers should be a point of personal transformation; they agreed to accept upon themselves particular assignments pertaining to the particular character traits which they, as individuals, needed to develop; they agreed to follow Simḥah Zissel's practice of "tithing days," setting aside every tenth day as a day for special contemplation; they agreed to meditate on their own deaths; and they agreed to regularly correspond with a partner and also to write to Simḥah Zissel on a regular basis.[95] Simḥah Zissel, in turn, wrote out discourses for the Devek Tov group to read, and he asked the members of the group to circulate the discourses among themselves and to respond to him with their comments and questions. The discourses written for Devek Tov are among the central texts written by Simḥah Zissel, and the following chapters of this book draw heavily on them.

In addition to focusing on the students in Kelm, and on the Devek Tov group that was spread out across Europe, Simḥah Zissel also gave some attention during this period to setting up other institutions that would spread his teachings. His most ambitious project was to set up a yeshiva in the land of Israel, a task that he assigned to his students Baruch Markus and Shmuel Shenker. Markus and Shenker set out from Lithuania in 1891 and settled in Jerusalem, where they established a musar house. In 1896–1897, they founded a full-time yeshiva for young men, Or Ḥadash, the "New Light" yeshiva, which was made possible with funding from Samuel Strauss and from Baron Edmond de Rothschild. Simḥah Zissel himself expressed a longing to join his followers in Jerusalem—"if I had the wings of a dove, I would fly to dwell with you," he wrote—but his ill health prevented him from doing so.[96]

The land of Israel seemed to Simḥah Zissel to be a place where the Musar movement could successfully take root. Lithuania, on the other hand, was becoming increasingly less hospitable. At the same time that Or Ḥadash was founded in Jerusalem, a new wave of contempt for the Musar movement erupted in Lithuania. At Natan Tzevi Finkel's Slobodka yeshiva, and at the Telz yeshiva, now directed by Eliezer Gordon and supervised by Simḥah Zissel's student Leib Ḥasman, students protested against the study of musar, which they saw as infringing on their study of Talmud and as demeaning them, treating them "like children who needed to be trained to behave" (as Shaul Stampfer has put it).[97] Building on the protests, a wave of newspaper articles emerged in the Hebrew press attacking the Musar movement, which was portrayed as a divisive sect, detached from tradition and lacking respect for the study of the Talmud.[98] One newspaper report from the summer of 1897 condemned those devotees of musar who streamed to the Talmud Torah in Kelm each fall, focusing themselves on musar while ignoring the Talmud. Furthermore, the article noted, the study of musar damaged their souls by filling them with worry, regret, and despair.[99]

The sorts of responses that Simḥah Zissel offered to these criticisms sounded consistent themes. While he welcomed informed critique, he thought that opponents of the Musar movement were often misinformed. He saw worry and regret as essential moral emotions, and he did not think that musar work led to despair. He criticized his opponents for emphasizing Talmudic learning over the performance of deeds, and he argued that the Talmud itself counsels students to do more than study Talmud. Simḥah Zissel strenuously objected to the characterization of his efforts as innovative reforms that failed to respect tradition; indeed, he pointed out, he was simply trying to take seriously the teachings of the widely respected rabbis who had urged the cultivation of virtue in the rabbinic period and throughout the Middle Ages—the teachings of figures such as Baḥya Ibn Pakuda, Maimonides, and many others.[100]

These arguments were largely ignored. Though the Musar movement may have been building on earlier precedents, it continued to be viewed as a radical challenge to the norms of Lithuanian rabbinic culture. The controversy over the Musar movement raged on and Simḥah Zissel's health, meanwhile, continued to decline. Ever since he had been diagnosed with a heart condition in Grobin, he had been cautioned against exerting himself to the degree that he did. While he did give up his administrative responsibilities upon leaving Grobin, he continued to lecture despite the counsel of doctors that he should not; he argued that he was engaged in the work of saving souls, and that such activity justified risking his life.[101] Simḥah Zissel also continued to write, especially to the members of the Devek Tov group, despite the fact that writing caused him great pain.

Simḥah Zissel died at age 74 on July 27, 1898, the day before the traditional fast day of Tisha Be-Av. Among his final requests, according to his students, was that his clothes should be laundered after his death so that they would be clean when they were given to the poor.[102] Some students recalled that, at the end of his life, he was grateful to have been able to teach the path of musar to the degree that he did; others recalled his disappointment that his vision had limited influence on Jewish culture.[103] Simḥah Zissel did cultivate students lauded for their moral standards who ended up as leading figures in the Musar movement; but indeed the influence of the Musar movement was limited, and Simḥah Zissel did not reshape the Jewish world as he had hoped to do. He deserves our attention less because of his historical influence and more because of the value that might be found in his thought. Simḥah Zissel's thought offers a serious but neglected moral vision that addresses perennial human questions about the nature of virtue and human flourishing that we would do well to take seriously. I will consider the character of that vision throughout the remainder of this book.

2

# Virtue and the Path of Happiness

Most premodern approaches to ethics in the Western tradition were grounded in a vision of what human nature is like and a vision of what human beings should be; the purpose of the human being, from these perspectives, is to transcend one's initial nature and to move toward the ideal human life. In Aristotle's influential theory, human beings cannot be said to possess virtue by nature; their purpose is to build on their preexisting natures by habituating themselves to certain essential virtues. But there is a sense in which this process is "natural," for it is also human nature to be rational, and to cultivate one's character in accordance with reason, thus achieving *eudaimonia*—a state of "flourishing," or "happiness."[1]

As Jonathan Schofer has argued, a similar paradigm exists in classical Jewish thought: the rabbis of the Mishnah and Talmud tend to depict human beings as born under the rule of their "evil inclinations," while they depict a life dedicated to the Torah as a path for overcoming that inclination, developing certain virtues, and achieving an ideal of character. As Hava Tirosh-Samuelson has argued, the rabbis often depict overcoming evil and cultivating virtue as fostering a state of "happiness." With the Jewish encounter with ancient Greek philosophical terminology, Jewish thinkers also began to frame this path in terms of human nature, reason, and purpose. Maimonides, most prominently, embraced Aristotelian language in describing the human being as naturally unformed and as fulfilling his purpose (and finding happiness) by cultivating the virtues in accordance with reason.[2]

This sort of framework also fills Simḥah Zissel Ziv's writings. Simḥah Zissel uses classical rabbinic language as well as Aristotelian language regarding nature, purpose, and happiness. He stresses the importance of understanding the baseness of human nature under the rule of the evil inclination, while also stressing the importance of focusing one's attention on the moral ideal. For Simḥah Zissel, human beings have a purpose, which is grounded in our nature as rational beings: to cultivate moral character in accordance with reason. The work of cultivating character, of closing the gap between original human nature and ideal human excellence, is the work of musar.

## Wisdom and Musar

Simḥah Zissel's written explorations of the concept of "musar" often include discussions of "wisdom" and how wisdom is related to musar. The pairing of these words stems from the opening of the book of Proverbs (1:2), which describes "knowing wisdom and musar" as the proper goal of human life. Recognizing the centrality of these terms in Simḥah Zissel's thought, *Wisdom and Musar* (*Ḥokhmah U-Musar*) was the title that Simḥah Zissel's students assigned to the volumes of his writings that they compiled after his death. Those writings suggest that wisdom and musar are distinct but interrelated elements: human beings are obligated to acquire wisdom about human nature, often described as "the wisdom of musar," a prerequisite for successfully engaging in the work of musar; the work of musar, in turn, can serve as an aid for recognizing, acquiring, and internalizing that wisdom.

Simḥah Zissel sees two forms of wisdom as especially important to moral development. First, a person is required to obtain wisdom about human nature as it ordinarily is, in its nonperfected state. Second, a person is required to obtain wisdom about the ideal character of the human being, about how human nature is properly fulfilled. Rather than overemphasizing either human depravity or human excellence, Simḥah Zissel seeks to maintain a balance in his teaching, reminding his students that human beings are in many respects ignoble and in many respects primed for virtue. And it is essential, in his view, to obtain wisdom both about the corrupt nature of the human being and about the human being's potential excellence.

### *Wisdom about Human Lowliness*

Traditional modes of Talmudic scholarship, Simḥah Zissel cautions, are inadequate for learning about ordinary human nature. Rather, one must study "wisdom about the soul" (*ḥokhmat ha-nefesh*)—or, as one might alternatively translate it, "the science of the soul" or "psychology." He explains the importance of understanding human psychology with the following analogy:

> Just as it is not possible to be a physician for the body without a knowledge of anatomy, so too it is impossible to be a physician for the soul without a knowledge of the anatomy of the soul—knowledge of the faculties of the soul [*koḥot ha-nefesh*; psychological forces]—so that one may recognize the paths of deceptions that flow forth from the evil character traits naturally impressed in the human being. And for one who does not have knowledge of the faculties of the soul, it is impossible not to be harmed by its deceptions.[3]

This sort of medical analogy is a staple of Aristotelian and Maimonidean ethics, and the passage here echoes a passage from Maimonides's writings. Maimonides, however, sees souls as commonly sick but as sometimes healthy, whereas Simḥah Zissel here depicts souls as fundamentally and inevitably sick. For Simḥah Zissel, the most important thing to know about the soul's anatomy is that it naturally inclines toward evil, deception, and harm.[4]

Maimonides, to be sure, also sees human beings as deeply marked by imperfection; but the pervasive sense that human nature is deeply bent towards sinfulness does not mark his writing. Simḥah Zissel, on the other hand, fills his writings with meditations on the corrupt nature of the human being, drawing on sources from rabbinic and medieval musar literature. Knowing one's soul, for Simḥah Zissel, requires knowing that "man is born with flaws and needs mending [*tikkun*]," in line with the teaching from the book of Job (11:12) that "man is born a wild ass."[5] "The righteous person knows the soul of his animal," the book of Proverbs (12:10) teaches—meaning, Simḥah Zissel explains, "his own animal soul," the inhumane tendencies that pervade human nature.[6] Human nature is "polluted," such that human beings cannot naturally see the consequences of their own deeds and cannot properly express love for others.[7] It is "natural" for human beings to be self-absorbed and insensitive to suffering, such that it would have been natural for Moses, at the start of the book of Exodus, to remain "joined with Pharaoh" rather than feeling compassion for the Hebrew slaves around him.[8] Indeed, "the human being can in no way walk in accordance with his nature, for then he is very likely to turn aside from the path of the Torah"; rather, the greatest sages of the past sought "to distance themselves from [human] nature, for they were expert physicians regarding the anatomy of the soul, and they knew that [human] nature is 'simply evil, all the time'" (Genesis 6:5).[9]

A tendency to evil is sufficiently engrained in human nature that even very good people easily revert to their natural brutishness.

Among those who consistently act with love and beneficence, and who have been trained by expert physicians of the soul, "even the best of them can revert to being reborn [*yashuvu le-hivaled*] with a cruel nature." This is, Simḥah Zissel explains, because "human nature inclines more towards being 'evil, all the time.'"[10] In another passage, using the philosophical language of Aristotle, Simḥah Zissel suggests that human beings have a proper "form," a final purpose characterized by reason, but that our "matter," our original state, consistently obstructs the realization of that form.[11] Our materiality is so deeply embedded in our nature that even Adam, in the Garden of Eden when "his materiality was very, very pure," was afflicted by the baseness of human nature.[12]

Given the strength of our inclination to evil and the weakness of reason, the fight against our evil nature is incredibly difficult: it is "a war against nature, against the brutishness with which the human being is born, and it is a great war to conquer a power as strong and mighty as nature and bring it under the governance of reason."[13] Fighting the war properly begins with recognizing one's individual condition, including the particular character traits that are most in need of repair; moreover, one must recognize "the paths of deception that flow forth from the evil character traits," as Simḥah Zissel put it in the passage quoted at the start of this discussion. As he writes elsewhere, the essential wisdom needed for the "war against nature" is "recognizing the paths of cunning by which the evil inclination deceives the human being with all sorts of cunning, ensnaring him by means of knowing the nature of each and every one according to his way, as it is written: 'In this path where I walk, they have laid a trap for me' (Ps. 142:4). Therefore, it is a necessity to know the cunning of the evil inclination, in accordance with the faculties of the soul, and this is the wisdom of musar."[14] In Simḥah Zissel's view, the evil inclination—the inclination to fulfill selfish desires—works differently in each one of us, depending on our individual temperament; it often exploits our individual weaknesses and seeks to rationalize whatever we do. We cannot be effective in the war against our base nature unless we understand its "cunning" and "deceitful" tendencies, and, ideally, find ways to outwit it.

Indeed, the human intellect is not strong enough to overcome the evil inclination without learning from that inclination's example in devising ways to deceive it. Explaining a Talmudic dictum that "when wisdom enters a person, cunning enters along with it" (BT Sotah 21b), Simḥah Zissel writes that "one who wishes to fulfill the Torah and to divert the uncircumcised heart to the paths of wisdom cannot do this without cunning, for reason does not rule over the heart. . . . To divert the brutish heart with which a person is born is not possible without cunning, in accordance with the way of the brute." To gain wisdom, from this perspective, one's reason must go to school with the evil inclination and learn to emulate its cunning, "waging war with the strong and cunning enemy using all sorts of cunning," learning to be "cunning in one's reverence" (BT Berakhot 17a).[15] One might, for example, placate the pleasure-seeking parts of the soul by emphasizing the pleasures of virtue, as Simḥah Zissel's writings often do.

### *Wisdom about the Human Form*

But knowledge of the cruel and devious tendencies embedded in human nature is only part of the wisdom that human beings are required to obtain, in Simḥah Zissel's view. We are also required to obtain wisdom about what is ideal for human souls, a wisdom that Simḥah Zissel sees as reflected not only within the Torah but also in the "form" of the human being.[16]

Simḥah Zissel describes that form as a true "self" that lies hidden within the human soul, generally obscured by the "materiality" of the selfish, evil inclination. This description follows a standard Neoplatonic view that is often echoed in medieval Jewish philosophy. As Simḥah Zissel puts it at one point, a person typically "does not recognize oneself, and does not know what one's 'I' [*ha-ani, der Ich*] is, because the true 'I' is hidden in the human being." As a result, people mistakenly think of themselves "in accordance with the 'I' that they recognize—the appetite and the will, which a person can feel."[17]

One's appetites, here, do not reflect one's authentic self; rather, the true self is the part of the soul known as "reason" (*sekhel*). Reason should not be confused with the faculty of "cleverness" that can come up with explanations and justifications; the evil inclination itself is capable of (and expert in) doing such work. Reason is, rather, the faculty that is directed toward wisdom—the faculty that sees things as they really are, and that can apprehend the attributes of divine, perfect moral goodness. Reason is essentially perfect, unsullied by materiality. Simḥah Zissel describes reason as "a part of God" and as "the image of God," generally obscured by the selfish appetites that dominate the human soul.[18]

The identification of reason with "the image of God" follows a longstanding tradition, well supported in medieval Jewish Aristotelianism (e.g., Maimonides) and in Jewish Neoplatonism.[19] Being created in the image of God, the human being has the capacity to reflect divine attributes through reasoning well—above all, for Simḥah Zissel, by clearly perceiving and imitating God's central attribute of "love for all creatures."[20] The image of such rational and moral perfection is buried within the human soul, and recognizing this image is an experience of "knowing God." Commenting on a statement by the Neoplatonic Jewish philosopher Abraham Ibn Ezra that "one who knows his soul knows God," Simḥah Zissel explains that

> "He made the human being in the image of God" (Genesis 9:1)—and therefore one who looks upon the image will understand Divinity (*Elohut*). One who looks upon his soul will, from its image, understand God. "To what likeness can you compare Him?" (Isaiah 40:18)—and yet from the faculties of the soul which are unbounded, we can rise above the paths of the material, and see how supreme God's faculties are: "God alone is supreme" (Isaiah 2:11). This is the intention of the verse, "From my flesh I can see God" (Job 19:26), meaning that from one's image, the image of God, one may see reflections of God. Just as one who looks at a map can understand the land, even though there is no comparison in value between the two, one may understand from this [map] what one needs to understand—and that there is no comparison at all. . . . Just as it is not possible to know the lay of the land without studying a map, so too it is truly impossible to recognize the divine faculties without looking upon the map—the image of God.[21]

There are, here, "unbounded" and immaterial capacities within the human soul that reflect the image of God. The reflection of God that exists within the human being is an imperfect image, which cannot be properly compared to God's perfection. But traces of divinity within the human being can nonetheless guide us in our attempts to understand God's attributes. Our rational capacities can indicate the contours of moral perfection that are found within God.

In this passage, Simḥah Zissel builds on the Neoplatonic tradition, which sees the rational soul as an immaterial, divine entity trapped within the human body. Elsewhere, he uses Maimonides's Aristotelian language, describing reason as the "form"—the essence—of the human species. For Simḥah Zissel, as for Maimonides and Aristotle, reason distinguishes humans from other animals, properly governs the "matter" of which they are made, and guides their purpose in the world; those who do not utilize reason are less than human. Humans, in this view, are commanded to fulfill their purpose by using their reason to its fullest potential; those who reject this purpose are better described as animals than as humans. In one passage Simḥah Zissel notes that animals are superior to such people—animals generally fulfill their purposes, whereas these people are far from fulfilling them.[22]

One paradigmatic example of a person who lost his humanity, for Simḥah Zissel, is Titus, the Roman general and emperor who engineered the destruction of the Temple in Jerusalem. Simḥah Zissel sees Titus's crimes against the Jewish people and against God as having developed from his irrational rage—Titus "raised up his hand in anger and rage against Heaven, and he left the boundaries of humanity."[23] Simḥah Zissel describes others as losing their humanity when they lose their powers of thoughtfulness, fail to control their appetites, and fail to empathize with the suffering of others.[24] Simḥah Zissel teaches that those who are less than human still deserve love and empathy, as do animals, but he castigates them for surrendering to their animal appetites and failing to respect the rational, moral purpose for which they were created.[25]

Simḥah Zissel often describes the human being as "born a wild ass" and commanded to leave behind his original nature. But elsewhere he offers an alternative narrative: the human being is born in a rational form, created in the image of God, such that one needs "to preserve the image of God that is upon him."[26] Along these lines, Simḥah Zissel also urged his students to recognize the human being's "angelic" nature:

> The truth is thus: that it is possible for a person to reach the height of virtue. It is not as people in the world think, that a person is a person and it is good for him to learn to become an angel. This is not so. Rather, on the contrary, a person is truly an angel and, without learning, he will become an animal. This is as scripture says: "I had said that you are angels" (Psalm 82:6). If people were not angels, then how would it be possible to say this? Behold, a person truly is an angel, but in following after the evil impulses of his heart he becomes an animal, and thus the verse continues: "Therefore you will die as men" (Psalm 82:7). Thus it is better to learn when one is young, for then the animal within one will not grow further.[27]

Simḥah Zissel is here building on classical rabbinic teachings that indicate that the human being is partly angelic, partly human, and partly animal. But whereas rabbinic sources tend to depict children as born like animals who need to be "broken" to become fully human (or to develop "angelic" qualities), Simḥah Zissel here depicts children as like angels who must be nurtured properly so that they don't turn into animals. And whereas the typical rabbinic trope depicts children as under the sway of their evil inclinations until they are transformed by words of Torah, Simḥah Zissel here depicts the study of Torah as staving off the evil inclination before it embeds itself in children's hearts. Simḥah Zissel certainly endorses the classical rabbinic vision of taming animal impulses, as we have seen, but he also acknowledges an intrinsically good side to human nature that must be nurtured.[28]

As Simḥah Zissel explained in one letter regarding his vision for his Talmud Torah school, "there are great riches hidden in the human being, in his nature"; as an educator, he explained, he sought "to bring out the faculty to love wisdom which is hidden within the human being."[29] While he viewed human beings as created with their appetitive matter, he also viewed them as created with their rational, wisdom-loving form. He saw the work of musar as requiring not only offensive battles against the evil inclination but also defensive efforts to protect the natural "riches" of the human soul.

### *The Limits of Wisdom*

Simḥah Zissel more often applies the word *natural* to our base nature, though, not to our higher nature. In a certain sense, the pursuit of virtue is "natural" for our species, since we possess the capacity for virtue and the virtues define our purpose; but it is clear to Simḥah Zissel that we are dominated by selfish drives, and disciplining (bringing musar to) those drives does not come "naturally" to anyone. "Disciplining oneself," as he says at one point, "is the opposite of nature."[30] It may be difficult to attain wisdom about human nature, but it is all the more difficult to fulfill the central task of musar—putting that wisdom into practice.

Following Israel Salanter, Simḥah Zissel stresses that wisdom by itself is insufficient. He notes that many people gain wisdom about human nature but fail to use that wisdom for its proper purpose—for example, the biblical characters of Laban and Esau, who "were great wise men" but "who did not bring [their wisdom] to serve as moral discipline [*musar*] for their hearts." In the end, then, we should conclude that their wisdom was impaired, "for one who is truly a sage would of necessity take up the study of musar, for he would see that wisdom is not complete without musar."[31]

In one good late-nineteenth century metaphor that Simḥah Zissel employs, wisdom is like a powerful locomotive train engine, but the work of musar is the necessary work of laying and repairing tracks on which that engine can run. "One who fixes the locomotive must, by necessity, fix the path of the tracks," Simḥah Zissel writes. Here, musar involves guiding and inculcating human wisdom so that it can find expression in stable virtues—qualities such as love, humility, generosity, reverence, honesty, and equanimity, among many others.[32]

## What Is a Virtue?

Simḥah Zissel conceives of "virtues"—in Hebrew, *ma'alot* (or *middot tovot*, "good character traits")—along classical Aristotelian lines.[33] Like Aristotle and many other ancient and medieval thinkers, he emphasizes that virtues are excellent, stable dispositions acquired through habit and affirmed by choice, and he emphasizes that virtues are dispositions formed through the training of the nonrational parts of the soul by reason.

In this view, first of all, we can speak of people as possessing virtues only when these dispositions are deeply embedded in their souls. If a person has truly habituated himself to a virtue, his behavior will consistently express that virtue—"on any occasion, whether he is on the road or in his home, whether he is by himself or in public," as Simḥah Zissel puts it in one discourse on the virtue of reverence.[34] Virtue in general, he says, should be like "a wall" (Song of Songs 8:9–10)—stable, reliable, and visible in every dimension of a person's life. It is not that a person should act the same way in all situations, but that his virtue should be expressed in all situations according to what the situation calls for. A person who is consistently honest, for example, will be honest in the way that is appropriate for all situations, rather than being tempted to lie for the sake of personal gain. The ultimate exemplar of consistency is God, the ideal of consistent goodness. It is impossible for human beings to attain perfect moral stability, but virtue may be attained to a certain degree, and "to the extent that a person habituates himself so that there is no changeability in his words and deeds, and he will be reliable in accordance with human ability, he will have some resemblance to the Blessed One."[35]

Simḥah Zissel follows the Aristotelian view that virtues may be cultivated through habit—through performing activities that instill virtues in us—and that they can become so much a part of people that they become our "second nature." As corrupt as our "original" nature may be, that nature can be transformed when people develop new traits that express themselves naturally and consistently. Simḥah Zissel saw such transformation as most possible in youth, and so he hoped that educators like himself could train students, for example, to refrain from pernicious speech, for "in a place where they train and teach from youth, these things are like second nature, to such an extent that [evil speech] is almost not heard among them."[36] But even those who grow up with bad habits, in Simḥah Zissel's view, can acquire a "second nature." Thus Simḥah Zissel describes the biblical patriarch Abraham as accustomed to evil in his youth, but as having worked so hard to "change his nature" that he came "to have all the virtues by nature." With his dedication to musar and "the great labor of repairing his character traits," Abraham developed a second nature from which moral goodness could naturally flow.[37]

### *Choosing Virtue*

This Aristotelian ideal of a virtue as a disposition to which we are habituated to such an extent that it emerges naturally has been forcefully critiqued by many modern philosophers. Immanuel Kant, most influentially, contended that this ideal encouraged mechanical, thoughtless behavior, discouraging accountability and thoughts of one's duty.[38] As many subsequent philosophers have shown, however, this sort of condemnation of the Aristotelian virtue-centered tradition is not a fair critique: Aristotle and his followers put a good deal of emphasis on the importance of thoughtfulness, choice, and moral accountability. Indeed, Aristotle indicated that virtues are always the products of choice, reason, and continued reflection.[39] This sort of conception is present in Simḥah Zissel's writings as well.

First, Simḥah Zissel sees virtues as the product of choices. He does not see human beings as possessing virtues simply because we are created in God's image, nor does he see us as possessing vices simply because we are created with a powerful inclination toward moral evil. Virtues are qualities for which we can be praised or blamed, and Simḥah Zissel indicates that we should not be praised or blamed for things we cannot control—"when someone is compelled," he writes, "it is not considered a source of praise for him."[40] For Simḥah Zissel, human beings should not be judged for our nature as a species, nor should individuals be judged for their particular inborn temperaments; for instance, someone who "is not inclined to be quarrelsome by nature, rather than out of love of God's creatures" shows no virtue.[41] Virtues, rather, are dispositions of the soul formed by choices.

And proper virtue, in Simḥah Zissel's model, seems to require *autonomous, reasoned* choices, not just obedience to established religious norms. Obedience that does not rest on reasoned thought is, in Simḥah Zissel's language, mere "piousness" (*frumkeit*). A primary motivation of pious obedience will not lead to the creation of firm virtues in a person's heart; merely "pious" people will be inclined to change their behavior whenever they are away from those who might be watching them. The ideal model for behavior is instead the path of the philosopher, exemplified by the figure whom Simḥah Zissel sees as the archetypal philosopher—Abraham. Abraham did not act "out of piety," but, rather, was bound by his reason to live a life of virtue.[42] Other prophets, in Simḥah Zissel's view, also realized that one should serve God from this sort of autonomous posture. Thus Simḥah Zissel interprets the prophet Isaiah's proclamation that God "awakens my ear to hear the learning" (Isaiah 50:4) as follows:

> "He awakens my ear to hear *for myself* the learning *that I have learned*"—so that I understand things well, as if I had authored them in my own mind. And this is the task of a person: to understand all his learning, to hear them as if he had authored them—both with the Talmud and with musar, it should all be in this way. And this is the intent of R. Ḥayyim of Volozhin in answering "Which is the straight path that a person should choose?" (Mishnah Avot 2:1) [by saying that he must choose it] *on his own*. For when one receives a gift and is not able to earn it by himself, this is worthless, for, God forbid, he may lose it the next day. But one who earns—if he loses it, he may earn it again. So too with serving God.[43]

God, here, does not want humans to be passive recipients of God's teachings, but to understand them to such an extent that one can view them as if one has authored them oneself. A person must *choose* to follow those teachings by means of his own understanding—"on his own," as Simḥah Zissel interprets the comment of R. Ḥayyim of Volozhin. Simḥah Zissel presents the reasoned approach as superior especially because it will produce a more lasting state within a person. If one's service of God is based on mere acceptance of what one has received, one's devotion will not persist; but if one can see the reasoning behind one's service—if one can see oneself as its author—then one's devotion will persist.

This should not imply that Simḥah Zissel does not also have a place for accepting teachings based on authority. Indeed, he embraces a classical interpretation of the people of Israel's declaration at Mount Sinai that "we will do and we will hear" (Ex. 24:7)—that they agreed to follow God's commandments even before hearing them, let alone understanding them. They trusted that, God being God, God's commandments would be perfect, the epitome of rationality; Israel could, therefore, accept the commandments "on faith" before understanding them. But Simḥah Zissel adds to this teaching his hope that "we may merit to understand the reasons for the commandments."[44] From his perspective, it is admirable to embrace divine commandments without hesitation, but it is ideal to practice them with rational understanding ("as if he had authored them") rather than passively and mechanically. Putting virtues into practice requires reasoned choices and ongoing reflection. As Simḥah Zissel writes in another passage, "every movement that a person makes needs to be done with consideration [*ḥeshbon*]"— one must consistently evaluate one's behavior, as well as one's words and one's thoughts.[45]

## *The Repair of the Soul*

There are parts of the vision outlined above that may sound deeply Kantian; Simḥah Zissel's language about viewing rational ideas "as if I had authored them in my own mind" sounds like it could well have been lifted from Kant's own writings.[46] But Simḥah Zissel's stress on the importance of reasoned choice is as Aristotelian as it is Kantian; indeed, he cites Aristotle's *Ethics* as a source that teaches the necessity of learning wisdom through one's own experience.[47] And, ultimately, his vision of virtue is much more Aristotelian than Kantian.

The central theoretical disagreement between the Aristotelian and Kantian traditions, when it comes to virtue, regards the role that emotions play in virtue. Kantian thinking has tended to emphasize that virtues are achieved when one has the strength of will to overcome one's emotions. One's reason must rule over one's emotions and keep them at bay, but vicious emotions and desires always remain present in the heart of a virtuous person, and they must always be restrained. For the most part, emotions cannot be transformed to help the cause of virtue.[48]

For Aristotle, as for most other ancient Greek thinkers (and the medieval Christians, Muslims, and Jews who followed them), virtues are achieved when emotions cooperate with one's reason. One's reason must train one's emotions so they can be expressed in appropriate ways, taking their rightful place at the center of one's moral life. Truly virtuous people do not have vicious emotions and desires that remain in their hearts and that they need to battle; rather, they transform their emotions so that they can work hand in hand with reason. One who continually battles vicious emotions is a person whom Aristotle views as merely "continent," or "self-controlled," rather than being fully virtuous. This Aristotelian contrast between virtue and mere self-control is upheld in medieval Jewish philosophy—most clearly in the writings of Maimonides.[49]

Israel Salanter's writings, in turn, view Maimonides as the authority on this question, though Salanter is even clearer in defending the Aristotelian ideal of transforming and directing all parts of one's soul toward the good. But Salanter also adds an important corollary that does not appear in Aristotle or in Maimonides, emphasizing that even people who have achieved true virtue, who have repaired their character traits, must nonetheless continue to be prepared for the appearance of inappropriate desires and emotions that need to be controlled. Simḥah Zissel shares this concern: as we saw above, he warns that "even the best" of people "can revert to being reborn with a cruel nature." For Simḥah Zissel, as for his teacher, the work of achieving full virtue is extremely difficult, and perhaps impossible. But the ideal remains for him, as for Salanter, a virtuous person who repairs all of the faculties of his soul—including his appetites, emotions, and imagination—so that they are in line with reason.[50]

At the center of this vision is the idea that one's appetites (*ta'avot;* alternatively, "lusts" or "cravings"), which are normally directed toward selfish material benefits, should be transformed so that they can serve God instead. For the true sage, Simḥah Zissel writes, "appetite is given over into his hand, so that his appetites themselves [*davka*] have a desire for wisdom."[51] For a person to be fully virtuous, his reason must reach all the way down, repairing even the most appetitive parts of his soul.

When it comes to the virtue of honesty, for example, Simḥah Zissel describes a truly honest person as one "who has already conquered his character traits to such an extent that it comes to be his second nature that he has no desire for evil." Such a person still has appetites, but the appetites are completely aligned with reason. He longs for the truth, and there is nothing in his soul that challenges this longing.[52]

Few people are able to transform their appetites in this way, however. More common are those at a lower level, who possess "self-control" but not "virtue." They "long for evil character traits," but they "subdue their wills to follow the advice of their pure, strong reason." People who are at this level when it comes to truth-telling have the desire to lie, but they have the wisdom to recognize that this is wrong, and they are able to stop themselves from doing so. They have not transformed their appetites, but they are able to control them.[53]

At a still lower level—a very common level—are people who are incontinent, lacking self-control: "their reason is weak, and their appetites and their will and their character traits blind the eyes of their reason to think that they are good."[54] Persons at this level try to behave virtuously, but their aspirations to act in accordance with reason cannot overcome their appetites. Such a person "wants to walk in the path of the Blessed Lord, but then when it is in his power to act, he is not able to conquer his appetite."[55] He has the desire to lie, and is unable to stop himself from giving in to that desire, though he still has the admirable quality of valuing truth. He is not truly vicious; rather, he lacks self-control.

At the lowest level are those who are truly vicious, who do not seek the truth at all, but who instead assert that "their wills are themselves the truth." Rather than seeking to "align their wills with the truth," they seek to "align the truth to their wills." "Their wills rule over their reason," such that reason has no power to push them toward the good. Simḥah Zissel sees this state of being ruled by appetite as widespread, but he suggests that even people at this level can gradually develop virtues by gaining wisdom and self-control and eventually redirecting their desires to serve God.[56]

Just as appetites can be governed by reason and redirected to serve God, so too can emotions be redirected; a person can be trained, in Simḥah Zissel's view, to feel the right way at the right time. "A master of inner feeling," as he puts it, "will arouse himself to feel the necessary feelings."[57] Thus when Moses was a prince in Pharaoh's palace, for example, he showed the virtue of love for the people of Israel not only by recognizing their suffering but by "feeling their pain as if he himself was in this pain." Proper reasoning was essential to Moses's love, but that reasoning was grounded in feeling. For a virtue to be a virtue, it must be supported not only by cognition but by emotion.[58]

Other parts of the soul should contribute to virtue as well, including the imagination (*ko'aḥ ha-tzi'ur*), the faculty that forms mental images (*tzi'urim*) that are not directly perceived. Simḥah Zissel consistently emphasizes the need to repair one's imaginative capacities so that they are aligned with reason; in fact, he describes the use of the imagination as "what separates a righteous person from a wicked person."[59] One must, for example, be able to use one's imagination to visualize the rewards and punishments in store for one's soul after death.[60] So too, qualities of compassionate love depend on imagination: Moses's empathy toward Israel was made possible by his ability to imagine their suffering. In such cases, Simḥah Zissel sees imagination as guided by reason. Imagination can be an irrational, destabilizing faculty, creating false representations that lead human beings astray, but the truly virtuous person can repair, transform, and guide his imagination in line with reason, so that imagination can play its crucial role in the development of virtues.[61]

In sum, virtue requires the "repair" of all parts of the human self to the degree that it is possible. Simḥah Zissel holds out the potential for reason to reign supreme over all of one's appetites and emotions, one's imagination, and indeed one's very body: ideally, "one's body will become like a field cultivated for reason."[62] This vision of what reason can do makes Simḥah Zissel's ethics highly rationalist in a key respect. Unlike Kant, who concedes that irrational parts of the soul cannot be tamed by reason, Simḥah Zissel sets out an ideal of empowering reason to completely transform human beings in their entirety. This is the sort of demanding Aristotelian approach that, as Martha Nussbaum has put it, "gives reason an extremely ambitious role."[63]

On the other hand, Simḥah Zissel's vision of virtue, like Aristotle's, also gives an extremely ambitious role to the irrational parts of the soul. Appetites, emotions, and imagination all must cooperate with reason in the work of shaping virtue. For Simḥah Zissel, reason must rely on these various forces in large part because human reason, by itself, is weak. It must bring all nonrational parts under its command; to wage the "great war" that he sees as necessary, our rational capacities need all the reinforcement they can get.

### *Practical Wisdom*

Part of the work that reason should do, in Simḥah Zissel's view, is to seek wisdom regarding God, the rational human form, and the moral ideals of the Torah, directing the soul toward those ideals. Part of the work that reason should do is to see human nature clearly, and to devise appropriate strategies for ruling over the irrational parts of the soul. And part of the work that reason should do is what the Aristotelian tradition describes as the work of "practical wisdom" (or "prudence," as it is often translated): applying general moral ideals to particular situations. This third function of reason is, like the other functions, crucial for the development of virtue. The Torah, as Simḥah Zissel sees it, is "simple reason"—it offers perfect, rational ideals that need to be applied by "the reason of man, who is compound."[64] Practical wisdom is necessary for applying the pure spirituality of the Torah to a human world that is marked by complex material realities.[65]

As mentioned above, Simḥah Zissel suggests that ongoing reflection is central to moral life, because "every movement that a person makes needs to be done with consideration [*ḥeshbon*]."[66] Part of this consideration, for Simḥah Zissel, involves being sensitive to how ideals of virtue should be expressed, a sensitivity developed through one's own ongoing experience. He quotes Aristotle directly on this point: "one will not find [young people] who are prudent; the reason for this is that prudence deals with the knowledge of particulars which are known through experience, and the young person is not experienced, for one acquires experience over a long time."[67] Nobody can simply be told how to act rationally in the diverse circumstances that life presents; one must rather develop practical wisdom through one's own experiential learning.

The importance of practical wisdom is particularly clear in some of Simḥah Zissel's discussions of love. While Simḥah Zissel often describes love as the central virtue of the Torah, he cautions that love may be expressed in many different ways, depending on the situation. He sees this sort of sensitivity to circumstances as exemplified by a number of figures, including the rabbinic sage Shammai, who is described in rabbinic sources both as "acting with strictness" and as teaching friendliness. In Simḥah Zissel's understanding, Shammai taught that "character traits do not go according to a single style, but rather the character trait should be in accordance with the matter, [and] one needs to study and to estimate it. . . . All needs to be done in accordance with a measured-out character trait." While his colleague Hillel taught broad principles, Simḥah Zissel imagines Shammai as having preferred to emphasize the need to act differently in different situations, according to one's "measurements" and "estimations."

Why all this talk of "measuring" and "estimating"? In a Talmudic story (BT Shabbat 31a) about a prospective convert who asks Shammai about the overarching principle of the Torah, Shammai is said to have pushed the questioner away "with a builder's measure." In Simḥah Zissel's interpretation, Shammai was seeking to make a point about the need for carefully measuring how to apply character traits in particular situations.[68]

The Talmudic story recounts how the prospective convert also approached Shammai's rabbinic counterpart, Hillel, and how Hillel summed up the Torah for him in a concise formulation: "do not do to your fellow what is hateful to you." Simḥah Zissel applauds Hillel for, as he sees it, correctly emphasizing love as the overarching virtue of the Torah. But he also admires Shammai's insight that the ideal of love must be applied very differently in different circumstances. Following Shammai's model, Simḥah Zissel often emphasizes "strictness" as an appropriate way to show love; sometimes, in fact, he even sees circumstances demanding "cruelty" (*akhzariut*). "The obligation is on the human being," Simḥah Zissel writes, "to teach oneself cruelty and mercy for times of need." He sees the seemingly "cruel" commands of the Torah as designed to teach the appropriate use of character traits that are generally categorized as "evil character traits." The use of a certain level of cruelty, for example, is appropriate in certain cases.[69]

To be prepared for such cases, Simḥah Zissel argues, one needs to cultivate a wide spectrum of dispositions within one's soul. Just as God is depicted in the Torah as displaying both more tender and more harsh virtues when appropriate, so too human beings need to emulate this model of perfection by cultivating "contrary powers" (*koḥot hafukhim*) within themselves. And they need to use their reason to figure out when it would be appropriate to display the appropriate virtues: "It is a test for human wisdom, when contrary powers emerge from him, to be merciful in a place where one needs to show mercy and to be cruel in a place where one needs to show cruelty. Therefore, how pleasing are the words of Solomon in Ecclesiastes, chapter three: 'there is a time [for this] and a time [for that].' This is because one needs to imitate the ways of the Blessed One."[70]

Simḥah Zissel's model of a human being who holds such "contrary powers" within himself is Moses. Moses is "very humble, more than any man on the earth" (Num. 12:3), but he understood that humility should not always be equated with submissiveness. All depends on the circumstances: "The character trait of humility is extremely praiseworthy, but if one always behaves with humility without any change, this is a sign that this is simply the submissiveness of animals."[71] The submissiveness of animals is not guided by reason, and so it does not change according to the circumstances; properly humble human beings, however, are guided by reason, and so are sometimes "submissive" and sometimes not.

Simḥah Zissel points to one example where Moses clearly rejects a submissive posture: Israel's war with Midian, recounted in Numbers 31, where Moses leads a campaign to "wreak the Lord's vengeance on Midian." Israel's troops kill every adult Midianite man, while taking women and children captive. Moses is incensed, claiming that the nonvirginal women and male children also deserve to die. Following the Torah and midrashic tradition, Simḥah Zissel concludes that this must have been the correct decision. Moses followed the "advice of wisdom," in Simḥah Zissel's view, by drawing on "the contrary side" of humility "in accordance with the need." Moses had the practical wisdom to see, apparently, that the people of Israel were under a tremendous threat from the people of Midian; rather than show an unjustified form of "mercy," he humbly submitted to God's will to exterminate Midian.[72]

Simḥah Zissel cautions that commandments to engage in mass slaughter should not be followed in practice in the present day. But like other Jews committed to the divinity of the Torah, he endorses Moses's approach, and he sees the Torah as teaching a valuable lesson: that certain circumstances call for human beings to show harshness and even cruelty for the sake of the good.[73] While Simḥah Zissel's writings generally emphasize compassion, empathy, and mercy, he cautions that even these good character traits may be taken to extremes, such that they no longer reflect the guidance of reason. Every character trait (*middah*), he writes, should rather be expressed according to its proper "measure" (*middah*). Passing along wisdom that he claims to have learned from "the sages of musar and character traits" and especially from Israel Salanter, Simḥah Zissel writes the following:

> Mercy is a very, very good character trait, as is known, and there is no need to expound on this; nonetheless, Saul, the Lord's chosen one, was removed from his kingship because of [an excess of] mercy (I Samuel 15). Anger leads to many sins, and "so many of [the torments] of Gehinnom have dominion over [an angry person]" (BT Nedarim 22a); nonetheless, they said to "throw out one's ill-temper upon the students" (BT Ketubot 103b). Submissiveness is a very, very praiseworthy character trait; nonetheless, "a righteous man who falls down before the wicked [is like a muddied spring, a ruined fountain]" (Proverbs 25:26), meaning that if a person of virtue submits to people of vice, there is no vice greater than this, and he should instead have utilized magnanimity [*hitromemut ha-nefesh*]. This appears to be contrary to submissiveness, but he needs to keep the character trait properly measured so that it will not enter the domain of the [true] opposite, the extremity of the character trait.[74]

A generally negative character trait like anger can be good within certain bounds, as long as it is applied in the right time and place and in the right amount; so too, "very, very good" character traits such as mercy and submissiveness can be misapplied with some deficiency or excess.

Simḥah Zissel is working here with the Aristotelian concept of the mean. He imagines incorrect dispositions as excessive or deficient: an excess of submissiveness when confronting an evildoer is wrong, as would be a lack of submissiveness and an excess of pride. Both sorts of extremes reflect failures of practical wisdom—insufficient thoughtfulness about what sort of virtue is required in any given situation. Determining the mean requires constant reasoning, since, as for Aristotle and Maimonides, the mean is not simply a fixed median but is a "relative mean," measured relative to changing circumstances and to a person's preexisting dispositions. Thus, in one of Simḥah Zissel's examples, "one who is naturally cruel needs to heal his nature with the contrary trait, [doing] all with mercy." One should aim at the mean, calibrating what is appropriate in accordance with circumstance and in accordance with one's own nature and character.[75]

All expressions of virtue are, then, dependent on one's ability to use one's reason in finding the appropriate way to express them. Reason is, as Simḥah Zissel describes it, a force that properly balances and unifies disparate impulses: when dealing with the many opposites "on which all the Torah is built," "there truly is a mediator between them, and this is reason. For just as they were created from one source, so too reason, which is a part [of God] from above, can bind them and mediate between them, so that they can be unified rather than two opposites."[76] Reason does the divine work of integrating the virtues, which may seem to conflict, into a seamless whole. Though Simḥah Zissel is aware of the difficulty of integrating the virtues together, he follows the Aristotelian idea that practical wisdom should integrate the virtues and illustrate their unity, so that thoughtfulness can serve as "the foundation upon which all of the regimens of [the soul's] health are built."[77]

### *Putting Virtue into Action*

Although Simḥah Zissel generally does not have a special term for what Aristotle calls "practical wisdom," this Aristotelian concept is found throughout his discussions of the work of reason. It is, notably, a concept that is more present in Simḥah Zissel's writings than in the writings of Maimonides. Maimonidean ethics may rely on practical wisdom to a great extent, but his writings say little about practical wisdom and the unity of the virtues that it makes possible. This may in part reflect Maimonides's emphasis on the fixed laws of the Torah, which (as Simḥah Zissel would agree) practical wisdom cannot be permitted to challenge. It may also reflect Maimonides's conviction (with which Simḥah Zissel would not agree) that the ideal life is a life of contemplation that does not require all of the moral virtues to be integrated together.[78] Maimonides takes moral virtue seriously, but he privileges the intellectual virtues over the moral virtues, and he views practical wisdom as the lowest of the intellectual virtues. Though there is significant scholarly dispute about Maimonides's approach to this matter, it seems on balance that Maimonides sees human excellence as better achieved through solitary, theoretical, metaphysical speculation than through displays of moral virtue.[79]

Contrary to this model, Simḥah Zissel does not describe the pursuit of virtue as culminating with metaphysical speculation; rather, he sees wisdom demanding that virtue culminate in action—and, above all, in socially oriented behavior.

The highest virtues, for Simḥah Zissel, are moral virtues, dispositions to act in certain ways in relationship to others. Virtue depends on thought, but virtue does not culminate in thought alone. For Simḥah Zissel, human beings are inescapably embodied, and so not only must reason depend on bodily faculties such as the appetites and emotions, but it must express itself through physical deeds.[80] These deeds include physical deeds of service directly offered to God, and above all physical deeds carried out for the benefit of one's fellows; "most of the Torah," Simḥah Zissel writes, "is built upon doing good for one's fellow—being good to people."[81] God seeks the improvement and the perfection of all human beings, and no one has the right to focus only on himself, avoiding God's call to apply one's capacities to this divine goal: "the human being was created not for himself but, rather, to engage in acts of lovingkindness for the body and for the soul."[82] The virtues that God requires of human beings cannot be expressed in solitary contemplation; they are expressed through care for others. Any implication, therefore, that one can perfect the virtues of one's soul without acts of care for others is necessarily false; the virtues would not permit this.

One of the targets of Simḥah Zissel's argument seems to be the Lithuanian rabbinic culture that saw all other activities as having limited value in comparison to the study of Talmud. That culture drew on rabbinic traditions that depicted study as being as significant as all other activities combined. Simḥah Zissel, on the other hand, drew on rabbinic traditions that saw the wisdom gained through study as good only insofar as it culminates in inner transformation, and then in proper action (*ma'aseh*). In a number of his discourses, for instance, he quotes the teaching of the Talmudic sage Rava that "the goal of wisdom is repentance and good deeds [*ma'asim tovim*]" (lest one think, Rava continues, that one can study Torah and simultaneously kick one's parents and teachers). Simḥah Zissel explains: "the goal of the person of reason [*ha-maskil*] should be that his wisdom match his deeds. This is the goal of wisdom: to be a 'master of the deed,' a master of understanding in one's deeds. Understand this! Therefore it emerges for us that someone who is not a master of musar is, without a doubt, not a sage in Talmudic learning, for he has not descended to the depths of the practical norm [*halakhah*] of the matter."[83]

To be a master of musar, here, requires applying one's insights to one's behavior; it requires virtues that express themselves in action. Talmud study that does not transform one's behavior is, by contrast, severely impoverished. While Simḥah Zissel sees some Jews as "accustomed to say that one should merit being a greatly learned person [*lamdan*], this is not the goal of creation, for this world is the world of action, and 'learning leads to action' [as the Talmud says], and this is the goal of creation." Simḥah Zissel sees such an emphasis written into the story of creation at the start of the Book of Genesis, which ends with the infinitive "to act" (*la'asot*)—that is to say, the world was created for action. Those who see the person who only sits and learns as the ultimate embodiment of virtue have, for Simḥah Zissel, failed to understand one of the Torah's most important messages.[84]

While some of Simḥah Zissel's rhetoric on this subject is directed against the rabbinic culture of scholarship from which he dissented, Simḥah Zissel also depicts himself as arguing against "the philosophers." These philosophers are, for him, those who argue that eternal life is gained "through concepts" and who do not trouble themselves with "action." Simḥah Zissel begs to differ, insisting that proper deeds are no less "spiritual" than proper thoughts; it is through deeds that "the essence of spirituality is attained."[85] Therefore, Simḥah Zissel argues, even the lowliest of the Jewish people may far surpass the greatest of philosophers in virtue, because they persist in performing the physical deeds demanded by God.[86]

What Simḥah Zissel describes as the ideal of "the philosophers" was the view famously ascribed to medieval Neoplatonic or Aristotelian philosophers in the opening pages of Yehudah Ha-Levi's *Kuzari*. It was also the ideal that was greatly esteemed by Maimonides, who privileged intellectual virtues that do not necessarily affect matters of conduct. Simḥah Zissel, by contrast, describes the very idea that virtues would not culminate in action as a "crazy" teaching of the philosophers. He joins the philosophers in affirming a rationally guided virtue ethics, but he does not see human goodness as culminating in solitary contemplation. Rather, "the essence of discerning whether a person is a sage is by means of his deeds. If he behaves in accordance with his wisdom, truly he is a sage. If he does not, he is crazy!"[87]

Simḥah Zissel seems to imagine that philosophers, lost in lofty realms of contemplation, are also oblivious to the ways that behavior is crucial to shaping human character. Thus, for example, when he tells of how Moses's and David's compassion was developed through their small acts of compassion while they shepherded their flocks, Simḥah Zissel concludes that "education in character traits needs to involve simple things, of small value, by means of which one can ascend to the crown of the virtues—and it seems that this insight is lacking in the philosophers."[88] The focus on habituation through simple deeds is in fact very Aristotelian, but Simḥah Zissel imagines "the philosophers" as they appear in the *Kuzari*—insufficiently concerned with action in general, and particularly oblivious to the importance of small acts of compassion.

Simḥah Zissel's virtue ethics is deeply intellectual (with its focus on reason) and deeply pietistic (with its focus on emotions and desires), but he is eager to show that reason and emotion must culminate in behavior. Neil Gillman has suggested that the "intellectual," "pietistic," and "behavioral" models are the three primary models of Jewish spirituality,[89] and it is worth noting that Simḥah Zissel tries to integrate these three models to a significant degree. He is certainly a pietist, focused on the transformation of human hearts, but he is a rationally oriented pietist who insists that all piety must culminate with proper action.

## Happiness and Virtue

Whether they believed that virtue culminated with action or with contemplation, premodern Jews generally believed that virtue led to happiness. As Hava Tirosh-Samuelson has shown, mainstream rabbinic Judaism took for granted that "only the one who possesses good character traits, which dispose one to do good deeds [*ma'asim tovim*], can experience the happy life."[90] Maimonides brought this vision into an Aristotelian framework, showing how the development of moral virtue and especially intellectual virtue was the best source of human happiness.[91] Simḥah Zissel drew on the rabbinic vision of happiness and on much of the language of Maimonides in articulating his own vision of how virtue leads to happiness.

Simḥah Zissel might seem an unlikely figure to argue on behalf of happiness. After all, his writings advocate a highly demanding ethical posture, allowing little room for repose. He applauds the Talmudic notion that righteous people tend to have troubling dreams; it is good to have troubling dreams, he argues, and to consistently worry about one's moral life.[92] Moreover, Simḥah Zissel cautions against the pursuit of pleasure to such an extent that it would seem surprising that he would encourage his students to pursue happiness.

And yet Simḥah Zissel, following the Aristotelian tradition, does insist that virtue leads to happiness and to a real sensation of "pleasure." He rejects the Kantian position that pleasure is deeply suspect and that virtue should not feel good. While Kant generally maintained that virtue is always characterized by the pain of restraining one's desires, Simḥah Zissel upheld the Aristotelian hope of transforming such desires so that pain would not need to be present. While Simḥah Zissel does have concerns about morality being motivated by a personal interest in achieving happiness, he is clear that virtue produces spiritual and lasting joy.

Simḥah Zissel imbibed this notion not only from classical Jewish sources but from Aristotle himself. He directed his students to the Hebrew translation of Aristotle's *Nicomachean Ethics*, which he saw as teaching that virtuous behavior leads to happiness and that such happiness, in turn, encourages continuing the behavior: "See Aristotle's *Ethics*, book 2, chapters 1–2: happiness is acquired from one's activities. See there. And if so, one will acquire much of happiness in accordance with the preponderance of one's activities. Happiness will lead to further activities, and the activities [will lead to further] happiness, and [this cycle] will continue on."[93] The more that one engages in good deeds, Simḥah Zissel goes on to suggest, the closer one is to attaining the ultimate happiness of complete virtue—which is the ultimate happiness of closeness to God. God *is* perfect virtue, and moving toward the divine ideal can be described as an experience of ever-growing pleasure:

> The purpose of the human being is to draw close to the Source of good—"for me, being close to God is good" (Psalms 73:28). It is like with very pleasant music, the closer a person comes to it, he feels its pleasantness more. Therefore, to the extent that a person comes close to the Blessed One, he finds greater joy and greater pleasure. The opposite is also true: for one who is taken away from pleasant music, with every step further away he is pained—thus, "those who

> are far from you will perish" (Psalms 73:27). The more the Blessed Lord penetrates into one's innerness [*penimiut*], the better, and this is what the human being needs. On the other hand, if the opposite occurs, then he is contrary to God's purposes.[94]

The process of growing in virtue, here, is a process of drawing one's soul closer to God or bringing God within one's soul, a process marked by increasing pleasure, though this pleasure can be lost if one moves away from the path of virtuous behavior.

The analogy with the pleasures of music, of course, can only go so far. Though Simḥah Zissel considers music to be a higher-order pleasure than many other sensory pleasures, it is nonetheless a sensory pleasure that comes to an end. Simḥah Zissel devotes considerable energy in his writings to contrasting the limits of sensory pleasures with the lasting pleasures of morality. Echoing Aristotle, Simḥah Zissel is sure that all human beings aim at happiness, but he sees them as often erring by seeking temporary, external pleasures rather than the true, inner joy found through moral behavior. A typical person "learns a craft so that he will profit from it," and "he goes to concerts and his seat is never empty at places of amusement and he does not keep his soul from any pleasure at all," but these pleasures are only temporary, and the pursuit of such pleasure proves to be "vanity and striving after wind" (Ecc. 1:14). The intrinsic pleasures of virtue, on the other hand, provide lasting satisfaction, connecting a person with God's enduring perfection, allowing him to drink from the "'fountain of living waters' (Jer. 2:13), which do not stop and which are never diminished."[95]

One of the tasks of human reason is to distinguish between pleasures that are merely transient and pleasures that are lasting. Building on the Talmudic notion that a wise person is one "who foresees consequences" (BT Tamid 32a), Simḥah Zissel stresses that a wise person should be able to see which pleasures are lasting and which are not. One should be able to foresee the limits of bodily pleasures, how "with pleasure in sexual intercourse and the like, after the deed it goes away . . . for it is pleasure that lasts only for a moment. This is not so with the pleasures of wisdom, 'whose breasts satisfy you at all times'" (Proverbs 5:19).[96] In one of his analogies, a wise person should be able to discern that "the sweetness of sin" is liable to lead to spiritual death, just he knows that a leech may find blood to be a sweet treat but will ultimately die from gorging itself on blood. In general, Simḥah Zissel describes seeking sensual pleasures as pernicious or vain, while he describes a dedication to truth, wisdom, and moral goodness as providing enduring spiritual pleasure.

Simḥah Zissel does not deny that material pleasure has some value: finding joy in eating and drinking, for example, is permitted insofar as "they are the supporters for the tree of life in a person"; but the ultimate "tree of life," the rational teaching of the Torah, is itself the essence of real and lasting joy.[97] Insofar as he sees basic goods such as food and drink as necessary "supporters" for happiness, Simḥah Zissel does not seem to hold that virtue is entirely sufficient for happiness. But he is far closer to this Stoic view than he is to the Aristotelian view that material prosperity is necessary for happiness. Not only does Simḥah Zissel see material prosperity as providing little real joy, but he sees real joy as possible even amid great poverty and physical pain. Physical pain is, after all, merely temporary, and it can in fact be a proper source of joy, conveying a divine reproof and prompting attention to one's moral life; and Simḥah Zissel sees moral benefits to poverty, which he experienced firsthand, as well.[98] One can find a sense of inner happiness, then, even while one is deeply ill or destitute, so long as one cultivates the virtues, the sources of truly lasting pleasure.

This pleasure persists even when the virtues themselves demand an experience of pain. At the heart of Simḥah Zissel's vision of moral goodness is empathy in response to the suffering of others; perceiving pain is, then, at the center of the virtuous life that Simḥah Zissel characterizes as providing unending pleasure. Simḥah Zissel's prescription for finding pleasure involves turning away from one's own personal desires for pleasure and seeking to identify with the pain felt by others.[99]

Also perhaps surprisingly, focusing one's attention on one's own mortality is a significant piece of Simḥah Zissel's prescription for true happiness. In one passage, he argues that "remembering death brings one to the highest level of joy, for then one can feel in one's soul that he is connected to eternal life." Meditating on the fate of one's body and one's soul is crucial to understanding the vanity of seeking sensual pleasure and refocusing one's attention on God and the needs of others. "Remembering the day of one's death," then, becomes the key to finding "lasting joy which is free from sadness and grief."[100]

Unending efforts at moral discipline, empathic identification with the suffering of others, and meditations on the day of one's death are the sorts of activities that we will typically regard as joyless, and probably painful. Given its stress on these sorts of activities, it is hardly surprising that the Musar movement has often been characterized as joyless; in a formulation introduced by the novelist Chaim Grade, "it is said that he who has learned musar will never again have joy in his life, even after he has stopped studying musar."[101] But Simḥah Zissel insists that the person who properly immerses himself in musar is the person who is best able to find unending joy during his lifetime. There is nothing more joyful, in Simḥah Zissel's view, than virtue.

*The World to Come*

Not only does virtue bring intrinsic rewards, in Simḥah Zissel's view, but it also leads to far greater extrinsic rewards after one's death. While Simḥah Zissel describes the possibility of experiencing lasting joy in one's lifetime, he concludes that, inevitably, "the pleasures of this world are mixed with sadness," whereas the pleasures of the world to come are truly "free from any admixtures of sadness whatsoever."[102] Using one's reason—and following the commandments of the Torah, which Simḥah Zissel sees as ordained by reason—can provide a "taste of the world to come" in one's lifetime, but much greater joy is available to the virtuous soul that has left behind the body and entered the real "world to come"—a realm of pure reason.[103]

So too, while moral viciousness can lead to great spiritual pain in one's lifetime, Simḥah Zissel assumes that the pain in store for a vicious soul in the purgatory-like realm of Gehinnom after death is tremendously greater. Just as the world to come is a place of beholding "the illumination of the face of the Blessed Lord . . . without end," so too Gehinnom is a place where one experiences God's anger "without end."[104] While at times Simḥah Zissel seems to follow the common view of Gehinnom as more a place of purgation where all human souls spend a limited period of time than a place of eternal punishment, he sometimes depicts the purgation experienced in Gehinnom as unbearable and seemingly without end.[105]

In some passages, Simḥah Zissel stresses the intrinsic rewards of virtue and cautions against focusing too much on the rewards and punishments in the world to come. Thus, for instance, he writes that the path of Torah is "a straight path by which he can live a life of pleasure and satisfaction—not simply through his future reward, but through the path in and of itself being a 'path of pleasantness'" (Prov. 3:17).[106] But while discussions of the intrinsic pleasure of virtue and the intrinsic pain of vice have a prominent place in Simḥah Zissel's writings, the promises of even-greater otherworldly rewards and punishments have an even greater place. To a large extent, Simḥah Zissel follows Israel Salanter in that he seems uninterested in metaphysical speculations about the details of an afterlife, but quite certain that an afterlife may be very painful or very pleasurable. He particularly urges all people to fear for their potential suffering in Gehinnom—unlike Maimonides, and unlike most leaders of the Haskalah, who spoke of otherworldly rewards but had little to say about otherworldly suffering.[107]

Simḥah Zissel sees such talk as necessary, given his relative pessimism about human nature. Ordinary rational arguments are not strong enough to convince people to refrain from vicious behavior, he suggests; even "the philosophers admit that without faith in the immortality of the soul, there is nothing to stop a person from retaliating against his fellow." Morality depends on faith in immortality and otherworldly justice, making such faith "the cornerstone of religion" and "the peg upon which everything hangs."[108]

Such faith should not merely be intellectual, though, but must transform one's emotions, inspiring deep longing for the world to come and deep fear of Gehinnom. The intellect does not have great motivational power, in Simḥah Zissel's view, whereas genuine fear is perhaps the greatest of motivators, and so "a person needs to bring reward and punishment into his sense experience as much as is possible, to visualize sufferings [of Gehinnom], as if they are actually coming upon him (God forbid), and to contemplate well how hard it is to bear them." For all that Simḥah Zissel may have admired the Haskalah, he surely did not admire its tendency to shy away from offering threats of harsh punishment. These sorts of threats, Simḥah Zissel thought, were the best way to keep human beings from engaging in evil behavior.[109] While Simḥah Zissel emphasized the consequences intrinsic to such behavior, he saw teaching about extrinsic punishments as even more effective.

### *The Motivations for Virtue*

In advertising the great pleasures of virtue and the pains of vice, Simḥah Zissel was undoubtedly seeking to make the work of musar seem more attractive. But his emphasis on reward and punishment is clearly in tension with the concerns about moral motivation in his writings. Doing good deeds out of a self-interested desire for reward and punishment is clearly, in his view, a sign of viciousness. A truly moral person, for Simḥah Zissel, should pursue virtue "for its own sake" (or, to use other language that he sometimes uses, "for God's sake"), without any ulterior motives.

As Tamar Ross has pointed out, Israel Salanter had been rather less cautious about the self-interested pursuit of morality. Salanter was unapologetic in encouraging people to dedicate themselves to good deeds precisely because it is what self-interest demands, though he hoped that habituation to the performance of good deeds would eventually lead to performing them for better motivations. With this ultimate hope, he followed the Talmudic dictum that "a man should always occupy himself with Torah and good deeds, even when it is not for their own sake, for out of [doing good] with an ulterior motive comes [doing good] for its own sake."[110]

Simḥah Zissel often echoes this dictum as well, especially in suggesting that those motivated by the self-interested pursuit of pleasure will eventually discover that greater pleasure can be found when one does away with the self-interest. And, like Salanter, he sometimes makes a case for morality on the grounds of self-interest.[111] But Simḥah Zissel's writings sometimes take a different approach, describing those motivated by reward and punishment as "fools" susceptible to "the spirit of stupidity," and stressing that the work of musar must involve developing purer motivations.[112] Yes, one must often appeal to one's evil inclination, enticing it with promises of pleasure to convince it to support the path of virtue, he suggests—but one must also actively pursue a purer path. Yes, acting without concern for personal satisfaction will bring the greatest personal satisfaction—but one must work on not being selfishly motivated by this fact. Simḥah Zissel thus seems to follow the general approach of Maimonides, stressing the happiness that virtue can bring but counseling against being motivated by it; and beyond this, Simḥah Zissel offers his characteristic emphasis on describing the long, slow process of purifying motivations.[113]

Simḥah Zissel also places a distinctive focus on the ideal of doing the right thing even if it means giving up potential happiness. In a number of passages he offers his admiration for biblical figures who give up the pleasures of prophecy to focus on more mundane and less obviously pleasurable forms of moral action. At the start of Genesis 18, for example, Abraham is said to receive a prophetic visitation from God, but he seeks to delay the prophecy so that he can rush out to greet the strangers who are passing by his door:

> The prophecy appeared for him, as it is written: "God appeared to him" (Gen. 18:1), and nonetheless he requested of the Holy Blessed One: "Please do not pass by your servant," and he put aside the prophecy and went to greet his guests. Why? Surely prophecy is a wonderful pleasure, for

> the substance of prophecy is knowing God and there is no pleasure like knowing God—but nonetheless he left behind this pleasure on account of his guests, for "the central thing is not the study [*midrash*] but the deed [*ma'aseh*]" (Mishnah Avot 1:17). And our sages of blessed memory learned from this: "Receiving guests is greater than receiving God's presence" (BT Shabbat 127a).[114]

Prophecy is here depicted as providing the prophet with guaranteed spiritual pleasure, just as study (*midrash*) is a source of guaranteed pleasure. But Simḥah Zissel cautions against the potentially selfish pleasures of such contemplative activity. As he goes on to clarify, the content of prophecy—God's will—rightfully encourages prophets to turn away from spiritual contemplation and toward action, even when this requires giving up the immense pleasures of the contemplative life. Simḥah Zissel elsewhere indicates that proper action can in fact be the source of even greater pleasure, but here he does not reference that pleasure and instead emphasizes that Abraham chooses morality over pleasure.

Even more emphatically, Simḥah Zissel argues that what distinguishes the Jewish tradition from the Aristotelian tradition is its willingness to forgo pleasure for the sake of morality. In one polemical passage, immediately after mentioning Aristotle's name and acknowledging Aristotle's great intellectual achievements, he offers the following contrast:

> When you comprehend the words of the philosophers and the words of our sages of blessed memory, you will see the difference as the difference between light and dark. The philosophers: their words see the greatest excellence in happiness acquired through good activities and through good virtues, and so their goal is self-love. But our sages of blessed memory: they never speak about themselves, but rather about the will of the Blessed Lord—"let not the mighty man glory in his might . . . but let him who glories glory in this [that he understands and knows me, that I am the Lord who exercises lovingkindness, justice, and righteousness, in the earth] for in these things I delight" (Jeremiah 9:22–23)—the will of the Lord, and not one's own happiness. The proof is that the Vilna Gaon said that he would give away all of his [reward in] the world to come for one moment more of serving the Blessed Lord. And so one of

> the sages in the book *The Beginning of Wisdom* said: if I were to know that for fulfilling a commandment I would go to Gehinnom, and for committing a transgression I would go to the world to come, I would fulfill the commandment even though I would inherit Gehinnom on account of it. And this is because the love of the Blessed Lord, to do the will of the Blessed One, burns within them. Truly, this was the statement of our teacher Moses, peace be upon him: "Erase me from the book which you have written" (Ex. 32:32)—for the sake of Israel, the children of the Living God.[115]

Here is Simḥah Zissel's ideal vision of loving God: a dedication to doing the right thing that is so deeply embedded in one's character that one would not hesitate to endure the worst suffering on account of one's virtue. The Aristotelian philosopher, by contrast, is taken to be far more egoistic, motivated by the promises of happiness and unwilling to sacrifice his happiness for the sake of what is right. This is a critique that other modern Jewish thinkers (most notably, Hermann Cohen) and non-Jewish philosophers (most notably, Immanuel Kant) also leveled against Aristotle, and in many respects it is not a fair critique when applied to Aristotle himself: while Aristotle (like Maimonides) views virtue as central to human happiness, he views virtue as intrinsically good rather than justified on account of its rewards. As Julia Annas has argued, when Aristotle speaks of acting virtuously "for the sake of the fine," this is akin to Kant's notion of performing duty for the sake of duty—the point is that one should not be virtuous for the sake of an external reward.[116] On the other hand, Simḥah Zissel may be correct to think of Aristotelian virtues as somewhat more self-regarding; Aristotle may not give sufficient attention to the other-regarding virtues of "lovingkindness, justice, and righteousness," which are primary for Jeremiah. Notably, it is with reference to these very virtues, as Jeremiah described them, that Maimonides concludes his *Guide of the Perplexed*, a conclusion that may help to distinguish him from Aristotle by describing these other-regarding moral virtues as the culmination of the good life.[117] Simḥah Zissel pushes this emphasis further with reference to the Vilna Gaon, Eliyahu de Vidas's musar text *The Beginning of Wisdom*, and then Moses—the ultimate exemplar of a Jew willing to accept the punishment of being "erased" from the book of life rather than accept a seeming injustice.

Simḥah Zissel may have grounded his theory of virtuous action producing happiness in Aristotle's *Ethics*, but he sometimes seeks to distinguish his ethical vision as being more other-regarding and more deontological. While he may often seem to be a real hedonist, encouraging his students to pursue the greatest pleasures possible, he insists that they ultimately should not be motivated by the pursuit of pleasure. While he generally paints no conflict between happiness and duty, he sometimes insists on raising the possibility that they may conflict. While he wants people to care about saving their own souls, he wants them to care less about their own souls than about tending to the physical and spiritual needs of others. Tamar Ross has thus described Simḥah Zissel as a "semi-consequentialist," a label that is fitting for a thinker who tries to both emphasize the satisfactions of morality and to caution against them.

Salanter, by contrast, had fewer hesitations when preaching about the appealing consequences of morality and the fearful consequences of immorality. As Ross has suggested, Salanter was focused on outreach to the broad public, seeking to convince them to lead more morally and spiritually focused lives even if they lacked proper motivations. Simḥah Zissel, by contrast, focused on developing a small spiritual elite within a cloistered yeshiva environment, and it should not be surprising that he had a somewhat more idealistic emphasis on purity of motivation. Simḥah Zissel followed Salanter in seeking to harness the power of the "evil inclination," but he was even more relentless in his efforts to "repair" that inclination altogether.[118]

On the other hand, Simḥah Zissel tempered his idealism to a significant extent. For all of his hopes that his students would outgrow a concern with personal rewards and punishments, his writings do emphasize reward and punishment and often do focus on crude threats of otherworldly recompense. As I have indicated, these were the sorts of threats that leaders of the Haskalah disavowed. Simḥah Zissel would have viewed the Haskalah as far too naive about human nature: though he dreamed of transforming the human being entirely, Simḥah Zissel also realized that human nature was "simply evil, all the time," and that the animalistic tendencies in human nature needed to be controlled by any means possible.

# 3

# Simḥah Zissel Among the Philosophers

At times, Simḥah Zissel described how he learned from the teachings of Aristotle and other non-Jewish philosophers, while at other times he distanced himself from their teachings. Notably, he did not embrace the hostility of many traditionalist rabbis toward the Greek philosophical tradition, a view that had much support in his own family. A few generations earlier, Simḥah Zissel's distant relative Jacob Emden had castigated philosophers as selfish and licentious atheists who were "abhorrent unto God." In Emden's view, Jewish interest in philosophy had repeatedly provoked divine fury, leading to tragedies such as the destruction of the Second Temple, the expulsion of the Jews from Spain, and the Chmielnicki Massacre of the seventeenth century, during which approximately 100,000 Jews were murdered.[1] Lithuanian traditionalists were not all so hostile toward philosophy, but they generally depicted it as allied with the sinister forces of the Haskalah. Within the Musar movement, Israel Salanter's opposition to the pursuit of foreign wisdom was shared by his students—with the exception of Simḥah Zissel.[2]

Simḥah Zissel criticized Aristotle, Plato, and their fellow philosophers, but he was engaged with them to a striking degree—often mentioning "the philosophers" in his writings, and often approving of their insights. While some of his ideas about the philosophers probably came from simplified accounts of their thought, he also distinguished himself by reading some primary philosophical sources. We know that he read Aristotle's *Nicomachean Ethics* in its standard Hebrew translation, as he quotes from that translation and from the commentary on it by the Haskalah intellectual Isaac Satanow.[3] His students reported that, "had he not owned Aristotle's *Ethics*, he would have been prepared to pay the price of a hundred rubles for it."[4]

Simḥah Zissel's students claimed that their teacher in fact immersed himself in non-Jewish philosophy every evening—while taking care not to violate the Talmud's restrictions on the study of philosophy. The Talmud, considering a query about when Jews might study "Greek wisdom," responds with the biblical admonition that "the Book of the Torah shall not depart from your mouth; but you shall meditate on it day and night" (Joshua 1:8)—"go and find a time that is neither day *nor* night, and learn Greek wisdom *then*" (BT Menaḥot 99b). Simḥah Zissel creatively sought to follow this stricture by leaving his studies of Greek philosophy for a time that was "neither day nor night." As Dov Katz reports:

> He immersed himself in books of philosophy. In addition to books of Hebrew philosophy, ancient Greek philosophy was found by his side: for example, the books of Aristotle, Plato, Socrates, and so on. But for all the great value that he saw in them, he would say that a non-Jewish scent came from them. These books were placed on the lowest shelf of his bookshelf, and he would reflect on them while he lay on his bed, after he was worn out from the study of Torah. Apparently, he saw this situation as "the time that was neither day nor night," during which it is permitted to study Greek wisdom. Once he obtained a rare book of philosophy translated into Hebrew, known as the work of Al-Ghazali, for which he paid a price of nine rubles. But despite all of his esteem for this book, he also read it only at night on his bed. The books of philosophy served to help him in his investigations into the forces of the human psyche and the methods for learning character traits, and he relied on them regularly in his musar lectures and articles. These books enriched his knowledge and his thoughts, and on account of this his friends called him "the Godly philosopher."[5]

It seems that Simḥah Zissel did study from non-Jewish philosophical books and at times made significant efforts to attain them, while also trying to hew to the letter of the law that might seem to prohibit their study altogether. The writings of Aristotle and Plato and the Muslim theologian Al-Ghazali had a "non-Jewish scent," and they clearly could not count as part of the Torah, but Simḥah Zissel thought that they contained "great value."

Simḥah Zissel seems to have shared the Haskalah's openness to learning from sources beyond the Torah; he especially shared the impulse of the Haskalah's favorite medieval thinker, Maimonides, to learn from non-Jewish philosophers, following Maimonides's dictum that one should "hear the truth from whoever says it." Israel Elyashev reported that Simḥah Zissel relied on Maimonides, in particular, when he spoke of the philosophers to his students in Grobin; he praised Plato, Elyashev recalled, as "one of the saints of the nations of the world whom the Sages of blessed memory and Maimonides exonerated with their words of praise."[6]

## "Mocking" the Philosophers

As we saw in the previous chapter, though, Simḥah Zissel sometimes sharply criticized the philosophers. He criticized them for valuing personal happiness over morality, and for underestimating the value of action and overestimating the value of thought. What caused them to err in these matters?

One of Simḥah Zissel's claims is that philosophers are, too often, insufficiently philosophical. In defending the idea that moral action is no less "spiritual" than thought, for example, he claims that the typical philosopher has failed to thoughtfully critique his own bias toward the "contemplative life": "he does not consider in depth in his thoughts what seems to him to be what he knows—because *surely* he knows it." Simḥah Zissel depicts such a philosopher as overconfident, failing to "delve deep and understand that he does not know."[7]

Of course, a philosopher in conversation with Simḥah Zissel could easily accuse Simḥah Zissel of the same vice, especially insofar as Simḥah Zissel's praise of the "active life" often appears to rest on the Torah's praise for action—and on Simḥah Zissel's assumption that the Torah is the epitome of rationality. Simḥah Zissel might seem especially overconfident as he asserts that the Torah has made its rational conclusions available to the entire Jewish people, including those who could not reach its conclusions on their own—such that "the lowest among the people of Israel mocks and triumphs over the greatest of philosophers."[8]

Thus, in Simḥah Zissel's view, ancient philosophers' insights are especially deficient because they did not have access to the Torah. Simḥah Zissel sometimes mentions this even when he praises the philosophers for their wisdom. In one discourse regarding the importance of introspection, he refers to Aristotle's insights on the matter—but then he immediately pivots and claims that philosophers such as Aristotle, lacking the Torah, surely lack psychological insight: "This summer the insight became clear to me that the philosophers did not know the faculties of the soul at all in comparison with the sages of the Torah. And, moreover, a simpleton like me knows more than them in this matter. Why? It is not on account of my paltry wisdom; rather, I know more than them because I have looked into our holy Torah."[9]

Having praised Aristotle, Simḥah Zissel seems to want to cover his tracks and display his traditionalist credentials. He perhaps is reassuring his students that he is not like the Maskilim who value Aristotle over divinely inspired Jewish sages. Simḥah Zissel is confident—overconfident, one might say—in God's guidance of the Jewish tradition, and so he is sure that its psychological insights must be deeper than those of Aristotle.

In showing the weakness of the philosophers' approach, Simḥah Zissel sometimes also points to ways in which philosophy may encourage arrogance and inappropriate self-love. He argues that philosophers' lack of humility is especially visible insofar as they "do not rest upon their predecessors" and instead act "as if each invented the matter." Rather than acknowledging the wisdom of the past, they learn that one should "not trust what your fathers have bequeathed you."[10] Simḥah Zissel sees rabbinic sages, by contrast, as trained to take a more humble posture, connecting their rational discoveries with a broader tradition:

> For every single thing that reason demands, they nonetheless learn it from Scripture, because this is the root and essence for them: that one should not rely upon oneself, but rather upon what is received. For the sages of the nations it is the opposite: their whole aim is to devise new messages and principles from out of their bellies, and to place their names upon them. This is just as *The Kuzari* wrote about Aristotle: that he stole from the wisdom books of Solomon of blessed memory and put his name upon them.[11]

Jewish sages are expected to derive insights through the use of reason, but they do so in the context of a tradition, showing how their insights follow from the Torah and taking little pride in their own originality. Simḥah Zissel sees philosophers, by contrast, as motivated by self-love and the desire for personal honor. They work independently of a tradition, and when they do learn from a tradition, they deny it and claim that their insights are in fact their own.

The myth that the insights of Aristotle were taken from the Jews without attribution is not actually found in Yehuda Ha-Levi's *The Kuzari*, as Simḥah Zissel claims, but it does appear in sources that Simḥah Zissel read, such as *Torat Ha-Olah*, a sixteenth-century work by Rabbi Moshe Isserles. As Isserles tells it,

> The whole essence of the wisdom of Aristotle was stolen from the wisdom of Solomon, peace be on him, for when Alexander of Macedon conquered Jerusalem, he gave his teacher Aristotle authority over the collection of Solomon's books. [Aristotle] wrote his name upon every good thing that he found in them. And he mixed some bad opinions in with them, such as the eternity of the world and his denial of Providence, to protect himself, so that people coming after him would not know that he had stolen the wisdom of the Jews. Or it is possible that he did not believe anything in the words of Solomon for which he did not find a definitive proof.[12]

This fanciful legend, which Simḥah Zissel appears to embrace, depicts Aristotle as exceedingly proud and exceedingly devious. It also reveals the exceeding pride of those who have transmitted the story, who were seemingly unable to believe that valuable works of philosophy might have emerged from non-Jewish thinkers. At the same time, it conveys a view that Aristotle's writings are of great value; hence the need for the story explaining the origins of such valuable wisdom. Isserles himself certainly held such a view, as he was an ardent defender of studying Greek philosophy so long as its heretical teachings were ignored.[13] Simḥah Zissel joined Isserles in esteeming the ancient Greek philosophical tradition in many respects but in condemning it for corrupting some of the essentials of Jewish wisdom. Alongside his criticisms regarding the value of happiness, the value of action, and the value of tradition, Simḥah Zissel joins Isserles in condemning the philosophers' denial of God's creation of the world and providential guidance.

In speaking of creation, Simḥah Zissel is especially concerned by the philosophers' disparagement of the Sabbath, the weekly testament to God's creation of the world. Not only do philosophers fail to acknowledge the idea of creation, but they ridicule the effort to commemorate creation through physical ritual activity. Here, Simḥah Zissel points to the irony that philosophers do not understand how the Sabbath allows for the flourishing of human reasoning; they therefore condemn a practice that cultivates the very qualities that they prize.[14]

When Simḥah Zissel criticizes the philosophers for their denial of divine providence, he notes their inability to understand "the purpose of creation."[15] Simḥah Zissel has a strong faith in God's purpose for the world, and he has strong faith that God's providential guidance will eventually guide the world toward its proper ends—including restoring the people of Israel to its land and rebuilding the Temple in Jerusalem. This was a hope that, in Simḥah Zissel's view, the philosophers surely could not understand. According to one of his students, Simḥah Zissel illustrated the philosophers' position through another fanciful medieval legend, this one about a meeting between Plato and the prophet Jeremiah. Plato could not understand why Jeremiah was crying over the destruction of the Temple. Simḥah Zissel explained that, above all, Jeremiah's tears expressed a longing for future redemption. "A matter like this," Simḥah Zissel said, "which a common Jew can understand easily, could not be understood even by a great sage of the nations of the world like Plato."[16]

## The Philosophers as Musar Masters

Simḥah Zissel seemingly loved to tell his students stories about how the Jewish tradition was more profound than anything the philosophers could come up with on their own. But he also seems to have dedicated himself to the study of "Greek wisdom," and he taught his students that there was, in fact, a good deal of truth in the traditions that stemmed from Plato and Aristotle. As we saw in the previous chapter, many aspects of Simḥah Zissel's conception of virtue are deeply Aristotelian, and periodically throughout his discussions of these and other themes, Simḥah Zissel notes that he is following the approach of Aristotle or, more generally, the approach of "the philosophers."

Thus, as we have seen, Simḥah Zissel followed Abraham Ibn Ezra in accepting the "secret of the philosophers" that the divine form is imprinted on the human soul. So too, he made it clear that he was following in the footsteps of Aristotle and other philosophers when he used a medical analogy to describe the repair of the human soul. When he spoke of a belief in reward and punishment as necessary for morality, he pointed to the philosophers' endorsement of this idea. When he considered the joy of engaging in virtuous behavior, he referred his students to Aristotle's *Ethics.* When he considered the importance of practical wisdom, he urged that they must "contemplate the words of Aristotle" that explained how wisdom must be developed though experience over time.[17]

The very idea that reason must direct all activity within the soul is, for Simḥah Zissel, itself one of the most important lessons that rabbinic scholars should learn from the philosophers. Throughout his writings, he applauds the philosophers for teaching how reason can direct the imagination, the appetites, and all of the other parts of the human soul.[18] One folktale that Simḥah Zissel recounts tells of a poor philosopher, given great wealth by a king, who discovers that his peace of mind is destroyed by his thoughts of what to do with the money. His reason overcomes his desires for wealth, and he promptly returns the money to the king. Simḥah Zissel, considering his personal efforts to reduce his own attachments to possessions, admits that he is no match for the philosopher who can detect such agitation in his soul and act decisively to restore equanimity.[19] And Simḥah Zissel admires the training required to be a philosopher, training that, he notes, is the same as what Maimonides required for students of Torah: "they devoted their souls to conquer their appetites," especially their self-indulgent desires for sexual intercourse and sleep.[20]

Simḥah Zissel describes this philosophic regimen as a path of musar. He depicts Aristotle as a teacher in the musar tradition—as Alexander of Macedon's "special teacher for musar." Other philosophers who were true sages must have also been masters of musar, he argues: "it is not possible to be called a sage without musar; therefore, all the philosophers immersed themselves in musar."[21] And in a letter to his colleague Eliezer Gordon, urging Gordon to give more prominence to musar at his yeshiva, Simḥah Zissel pointed out to Gordon that "it was not for nothing that the philosophers exerted themselves in 'wisdom and musar'—though they did not have the Torah, they stuck to their conviction that musar was the great gateway to wisdom, and their souls longed for wisdom." Simḥah Zissel goes on to suggest that, therefore, Jews who possess a tradition deeply concerned with musar should certainly be committed to it. The implication here is that many Jewish leaders (like Gordon) were not sufficiently committed to musar and were, in key respects, inferior to the philosophers.[22]

In another passage, Simḥah Zissel concludes that non-Jewish communities have outdone Jewish communities in taking the philosophers' musar teachings seriously. He notes the failure of his fellow Jews to internalize the Mishnah's teaching that the human being has the most humble of origins, "born from a putrid drop" of semen—"this awareness doesn't automatically help him regarding himself, unless he becomes habituated to it in action, as Aristotle, the sage of the nations, also wrote."[23] Other nations, Simḥah Zissel indicates, took Aristotle's focus on habituation much more seriously: "the rest of the enlightened nations are habituated to considering themselves [in this way], and inevitably they are accustomed to honor people, since because of this they are accustomed to moral decency [*derekh eretz*]."[24] Such praise for Aristotle and the non-Jews who took his wisdom seriously, coupled with critique of his own nation, may reflect Simḥah Zissel's own efforts to adopt a humble posture; it may, of course, also reflect an effort to motivate his students to improve their efforts to take musar seriously.

As I pointed out in chapter 1, Simḥah Zissel was particularly aggrieved that his fellow Russian Jews were insufficiently dedicated to "moral decency" and "the civilizing of the world." By contrast, he praised those German Jews whose general education had helped them to appreciate "the work of musar," which was key to "moral decency as is known among the philosophers."[25] Such philosophers, he implies, engaged in musar as part of their interest in "civilizing" the societies in which they lived.

In other passages as well, Simḥah Zissel praised philosophers for their social concern, often reminding his students of the Aristotelian (and Maimonidean) insistence that the human being is a "political animal." In such passages, Simḥah Zissel rejects the characterization that we have seen of philosophers as contemplatives who reject human action; rather, he depicts philosophers as understanding how civilization is sustained through social and economic cooperation. Thus, for instance, in a discussion of how "all philosophers describe the human being as political," he notes that "one who works the earth is concerned to prepare bread for people, and this is a preparation for himself [as well], since he will profit from this, and will come to have other human needs (for clothing, etc.) fulfilled. So too the merchant travels to far-off places to prepare clothing for people, and this is a preparation for himself. So too with all of the goods of the world."[26]

Though there is also Talmudic precedent for this sort of meditation on political economy, Simḥah Zissel's discussions along these lines show his appreciation for the philosophers—perhaps even for modern philosophers such as Adam Smith whose ideas are echoed here. Though at times he derided the non-Jewish philosophical tradition for its lack of moral concern and for "stealing" its best insights from the Jews, he also admitted that the philosophers had much wisdom to offer, including insight about "civilizing the world" and sustaining moral societies.

## Reborn Like a Philosopher

We have seen how Simḥah Zissel criticized the philosophers' principle that one should "not trust what your fathers have bequeathed you." But in other passages he admires the philosophical model of questioning inherited assumptions. In one discourse, for example, Simḥah Zissel expresses his desire to emulate how "the philosophers, when they began to learn with their students, began by uprooting their prior knowledge, so that it was as if they were born on that day." This, he sees, is precisely what God demanded of the Jews at Sinai—that they overcome their prior, false assumptions and dedicate themselves to God—and this is what God continues to demand of Jews every day. Our childhood assumptions, Simḥah Zissel notes, are generally foolish; we need to approach them with skepticism and challenge our assumptions.[27]

Unsurprisingly, though, Simḥah Zissel's encouragement of skepticism only went so far. His Talmud Torah, after all, seems to have been more distinguished by its dogmatism than by its skepticism, such that students who were too suspicious of orthodox principles were asked to leave the school. Simḥah Zissel's writings likewise reveal no willingness to challenge childhood assumptions about the veracity and perfect rationality of the Torah; they suggest no reason to doubt "the true knowledge received from Sinai in our holy Torah, written and oral."[28] Philosophic skepticism is not to be directed against the Torah, given its perfection; it is, rather, to be directed against the alternatives to the Torah, which are imperfect. Challenging these alternatives will, then, increase commitment to the Torah, "uprooting" our tendencies to stray from its ideals and doctrines, so that we can be "reborn" and reexperience the Torah's goodness anew.

Still, Simḥah Zissel admits that human knowledge of the Torah is never complete; though the Torah that God revealed is perfect, in Simḥah Zissel's view, no human has a perfect grasp of it. One must, therefore, always seek to learn more and to challenge one's assumptions about what one knows. Socrates, with his stress on epistemic humility, serves as one of Simḥah Zissel's inspirations:

> It is an amazing thing that the philosopher Socrates said: "There are people who need to [claim to] know everything that is asked of them, for without this one is not a wise man. But I do not say this; [rather,] all of my wisdom is that I know that I do not know." These are the words of the sage, Socrates. Accordingly, we have said, this is the reason that the sages in the Talmud are always called "the disciples of the sages" [*talmidei ḥakhamim*] . . . for all of their days, they are like disciples who are learning.[29]

Simḥah Zissel sees Socrates's tendency to doubt his own wisdom reflected in the Talmudic model of rabbis who doubt their wisdom and always seek to learn more. The ideal posture of the rabbi is not to claim wisdom, but to love wisdom—that is, to be like a "philosopher"—and to seek wisdom wherever it may be found:

> We have said that the essence of wisdom is to know that one is not wise, but rather that one loves wisdom, and who is this? The one who learns from every human being—this is a sign of his love of wisdom, and therefore [Mishnah Avot teaches]: "Who is wise? The one who learns from every human being" (4:1). . . . [On the other hand], he who is conceited no doubt says that he is a sage who knows everything. But Socrates said: he who says, "I know everything"—this is a sign that he knows nothing.[30]

Socrates is, here, an exemplar of the kind of wise man envisioned by the Mishnah, and he is Simḥah Zissel's ally in the war against conceit.

Recognizing the limits of one's wisdom, from Simḥah Zissel's perspective, means refusing to impose one's assumptions on the world, resisting the urge to see what one wants to see, but instead approaching the world with clarity of vision—like a philosopher. In one discourse he stresses to his students that, at times, they should strive after this ideal of the philosopher *rather* than the conventional Jewish ideals of the "sage" (*ḥakham*), the "righteous person" (*tzaddik*), or "pious person" (*ḥasid*). As he explains:

> Why do I say "a philosopher" rather than "a sage" or "a righteous person" or "a pious person"? I have intended this: that the way of the world is to turn things around in accordance with their wills. If it was possible to turn things around such that two times two were three—then, certainly, they would do so for the needs of their appetites. But this is not possible, for experience denies this. But anything in this world of which it is possible to deny the existence, they surely do so. The things that the philosophers acknowledge, seeing through their reason, a person is not able to deny these. By contrast, with what we have received which is beyond reason, surely the will is able to turn dark to light, and so on, for the sake of the appetite. But with God's help, we will clearly demonstrate that most of the Torah is based on natural human reason, and from such [reason] we can understand the depth of that which goes beyond human reason and is only known from being received at

> Sinai. And therefore I say that this is the language which a person cannot contradict, for it is good.[31]

Simḥah Zissel does want his students to be pious, righteous sages; but he stresses that they should be as dedicated to reason as ideal philosophers would be. Most people prefer to bend the truth to their desires, but this is not the path of the Torah, which Simḥah Zissel sees as firmly grounded in rationality (even when it goes beyond what "human reason" can comprehend). The ideal path that students of Torah must walk must be characterized by mental clarity and rationality—the path of the philosopher.

## The "Clear View of What Is Good"

Overcoming the tendency to see the world as one wants to see it, and learning to see the world clearly and objectively, especially requires the virtue of equanimity—what Simḥah Zissel describes in Hebrew as *menuḥat ha-nefesh* ("restfulness of the soul") or *yishuv ha-da'at* ("a settled state of mind"). The virtue of equanimity is not a central virtue in traditional musar literature, though it has a place in the writings of Maimonides, among some figures in the Hasidic movement, and among Haskalah leaders, including Menaḥem Mendel Lefin.[32] Israel Salanter's writings also touch on ideals of mental clarity.[33] But the virtue of equanimity becomes absolutely central in Simḥah Zissel's writings, where it is praised as "the crown of the virtues" and as a state of *shalom* (peace, perfection), which is "the purpose of all creation."[34]

Equanimity is a state in which one's desires and emotions are controlled by reason so that one can see the world as it really is. The opposite of equanimity is "distraction of the soul" (*pezur ha-nefesh*), which Simḥah Zissel characterizes as a state of being focused on one's own desires rather than focusing on God's desires. Those who are driven by their desires for pleasure, wealth, and honor are "like the troubled sea (Isaiah 57:20)—always raging and tempestuous." Their moral vision is blurred, in contrast to the righteous, whose thought is as clear as the "pure olive oil" that Israel was commanded to use to kindle the lamp in the ancient Tabernacle (Ex. 27:20). Just as one must use clear oil for such a lamp, so too "one should light reason with a clear light, keeping the grit of this world out of reason insofar as this is possible."[35]

The grit of this world (*afruri'ut olam ha-zeh*) is what Simḥah Zissel elsewhere calls "matter" (*ḥomer*) or "materiality" (*gashmiut*). As we have seen, matter naturally inhibits reason, but human beings can seek to "repair" their material urges so that they do not interfere with one's clarity of vision: "In truth, real contemplation is simply when a person succeeds at stripping away materiality, for without doing this, the nuisance of materiality and his appetites interfere with his clear view of what is good. Thus, the entire goal of contemplation is to succeed at stripping away materiality; from this, he will have the understanding to distinguish between good and evil. The matter of musar and the matter of prayer revolve around this."[36] The work of musar, and especially prayer, is fundamentally directed at achieving a state of equanimity allowing a person to see clearly and objectively. We usually see through our own eyes, which are colored by our subjective, material appetites. The ideal is to do away with such material obstructions and to achieve an objective view, so that one can "distinguish between good and evil" and, as Simḥah Zissel goes on to indicate, move closer to "the truth," "to God."[37] Whereas most people make judgments according to their own deep-seated biases, he notes elsewhere, God judges with perfect reason, "according to what is." The ideal form of vision is seeing like God sees: calmly, objectively, without bias.[38]

Reaching such a state of perfect objectivity would seem to be impossible for a human being, because humans are always bound by their subjective, material state to a certain degree; as Maimonides taught, even Moses could not see God perfectly, because of his embodied state. But in Simḥah Zissel's view, significant equanimity can still be achieved if one "slowly, slowly" pursues it. Thus, when he tells of the legendary philosopher (described above) who calmed his troubled heart, Simḥah Zissel notes that the philosopher's ideal of equanimity is possible. The Torah also commands the cultivation of equanimity, he points out, in its injunction to "circumcise the foreskin of your heart" (Deut. 10:16). "The foreskin is confusion [*bilbul*]" Simḥah Zissel writes, "and we are obligated to 'circumcise' it, using all possible stratagems."[39] Prayer, meditation, and the observance of the Sabbath are among the practices that he believes are helpful for cultivating equanimity; so are the disciplines of introspection and self-control favored by the philosophers. Achieving equanimity, after all, was at the heart of the work of "the philosophers"—and it is foundational to "the path of the Torah."[40]

Equanimity is central to the aims of the Torah, and Simḥah Zissel also sees it as essential for the study of the Torah. The Torah cannot be understood by a person who does not take the time or have the presence of mind to approach it through the lens of reason: "This is a common vice which opposes the entire Torah, which is only built upon equanimity. . . . Hastiness and anxiousness distance him from equanimity, and because he is without equanimity, he is distanced from the whole Torah—as our sages said, 'if you lack this, you lack everything' (BT Nedarim 41a). And he is distanced, God forbid, from the Holy Blessed One, and not only from the Holy Blessed One, but from every holy thing."[41] Without a settled mind, in this view, one cannot hear and properly interpret God's teaching.

But, for Simḥah Zissel, equanimity is not just "a scholar's virtue," which is how Don Seeman describes its function in the writings of Maimonides.[42] It is the foundation of practical reason as well as theoretical reason, action as well as contemplation. For Simḥah Zissel, equanimity is foundational for the central moral virtues of love, kindness, and the compassionate "sharing the burden of one's fellow." Seeing and responding to the suffering of the world requires clarity of mind and the repair of the selfish, material appetites that obscure one's vision. Thus "it is not possible to love one's fellow as oneself," Simḥah Zissel writes, "until one has removed all of the material impurities from one's soul, [so that] it will be pure, without any of the grit of materiality [*afruri'ut ha-ḥomer*] mixed in."[43] Noah, as one exemplary "man of equanimity," was able to set aside his own appetites and instead care for the sinful people of his generation (seeking their repentance) and, then, for the animals on his ark. "Behold, how anxious he was" to care for them, Simḥah Zissel writes, "for he habituated himself to the trait of equanimity, more than sufficiently."[44]

Notably, Noah's equanimity leads to anxiety: while equanimity requires doing away with anxieties felt for the wrong reasons, it generates anxieties felt for the right reasons. Having clarity of mind, for Noah, meant not being anxious about whether his own appetites would be fulfilled, but instead being anxious about the more significant needs in the world.

Equanimity, then, is not a state of being untroubled. Simḥah Zissel did not want his students to be free from concerns; he wanted them, rather, to have the tranquility of mind to see just how concerned they should be about a world filled with sin and suffering. Thus he decries those who seek to "walk with serenity" or "live a life of rest" in a world that requires their concern.[45] A state of spiritual tranquility must instead lead to spiritual wakefulness: the state of equanimity is a sort of "restfulness within the soul," Simḥah Zissel explains, which in fact demands wakefulness "from the sleep of foolishness."[46] Equanimity is anything but indulgent; it is a state of clear-mindedness that allows for little rest and that fosters concern for the world. Reason demands no less, and so the Torah demands no less.

## The Rationality of the Torah

A soul characterized by equanimity, where reason reigns supreme over the other faculties, seems to have ready access to hearing God's instruction. Does Simḥah Zissel then see revelation as simply a natural process whereby a prophet with great equanimity can rationally uncover God's teachings? Can all of the content of the Torah be described in rational terms?

Simḥah Zissel does generally describe the Torah as fundamentally rational. Though he describes the Torah and the process of revelation as beyond human comprehension in some respects, his emphasis is more often on the ways in which "most of the Torah is based on natural human reason," as he puts it.[47] Though God transcends the limits of human reason, reason is fundamentally divine, and the vast majority of what God asks of human beings and of the Jewish people is rationally comprehensible.

As we have seen, reason allows human beings some level of insight into the divine ideal of moral excellence, and reason indicates the path by which divine ideals may be actualized in the world. This is precisely what Simḥah Zissel sees the Torah as doing: actualizing divine ideals of moral excellence in the world, using divine reason to apply ideals to reality. For Simḥah Zissel, the Torah translates abstract rationality into terms that can be understood by concrete human beings. Embellishing one Talmudic story about a conversation between God and the angels, Simḥah Zissel imagines the angels objecting that a Torah of "reason in its simplicity" (or "disembodied reason") could not be appropriate for "composite," embodied human beings. God responds that "the commandments are behaviors, tools for the soul, which are composite." The commandments of the Torah are the product of translating abstract rationality into concrete forms that can be practiced by embodied human beings. The Torah is reason that is made accessible for humanity.[48]

Given this theory, Simḥah Zissel is confident that the commandments recorded in the Torah must be rational—building on the Torah's own confidence that its rationality can be recognized by the nations of the world. The book of Deuteronomy offers the commandment to "guard [the commandments] and do them, for this shows your wisdom and understanding in the eyes of the nations, as they will hear all of these statutes and they will say, 'Surely this great nation is a wise and understanding people'" (Deut. 4:6). While Jews have often interpreted "statutes" (*ḥukkim*) to refer to inexplicable commandments (as opposed to "ordinances," *mishpatim*, which are clearly rational),

Simḥah Zissel notices that this verse claims that the nations will see even the "statutes" as containing great wisdom:

> Indeed, truly, the way of Torah is that it is "most understandable" (Deut. 27:8), for scripture obligates the man of Israel to grow in wisdom and understanding, to contemplate the Torah with reason and understanding, in a manner that he can also understand through reason, to see that the Torah offers the human being a straight path by which he can live a life of pleasure and satisfaction—not simply through his future reward, but the path in and of itself being a "path of pleasantness" (Prov. 3:17). It is only before one understands its depths that it will seem like a yoke upon the necks of Israel, but while the beginning is suffering the end is very, very pleasant—not simply with the wondrous reward but in and of itself. This is the basic meaning of scripture: "guard them" (Deut. 4:6)—meaning, study using reason, in such a manner that also the doing ("do them") will be in a manner which the other nations will understand as showing wisdom and understanding. And they will necessarily understand that [even] the "statutes" [not immediately apparent to reason] have wisdom and understanding as their foundation . . . And therefore the Torah speaks in the following verses of the nation "who has righteous statutes and ordinances" (Deut. 4:8)—it is expressed like this because the "statutes" are placed in the same level as the ordinances in straightening human character.[49]

In this model, some of the commandments of the Torah may well seem irrational at first glance. They may seem to offer suffering and little reward, so that taking them on may feel like taking on a burden. But if one studies the commandments, using one's reason, one may come to understand their intrinsic rewards and how they may help in "straightening human character"—how, as Simḥah Zissel puts it elsewhere, "the virtues are the reason for the observance of the whole Torah."[50] When the commandments are seen in this way, Simḥah Zissel contends, their goodness will be apparent to all the nations of the world.

Simḥah Zissel is here arguing against those who would contend that it would be ideal to perform the commandments of the Torah in a spirit of submission to God's unfathomable will. He insists, on the contrary, that one must seek to find the rationality of the commandments insofar as this is possible. Simḥah Zissel takes his cue from Maimonides, as he explains how he seeks to bring Maimonides' approach to his students at the Talmud Torah of Grobin:

> In the responsa of Maimonides of blessed memory, I have found a statement upon which [our] House of Study can rely. He wrote as follows: "With all of our strength we must endeavor to bring matters of the Torah close to reason, though that which we are not able to bring close to reason we may place in the category of a 'miracle' or a 'statute.' But I have seen Torah-observant people whose entire goal is to explain all matters of Torah, whether past or future, as 'miraculous.' Their intent is that all should be foreign to reason"—and [Maimonides] mocks them, and his opinion is that this is not so. Anyone who knows the approach of [our] House of Study, surely he will bring matters of the Torah close to reason insofar as this is possible.[51]

In the widespread view that Maimonides mocked, God's commandments were seen as inaccessible to human reason; such a view continued to be widespread in the traditionalist Lithuanian society within which Simḥah Zissel lived, including among other figures in the Musar movement.[52] Maimonides saw some commandments as inaccessible to ordinary human reason, but he insisted that God wanted the people of Israel to think critically about the purposes of the commandments and to perform them with an understanding of those purposes. Simḥah Zissel seeks to follow in this tradition of Maimonidean rationalism.

When one understands the commandments, in this model, one can perform them willingly and joyfully, rather than with the submissiveness of an uncomprehending slave. Thus the Talmudic sage Hillel explained to one potential convert that the entire Torah aims at an ideal of loving one's fellow as oneself—and urged him to go and study further. Simḥah Zissel sees Hillel as exemplifying a rationalist stance, teaching that all of the Torah's commandments can contribute toward a rational goal, while emphasizing that one must study—applying one's reason—to understand how indeed the commandments contribute toward this goal. Hillel's teaching, as Simḥah Zissel sees it, is that "the commands of the Blessed Lord are not 'work'—for after deep examination [it becomes clear that] they are for man's welfare, and a person of reason [*ha-maskil*] should choose for himself what is good after examination, not what seems good without much examination. And in this he teaches him the simple way to keep all of the details [of the Torah], for they are all good for a person, and a person should receive the good willingly, joyfully, and open-heartedly."[53] The model here accords with what we saw in chapter 2: that Simḥah Zissel sees God as wanting people to be autonomous, understanding the reasons for their behavior, rather than acting without understanding. Our powers of reason must be utilized in seeking to understand the goodness of the Torah in general and of all of its particular details.[54]

Simḥah Zissel's rationalism, of course, following the lead of Maimonides and other traditional thinkers, begins with his assumption that the Torah is divine. Given this premise, he finds ways to understand the Torah as a rational document, teaching rational truths and commanding rational behaviors, but he does not allow reason to challenge the premise. To the degree that he can show the rationality of the Torah's commandments and of the truths it teaches, his faith in the divinity of the Torah is then fortified.

At times, Simḥah Zissel takes some of these truths for granted. He sees it as quite obvious that God exists, is the creator of the universe, and guides all that happens in the world—after all, Simḥah Zissel asserts (based on tradition), even animals know such things.[55] He does, however, admit that such principles need to be contemplated deeply and understood rationally: "self-evident things [*mefursamot*] which do not require proof nonetheless need contemplation, for one who does not contemplate such things will not understand with full understanding, but will only speak based on faith."[56]

Some of Simḥah Zissel's attempts to move beyond simple faith, and to rationally prove the truth of the Torah, fall quite flat. He appeals, for example, to the widespread acknowledgment of the Torah's historicity and divinity. He points to the continued existence of locations referred to in the Torah (the country of Egypt, the land of Israel, the Temple Mount, etc.), and he observes how various principles and institutions of the Torah (such as the observance of the Sabbath) are acknowledged as divine by other nations.[57] In discussions such as these, Simḥah Zissel sounds more credulous than rational, seeking to bolster his faith in the Torah's divinity rather than applying deep "contemplation."

Still, Simḥah Zissel's commitment to rationality within the bounds of orthodoxy is genuinely felt, and he defends it against those who value faith above reason. He insists that valid faith must rest on rational principles—it must be "the faith of reason" (*emunat ha-sekhel*), he says—and he critiques those whose beliefs are not subjected to critical scrutiny. Unfortunately, he notes, even the most rational people are easily duped into adopting irrational beliefs:

> The faith of the "simpleton [who] will believe anything" (Prov. 14:15) and the faith of reason are two [different] things. And, moreover, the faith of the simpleton is stronger within the human being himself—even in the person who possesses the greatest reason. . . . The faith of many people comes without rational contemplation, but is just faith, and this is the faith of the simpleton mentioned above, which has no foundation or endurance. We can understand its path from this and we can understand how much a person needs to bring his faith close to reason, so that it can settle in the human heart as an enduring premise.[58]

The role that reason plays in Simḥah Zissel's theological vision is especially clear in his reading of the Talmudic story of "Akhnai's Oven," a story that records a debate between Rabbi Eliezer and the Tannaitic sages about the purity of an oven. The Talmudic story is as follows:

> On that day, Rabbi Eliezer brought forward every imaginable argument, but [the sages] did not accept any of them. Finally he said to them, "If the *halakhah* agrees with me, let this carob tree prove it!" The carob tree was uprooted [and moved] 100 yards away from its place. (Others say: 400 yards.) They said to him: "No proof can be brought from a carob tree." Again, he said to them: "If the *halakhah* agrees with me, let the stream of water prove it!" The stream of water flowed backward. They said to him: no proof can be brought from a stream of water. Again he said, "If the *halakhah* agrees with me, let the walls of the house of study prove it!" The walls inclined to fall. . . . Again he said, "If the *halakhah* agrees with me, let it be proved from heaven!" A heavenly voice cried out, "What do you have against Rabbi Eliezer? The *halakhah* always agrees with him." But Rabbi Joshua stood up and exclaimed: "It is not in heaven" (Deut. 30:12). What does it mean, "It is not in heaven"? Rabbi Jeremiah said, "We pay no attention to a heavenly voice, since long ago the Torah was given at Mt. Sinai, and you have already written in the Torah: "After the majority must one incline" (Ex. 23:2).[59]

The story need not be read as showing how reason trumps faith; it could alternatively show that the power of the group, or of particular authorities, should trump the reason of the individual. But Simḥah Zissel, writing to his colleagues and students, interprets the story as follows:

> See now, my brothers, how great the Tannaitic sages were in walking down the path of those who had the strength of their reason. What appeared to them as being from the Torah was their foundation, and they did not look upon anything that would move them from their strong understanding. Let us imagine for ourselves: if there was one who said to us in a dispute about practical *halakhah,* let witnesses be heard and they will show that I am right as I argue, and the river was going from east to west, [and he said,] "If I am right it will change its course from west to east," and immediately the river turned, everyone would clap his hands and say, "Yes, yes, he is truly, truly right." But Rabbi Eliezer and the sages were arguing, and the river turned, and this matter did not impact them at all, as they said, "One does not bring proof from this." And not only this, but if a heavenly voice said, "He is right," surely everyone would become mute with fear and dread, and they would agree that the *halakhah* is like him. But these [Tannaitic sages] had strength of reason, and Rabbi Joshua stood up and said that we do not pay attention to heavenly voices. . . . Those who understand are astonished to see someone possess such strength of reason, which is truly, truly wondrous. All is from this foundation: that a person needs to possess strength of reason. . . . Contemplate how far we are from having this courage!

In Simḥah Zissel's interpretation, Rabbi Joshua and his colleagues display an exceptional commitment to the rational teaching of the Torah, and they refused to be swayed by miracles. Simḥah Zissel goes on to note that, following Rabbi Nissim Gerondi, he views these miracles as tests from God. Just as Israel should not abandon its commitment to reason and listen to false prophets sent by God to test them (Deut. 13:4), so too Israel should not abandon its commitment to reason and be swayed by heavenly voices sent by God to test them.[60]

## Rational Prophets and Rational Rabbis

Authentic prophecy, in Simḥah Zissel's view, rests on reason. Following Maimonides, he sees the great prophets of Israel's past as qualified to be prophets precisely because reason ruled over the other faculties of their souls and gave them great intellectual and moral virtue. Simḥah Zissel cites Maimonides in teaching that "the different levels of prophecy are all according to one's character traits," and he sees Moses as the greatest of prophets because of Moses's unprecedented humility, which indicates his overall moral excellence.[61] Simḥah Zissel also describes the whole people of Israel's access to divine revelation in such terms, as he notes that Israel merited God's attention only "because of the divine virtues found among them."[62] Israel does not seem to have a monopoly on high levels of virtue, though, and their uniqueness seems to be endangered by their moral laxity.[63]

It seems possible for any human being, not just Jews, to apprehend God to a significant extent. As we have seen, Simḥah Zissel endorses what he calls the "secret of the philosophers": that anyone created in the image of God "who looks upon his soul will, from its image, understand God."[64] One can know God by developing the clarity of vision to see and implement the ideals of moral perfection imprinted on the human soul. These are the ideals demanded by reason and, accordingly, accessible to all human beings. On the other hand, Simḥah Zissel often focuses his attention on Israel's unique relationship to God, indicating that Israel is particularly well primed to develop "the faith of reason," the virtues, and the ability to hear God's voice:

> A secret has been revealed to us, that the spirit of prophecy is buried within the heart of the Jewish human being; the conscience of faith is planted within, for it has a truly deep root. "Every single day a heavenly voice goes forth from Mount Ḥorev" (Mishnah Avot 6)—and not [only] on Mount Ḥorev, but in my heart and in the heart of every Jew, a heavenly voice goes forth from the *faith* of Mount Ḥorev. But "I am asleep, while my heart is awake" (Song of Songs 8:2)—meaning that the depths of the heart roar for the truth like the sea roars, but because I am asleep I cannot hear the wakefulness of the heart and its cries, the pangs of conscience, also in matters of faith. And therefore when they wake up [even] a little from their sleep, the heavenly voices of their hearts are heard, and this is the actual prophecy

> [*ha-nevu'ah mammash*] which is placed in the human heart. . . . This, for me, is actually [*mammash*] the gates of prophecy being opened up in this orphaned generation.[65]

In this passage, Simḥah Zissel is dreaming of the religious reawakening of his brethren; even those "orphaned" Jews who have turned away from the Torah, he suggests, have the potential to open up their ears to God's continuing revelation. God's revelation appears to be constant and always available to members of the people of Israel who open their hearts to God's message.

Simḥah Zissel here describes himself as revealing a "secret": that prophecy is possible in the modern era. In deference to the Talmud's teaching that prophecy ceased after the deaths of the final prophets of the Hebrew Bible—Haggai, Zechariah, and Malachi—later Jewish sources have generally cautioned against speaking of actual prophecy as an ongoing possibility. Israel Salanter, however, was one of the daring modern rabbis who did suggest that contemporary prophecy for Israel would be "possible, in accordance with the greatness of the exertion" were it not for the difficulties imposed on them in exile.[66] Simḥah Zissel seems to have had a similar hope for the renewal of "actual prophecy." Despite his regular reminders that human moral excellence is extremely hard to achieve, Simḥah Zissel proves himself to be extremely idealistic about human potential as he imagines the reemergence of true prophets among the Jewish people.

Simḥah Zissel would appear to have viewed the work of musar as key to unlocking the gates of prophecy, and he may have imagined that a musar master like himself could be a potential prophet. Indeed, he recalls how, when he was a young man living in Zagare, "immersing [himself] heavily in musar," Salanter suspected him of aspiring to prophecy. Salanter came to visit, Simḥah Zissel recounts, and "he worried lest I deceive myself and ascribe great things and wonders to myself, God forbid. Therefore he joked with me and asked me if I had received a vision of Elijah." Salanter was, apparently, cautioning against the haughtiness of aspiring to actual prophecy.[67]

But, Simḥah Zissel recalls, Salanter then proceeded to teach him an astounding lesson: that even if he could not become an actual prophet, he should remember that the responsibility of the rabbinic judge is in many ways akin to the task of the prophet. God tasks rabbis with interpreting God's will; thus, like prophets, they can develop God's Torah in every generation. But rabbis are only qualified to do this work if they submit to reason and achieve the incredible moral clarity characteristic of prophets. As Simḥah Zissel writes, recalling what he learned from his teacher:

> I heard from him something which he told me privately, and no other person heard it, and I was very frightened, for something like this had not been heard, and I had never seen this in any book. . . . He said: once it is known that the Torah is not determined in heaven, but rather that it is given over to the sages of each generation, dwellers on earth, who set the times for festivals and who judge divorce cases and who rule on capital crimes, all in accordance with how it seems to the court here on earth, and in accord with whose rulings practical law is determined in heaven, and yet a human judge can only rely on what his eyes can see (BT Sanhedrin 6b)—given this, surely, a judge first needs to perfect his character traits, so that he will not be biased. Then the judge will only rely on what his eyes can see—but he will have eyes that can see. On the other hand, if he does not perfect his character traits, then he is not fit to be a judge. Even if on one occasion he [only] aims at the truth, his Torah is not Torah at all. The Torah is not determined in heaven, as it is written: "It is not in heaven" (Deut. 30:12). . . . And this is what the sages taught: if a rabbi is like one of the angels of the Lord of Hosts, one should seek Torah from his mouth; but if he is not, then one should not seek it" (BT Ḥagigah 15b). . . . May the Merciful One have mercy upon us, that we may have a portion in the Torah of the Blessed One, that we may prepare ourselves through the character traits which are necessary for acquiring Torah—then one's Torah may be Torah, and one may have a portion in the Torah.[68]

In this passage, which Simḥah Zissel later describes as his own expansion on Salanter's insight, there is a sense that most rabbinic interpretations of Torah are, in fact, not true Torah. The moral vision of most rabbis is unclear, clouded by moral vices and biases, and so their rulings do not truly reflect God's will. As we saw above, Simḥah Zissel imagined that even the Tannaitic rabbis whom he considers to be spiritual giants made incorrect rulings when they failed to rely on reason alone; all the more so, then, ordinary contemporary rabbis would seem to be guilty of issuing incorrect rulings, as they would seem to easily fail the test of "being like angels." It is little wonder, given this sort of teaching, that the Musar movement was unpopular with many contemporary rabbis: Musar movement leaders such as Simḥah Zissel were suggesting that those who did not fully dedicate themselves to musar, whose vision remained clouded by moral vices and irrationality, were probably guilty of misleading the people of Israel.

The true rabbi, on the other hand, would seem to be much like a prophet. It is easy to see how this sort of teaching could evolve into the doctrine of *da'at Torat*, "*the* Torah understanding," an authoritarian doctrine developed by a number of twentieth-century rabbis—including a student of the Kelm Talmud Torah, Eliyahu Eliezer Dessler (1892–1953), who was the son of one of Simḥah Zissel's closest disciples. The doctrine of *da'at Torah*, as Dessler described it, is that all Jews must submit to *the* understanding of the Torah promulgated by the exceptionally great rabbis of their generation, rabbis distinguished by their intellectual and moral perfection.[69] As Dessler put it,

> Our Rabbis have told us to listen to the words of the Sages "even if they tell us that right is left," and not to say, God forbid, that they must be wrong because little I "can see their mistake with my own eyes." My seeing is null and void and utterly valueless compared with the clarity of their intellect and the divine aid they receive. . . . It is very likely that what [members of an inferior court] think they "can see with their own eyes" is merely imagination and illusion. This is the Torah view [*da'at torah*] concerning faith in the Sages.[70]

Dessler did view rabbis of exceptional character as essentially prophets, who must be obeyed even if their words seem to completely contradict commonsensical reason. In his discussion following this passage, Dessler goes on to support himself with a teaching from a figure whom he seems to have viewed as being on the level of such sages— "our master, that luminous personality, that genius in the understanding of human nature, Rabbi Simcha Zissel of sainted memory." The teaching in question is on the book of Esther: Simḥah Zissel applauds Israel's willingness to submit to the counsel of Mordechai, a prophet who had a great clarity of vision.[71] Dessler thus understands Simḥah Zissel to be teaching the doctrine of *da'at Torah*, urging his fellow Jews to submit themselves to the rabbinic authorities who had perfected their character traits, even if their teachings cannot be understood.

Dessler's use of Simḥah Zissel's teaching seems appropriate in some respects. Simḥah Zissel certainly believed that Israel should submit to the authority of its prophets, and he certainly wanted them to heed the authority of those rare rabbis who were masters of musar, distinguished by their excellent moral character. He generally thought that people with authority should be humble rather than authoritarian, but, as we saw in chapter 2, he thought that sometimes practical wisdom demanded more authoritarian stances: Moses, for example, was right to demand complete obedience in commanding the slaughter of the Midianites, because that was what reason called for in the particular circumstances. When Simḥah Zissel has full confidence that a given approach must be rational, he demands submission to that approach; above all, because of Simḥah Zissel's confidence that biblical prophets were truly conveying divine messages, he joins nearly all premodern rabbinic authorities in seeing submission to the prophets as the proper path.

But, nonetheless, Simḥah Zissel would be unlikely to fully endorse Dessler's doctrine of *da'at Torah.* Simḥah Zissel's stress on critiquing those with power, his strong sense of human fallibility, and his condemnation of those who bow to irrationality do not fit well with Dessler's doctrine.

Although Simḥah Zissel generally demands trust in biblical prophets, he also notes that even prophets need to be criticized. As he explains, even Moses needed to be rebuked by his father-in-law Jethro, who pointed out to him the weakness of the judicial system that Moses had designed. Moses, in taking the reasoned advice of a marginalized figure—Jethro had lived his whole life as an idolater and was a complete outsider to the Jewish people—was able "to show the [subsequent] generations that even the greatest needs to love rebuke from the lowliest."[72] Jethro is like the "little I" of whom Dessler speaks, who thinks that he can see the mistake of the greatest of sages with his own eyes; Dessler would tell Jethro to stop his criticism, for Jethro's ideas would be "null and void and utterly valueless."

Simḥah Zissel, on the other hand, applauds Jethro's dissent. As he notes, the Jewish tradition has encouraged the critique of other prophets as well—Simḥah Zissel singles out the criticism of Deborah and Phinehas for particular attention.[73] And if prophets make mistakes and in fact possess vices of all sorts, then certainly rabbis do; rabbis should certainly be subject to reasoned critiques rather than simply obeyed. The greatest of sages should thus focus on embracing the critiques of others, following the example of Socrates, who sought to continually learn from others rather than asserting his own authoritative wisdom. While Simḥah Zissel did see the value of more authoritarian approaches, he generally emphasizes humility and condemns the arrogance of figures who think too much of themselves. As he concludes one of his discussions of Moses's ability to listen to the critique of Jethro: "Happy is that generation in which the 'great' listen to the 'small' when there is need!"[74]

Simḥah Zissel also makes it clear throughout his writings that no human being is perfect. Human beings are commanded to strive for perfection, but we invariably fall short. Human nature inclines toward evil, and even the "best" people "can revert to being reborn with a cruel nature." Rabbis are certainly far from perfect, as Simḥah Zissel learned from Salanter. He suggests that the rulings of contemporary rabbis are often false, and that such rabbis need to engage in the work of musar to bring their rulings closer to the truth. This is not the view of a figure who would easily support Dessler's insistence that authoritative rabbis must be trusted.

Moreover, Dessler emphasizes that "even if they tell us that right is left," authoritative rabbis should be trusted. This is precisely the posture that Simḥah Zissel often opposes in his writings when he states his deep mistrust of those who offer demonstrably falsifiable teachings. As I noted earlier in this chapter, Simḥah Zissel demands turning to philosophic reason in the face of those who "turn things around in accordance with their wills. If it was possible to turn things around such that two times two were three—then, certainly, they would do so for the needs of their appetites." Those who "tell us that right is left" would seem to warrant similar suspicion.

Simḥah Zissel certainly hoped that his students, many of whom would become rabbis entrusted with the task of interpreting Torah, would make every effort to be guided by reason, and to follow the model of the ancient sages who rejected irrational "heavenly voices." Mere obedience to irrational rulings given by figures in authority would be "piousness" (*frumkeit*) of the worst sort, in Simḥah Zissel's view. While the descendants of Abraham should be open to truths that transcend ordinary reasoning, they should not embrace a simple posture of submission to irrationality. The children of Abraham, Simḥah Zissel taught, should be like philosophers who challenge irrational displays of authority, not obedient pietists who simply submit to them.

## "Reason Which Is Beyond Human Capacity"

Maimonides famously described Abraham as not only a prophet but a philosopher. Building on a midrashic tradition that sees Aristotle as discovering God through the contemplation of nature, Maimonides depicted Abraham as the first individual to develop rational arguments to prove God's existence.[75] Simḥah Zissel accepts and builds on this tradition, describing Abraham's rationalism as the necessary foundation for his becoming a prophet, and imagining his dedication to philosophy even amid persecution. According to midrashic tradition, Abraham was imprisoned and was nearly killed on behalf of his monotheism in his hometown of Ur Kasdim, and Simḥah Zissel takes this to be a sign of Abraham's unparalleled devotion to philosophy:

> Our father Abraham, of blessed memory, was the chief of the philosophers, understanding that there was a creator of all reality, the creator of the universe, as we have discussed, along with many other proofs that are explained in correct philosophy, and he understood that the essence of creation is to know and to come close to the Blessed One. And his philosophical reason was so strong in [laying] this foundation that we have discussed, that he built many strong buildings upon it. For ten years he was imprisoned in jail in chains of iron, and Heaven did not answer him at all during this long period—contemplate [even] one year in jail!—and all of this was to test if his philosophical reasoning was strong. . . . Moreover, he built on his philosophical reason to such an extent that he handed himself over in martyrdom to [the people of] Ur Kasdim, sanctifying the name of God. He was the first to understand from his own thinking, using his reason, that the Gracious One granted that "he made the human being in the image of God"—as Rashi explains, "to understand and to reason." And his reason was so strong that he built upon it fortified buildings to endure throughout so much time and to endure every kind of suffering—contemplate and imagine this lofty matter well, and be amazed at it!—and precisely then, when he had handed himself over in martyrdom to such an extent to serve his reason, then the Holy Blessed One saw that he was able to serve his reason to such an extent, the Blessed One saw that this wondrous philosopher, who could endure such suffering in the service of his reason, was fit to be a servant, sold to his reason—it was precisely then that the Holy Blessed One, the King of kings of kings, was revealed to him: "The Lord spoke to Abraham: 'Go forth. . . .'" (Gen. 12:1).[76]

Simḥah Zissel's discussion of Abraham resembles his discussion of Rabbi Joshua and the sages above, but Abraham is even more committed to reason, willing to risk death in Ur Kasdim rather than abandon his rational commitment to God. Abraham asserts the value of philosophical reasoning in a culture that despised it, and he favors service to God over personal happiness. Simḥah Zissel goes on to depict Abraham's willingness to risk his own death in Ur Kasdim as the most outstanding event of Abraham's life, because Abraham realized his duty "without being commanded" and instead acted autonomously on the basis of "his pure, philosophical reason."[77]

Abraham's philosophic path brings him extremely close to God. Simḥah Zissel depicts Abraham the autonomous philosopher as the model of the person who is able "to conquer one's crude inclination, to break one's material will, until one has changed one's evil nature, its appetites and its character traits . . . and one's body will become like a field cultivated for reason and for walking in the ways of the Blessed One."[78] Simḥah Zissel thus describes Abraham as seemingly achieving all that it is possible for human beings to achieve *before* God speaks to Abraham with the words recorded in Genesis 12:1; he reaches the height of moral excellence *as a philosopher*, before he becomes a prophet who directly hears divine revelation. Is there any reason, then, to rank the prophet above the philosopher? Is there anything that revelation contributes to human life that cannot be found through reason?

Simḥah Zissel answers these questions in the affirmative, and describes God as granting Abraham an additional, supernatural level of knowledge and closeness to the divine. After God reveals Himself to Abraham in Genesis 12, Abraham "understood his knowledge of the Blessed Lord beyond human nature"—that is, beyond what human reason can conceive of on its own. From Abraham's example, Simḥah Zissel learns that "after the Blessed One sees that a person reasons as far as he can reason, and he knows what is possible to know through his reason, then the Blessed One will bring him close and teach him wisdom that is beyond human reason."[79] There is such a thing as supernatural prophecy, then, which goes deeper than what "natural" human reason can comprehend, and which unfolds not only through human effort but through divine grace.

This supernatural wisdom is still rational, Simḥah Zissel clarifies; he would never accuse God, the epitome of reason, of authoring a teaching that is irrational. But human reason, with all of its weaknesses, cannot penetrate its depths. God's rationality transcends the limits of human reason; it is a level of "reason which is beyond human capacity." Simḥah Zissel generally assumes that this level of wisdom has only been accessed by the rarest of individuals—Abraham, Moses, and other acknowledged prophets—though, accommodating a midrash that depicts all of Israel as experiencing prophecy at the Sea of Reeds, he imagines that all of Israel caught a glimpse of this level at that time. In Simḥah Zissel's view, the people of Israel had collectively committed themselves to rationality at the Sea, and so they were worthy of directly accessing supernatural wisdom for that moment.[80]

Beyond that moment, ordinary Jews also have some limited access to "reason which is beyond human capacity" through the commandments that God gave to all of Israel. While Simḥah Zissel insists that "*most* of the Torah is based on natural human reason," he indicates that a small portion of the Torah's commandments point to a sort of rationality beyond what human beings can grasp. As we have seen, Simḥah Zissel argues that not only the obviously rational "ordinances" (*mishpatim*) but also the not-so-obviously rational "statutes" (*ḥukkim*) are accessible to natural reason—but elsewhere he suggests that there is a third category of material in the Torah, which he describes as "testimony to the Lord" (*edut Hashem*, quoting Psalms 19:8) and which is beyond that level. Simḥah Zissel writes that this aspect of the Torah consists of "divine knowledge, which is not like human philosophy, but far, far above human philosophy—beyond comparison—and is rather like the matter of the knowledge of the Kabbalists (the divine Rabbi Isaac [Luria] of blessed memory, and those like him). This is the perspective of the 'testimony' in the Torah—as with the Sabbath, the Exodus, and matters of that sort."[81]

The parts of the Torah that deal with what is beyond human reason are connected with miracles: paradigmatically, the miracle of the creation of the world (commemorated by the Sabbath) and the miracle of the Exodus from Egypt. Some of the commandments of the Torah seem to connect human beings with that supernatural realm, and Simḥah Zissel is at times inclined to see those commandments as giving Jews unique access to that wisdom. Hence, "as much as a human sage understands the greatness of God," Simḥah Zissel writes in another passage, "it is as nothing in comparison to a sage of the Torah."[82]

All Jews have some sort of contact with the supernatural realm, simply through their exposure to the commandments and principles that point to it. Sages with a greater exposure to those commandments and principles seem to have deeper access, and as Simḥah Zissel indicates in the paragraph above, scholars of Kabbalah—the Jewish esoteric tradition—are particularly suited to access this realm, which is "far, far above human philosophy."

## Simḥah Zissel Among the Kabbalists

Simḥah Zissel's writings devote relatively little attention to the mysteries of Kabbalah. He periodically mentions the various Kabbalistic texts with which he was familiar, but he seldom explores the esoteric truths that those texts seek to convey. His favorite Kabbalistic text appears to have been a work of Kabbalistic musar, Moses Cordovero's *The Palm Tree of Deborah*; one of Simḥah Zissel's letters dated to 1887 excitedly notes his discovery that *The Palm Tree of Deborah* can be incredibly valuable for musar work. [83] But his discussions of the book praise it for its attention to qualities of love and mercy, not its connection with the Kabbalistic doctrine of the *sefirot* with which such virtues were connected. [84] Simḥah Zissel's writings show little interest in the esoteric Kabbalistic tradition of viewing divine attributes as metaphysical entities. Indeed, he did not see himself as a Kabbalist concerned with such doctrines. He notes this explicitly in one discourse in which, after a brief discussion of Kabbalistic themes, he admits: "I do not know Kabbalah."[85]

And yet Simḥah Zissel does point to Kabbalah when he considers the mysteries of the Torah that transcend natural human understanding. While he sees philosophy as able to illustrate much of the Torah's perfection, he sees Kabbalah as the appropriate medium for discussing whatever parts of the Torah go beyond the natural realm. Philosophy can support one's faith in the Torah's perfection to a great degree, but Kabbalah can be an important supplement in fortifying such faith. And so, Simḥah Zissel writes, "Only when Kabbalah and reason are together is there a fortified wall of faith."[86] It would, then, be ideal to both be a philosopher and a Kabbalist, and this is an ideal to which Simḥah Zissel points, referencing rabbis such as Moses Ḥayyim Luzzatto whose writings sometimes combined philosophical and Kabbalistic themes: "One who wants to straighten his deeds in accordance with the Torah, he should make every effort to strengthen faith in rational proofs and in Kabbalistic proofs, together. . . . As it has been explained in the words of [Moses] Luzzatto, who was a divine philosopher and a Kabbalist together, all of the wisdom of the Kabbalah simply regards the scriptural verse 'and you should bring it into your heart that the Lord is God in heaven and on earth' (Deut. 4:39)—in order that faith may be well settled in the heart."[87] As he adds elsewhere, Luzzatto's Kabbalistic insights explain "the way in which the Lord guides the world, and also the reasons for the commandments, the way by which they bring repair (*tikkun*)."[88]

To build faith in the Torah, Simḥah Zissel is eager to make sense of all of the Torah's details even when they transcend ordinary human rationality, and he finds that Kabbalah is suited to this task. Much of Kabbalistic literature indicates ways in which the details of commandments can play significant roles in bringing redemption to the world through their effects on the divine order. Simḥah Zissel accepts the validity of such traditions. He accepts, for example, the Kabbalistic doctrine that there are three "spiritual worlds" that can be influenced by human actions within the "material world." The commandments, he writes, "make an impression and a great repair [*tikkun*] in all of the spiritual worlds." One can deepen one's commitment to the commandments, it appears, when one sees how they can aid not just the social world but worlds beyond human comprehension, though Simḥah Zissel does not depict himself as qualified to instruct his students in the details of these matters. Rather, "this is a secret hidden from us, and we only understand that it is so."[89]

Simḥah Zissel also points to Kabbalistic sources when confronted with various other mysterious facets of reality. In trying to understand the close relationship between physical deeds and spiritual life, for example, or to understand how it is that the physical body and the rational soul can be so bound together, he makes reference to Kabbalah. When it comes to understanding what he sees as the mystery of free will—namely, how it is that God seemingly surrendered his power to human beings—he refers to Isaac Luria's doctrine of "the breaking of the vessels." He also points to Lurianic Kabbalah when confronted with the problem of explaining Israel's long suffering in exile. In seeking to defend, more generally, the idea that sins lead to punishments and good deeds to rewards, he notes that this can be "proved in accordance with the opinion of the Kabbalists" who teach of the spiritual forces conveyed by one's deeds.[90]

In these passages, Simḥah Zissel indicates that faith in the Torah's commandments and central principles would be weakened were it not for knowledge of Kabbalah. Kabbalah appears as an important supplement to reason, attending to the dimensions that are beyond human capacity to understand; those who can combine Kabbalistic faith with philosophical and moral commitment would appear to be the wisest of all human beings. But Simḥah Zissel, hardly a systematic thinker, is not consistent in his approach to teaching about these matters; at other times, as we have seen, he reserves the highest possible praise for the ultimate philosopher, Abraham, at the point when Abraham did not have access to any supernatural knowledge. So too, in the same discourse in which he praises Luzzatto for combining philosophy and Kabbalah, he indicates that the most philosophical of rabbis—such as Maimonides—would not need Kabbalah at all:

> We see that the great early [medieval] sages did not yet know the wisdom of the Kabbalah, and these were wondrous saints [*ḥasidim*] such as Maimonides and those like him. Why? It was because they knew the way of faith through cause and effect, through human reason, and this is sufficient for a person to be a saint. Nonetheless, the commandment has come on the path of Kabbalah, which is the wisdom above human reason: how faith and the process of involvement with commandments may be settled even more in the human being.[91]

Those whose rational faculties are especially well developed—those who are most qualified to study Kabbalah—do not in fact need to be initiated into such secrets. And yet, as Simḥah Zissel makes clear, Kabbalah is clearly beneficial insofar as it can strengthen one's faith and commitment to proper patterns of living. It is not necessary, but it is extremely helpful, for the Jewish tradition to have recourse to the insights of the Kabbalists.

Simḥah Zissel seems to have appreciated and encouraged the study of Kabbalah more than Israel Salanter, who gave Kabbalah no attention in his writings. Nonetheless, he also differed from the Vilna Gaon and Ḥayyim of Volozhin, who made Kabbalah central to their approach. Simḥah Zissel showed limited interest in the secrets of Kabbalistic literature, and his emphasis on philosophic reason far outweighs his appreciation of Kabbalah. Though he appreciated Kabbalah as an aid to faith, especially when confronted with difficult commandments or principles, he did not think that significant access to the supernatural was possible without following the philosophical path of Abraham and immersing oneself in musar.

## Miracles and Nature

Simḥah Zissel sees God's Torah as generally aligned with natural human reason, while occasionally transcending natural human reason. His approach to God's providential guidance of history is similar.

God's control of history is generally reflected through the natural unfolding of events, while occasional miracles may transcend this natural process.

There are, as Simḥah Zissel puts it, two forms of divine providence: "miraculous providence" (*hanhagah nisit*) and "natural providence" (*hanhagah tivit*). Miracles transcend the rules of "earthly nature," and their causes cannot be understood by ordinary human reason, though Simḥah Zissel emphasizes that they are not a sign of divine irrationality. Miraculous providence rather works in accordance with the way of "supernal nature," a way of rationality that is simply beyond human understanding.[92]

"Miraculous providence," however, does not generally guide the world. Simḥah Zissel sees such providence as rare, and he sees blatant miracles as largely confined to the biblical miracles that were necessary for demonstrating God's sovereignty. As Simḥah Zissel learned from the Talmudic story of Akhnai's oven discussed above, miracles are not the means through which God generally works in the world. God, rather, works through "natural providence," guiding the world according to the laws of nature: "what we are able to do in a natural way, it is the will of the Blessed One that it be done, for He made it that most of the conduct of the world proceeds in this way."[93]

"But," Simḥah Zissel then goes on to caution, one must realize that "nature is also a miracle."[94] What we may call "natural providence" is, in fact, also miraculous. "In truth, nature is also a miracle—it is a hidden miracle."[95]

All that "naturally" happens in the world, in Simḥah Zissel's view, is ultimately caused by God. To properly acknowledge God's role in the world, we should see the inadequacy of speaking of natural "cause and effect," and describe God as the direct cause of everything that happens in the world: "What seems to be like nature, in truth this is not nature, but is rather also a miracle. And if so, we can learn from this that all of the paths of nature which seem to be effects necessarily proceeding from causes—this is not so, but rather it only appears so. Rather, truly, nature is also a miracle, and this is simply to teach us that the miraculous also applies to the path of cause and effect."[96]

Causality, then, is an illusion. It is useful illusion, Simḥah Zissel admits, for encouraging our human efforts; but it can also blind us to the daily miracles of the world. He bemoans how "scientists and doctors," for example, are blinded by their focus on causality: though thanks to the advance of technology they "can see the wonders of God more than those who crossed the sea," they are "like those who are blind" insofar as they fail to see the miraculous nature of the phenomena they study.[97] But Simḥah Zissel sees such blindness as afflicting not only modern scientists, but all people throughout history. He notes that the rabbis ordained blessings of gratitude thanking God "for your miracles which are with us every day" precisely to awaken Jews to the miracles of ordinary life that they would otherwise fail to see.[98]

In emphasizing ordinary miracles, Simḥah Zissel seems to want to combat the tendency to seek extraordinary miracles that defy the ordinary way of nature. "How foolish people are," he writes, "that they always seek miracles which contravene the ['natural'] way of the world [*minhago shel olam*]."[99] An opposition to those who seek after miracles was part of earlier polemics by Mitnagdim in Lithuania, often in opposition to the Hasidic focus on seeking to benefit from blatantly supernatural miracles; Ḥayyim of Volozhin reportedly claimed, in opposition to Hasidism, that "the source of true faith is in the hidden wonder [*nes nistar*] and not in blatant miracles [*nes nigleh*]."[100] Simḥah Zissel seems to follow in this tradition. He thinks that blatant miracles are extremely rare, and to seek after them reflects a certain level of irrationality.

He also seems to think that acknowledging hidden miracles can cultivate virtue in a way that seeking after blatant miracles does not. Above all, for Simḥah Zissel, seeing nature as miraculous can combat the pride that often results from human accomplishments. Simḥah Zissel is deeply concerned about such pride, following the concern of the book of Deuteronomy. Deuteronomy 8 expresses the concern that, when the people of Israel enter the land of Israel and become wealthy, "you will forget the Lord your God . . . and you will say in your heart, 'My power and the might of my hand has gotten me this wealth,'" when, in fact, it is God "who gives you power to get wealth" (Deut. 8:14–18). The problem, Simḥah Zissel explains, lies in our confused sense of cause and effect. When we do something successfully, we think that we have caused our success. When we think we caused wealth to be generated, it is exceedingly difficult to remember that God is ultimately responsible, that God "bestows upon [us] the strength to think and to gain wealth."[101] We want to take credit for things, and we resist acknowledging that we are in fact dependent on other forces in the world—"but the person of reason will understand that he receives nothing by himself."[102] Training ourselves to see God as responsible can help to diminish our unwarranted pride, increasing our humility and our sense of gratitude.

Simḥah Zissel's strong sense of divine providence also leads him to trust that what happens in the world will turn out to be for the good. But this does not lead him to the conclusion that one should adopt a generally passive posture in the world. Simḥah Zissel is clear that, when it comes to doing the right thing, one should exert oneself fully rather than trusting that God will provide supernatural assistance. One should, in doing so, acknowledge that one's own "natural" efforts are, in fact, a form of miraculous, divine assistance—since what we perceive as "natural" is in fact miraculous. God works through natural means, including through human beings. Thus, one should exert oneself to earn a livelihood—in fact, in Simḥah Zissel's view, ever since the expulsion from the Garden of Eden, God has *required* people to work to feed themselves. But one must realize that, while one is exerting oneself to earn a livelihood, this is in fact God acting through one's hands.

So too, when Simḥah Zissel reflects on Israel's mission to scout out the land of Israel in Numbers 13, he considers whether the people might have sinned by sending scouts at all; perhaps they should have had faith in God that things would turn out all right. Simḥah Zissel, following the commentary of Naḥmanides, answers that, "on the contrary, the Torah commands doing all that is possible by means of nature, and not relying on miracles at all."[103] Taking adequate precautions, in this case by engaging in a military reconnaissance mission, is precisely the sort of behavior that God demands. Exerting oneself in the world through natural means is anything but a denial of God.

Simḥah Zissel admits that there is a tension in asking people to make supreme efforts to cause things to happen while also attributing their efforts to God. But this is part of the challenge given to humanity after they were expelled from the Garden of Eden: that they would have to work in the world "by the sweat of their brows" (Gen. 3:19) and, at the same time, take no pride in their accomplishments. Meeting such a challenge, Simḥah Zissel admits, is very difficult, because it requires overcoming the "natural" human impulse to take credit for what one does, but he insists that seeking to transform such impulses is a central human responsibility.[104]

Simḥah Zissel makes it clear that human beings cannot rely on divine intervention. But he also holds out the possibility that, for rare individuals, "miraculous providence" may intervene. Just as it is possible to receive supernatural revelation that transcends human reason, it is possible to receive providential guidance that goes beyond what human beings can accomplish through their own exertions. As with revelation, such a miraculous occurrence is possible only after one has exerted oneself to the fullest: "'Know Him in *all* of your ways, and He will straighten your paths' (Prov. 3:6). This means: if a person does absolutely *all* that is in his power to do, and he immerses himself in effort and work until the point where nothing more is possible, then the help of God will come to straighten his paths, meaning to orient his character traits as they should be."[105]

On the whole, though, most people should not expect such supernatural grace. The obligation imposed on all human beings is to employ every effort possible toward becoming a virtuous person, and in fact, only the rare people who meet that obligation are able to experience supernatural grace. Though one should not take credit for one's efforts, one must make immense efforts in the world. The extent of such efforts will be the subject of the next chapter.

4

# The Great Effort of Musar

Simḥah Zissel viewed the work of musar, the work of bringing discipline to the soul, as arduous and endless. From his writings, we can see that there were two primary reasons why he thought that human beings must make such great efforts to cultivate virtue.

On the one hand, Simḥah Zissel saw such great efforts as morally required because human nature is properly oriented toward a divine ideal of moral excellence. As human beings are obligated to emulate divine perfection, individuals are obligated to continually strive for higher levels of virtue.

On the other hand, Simḥah Zissel saw great efforts as morally required because he saw human nature as corrupt and, in many respects, evil. Given the imperfection of human nature, individuals must continually guard themselves against vice.

As we saw in chapter 2, Simḥah Zissel stressed the importance of knowing both the weaknesses of human character and the divine ideal toward which human character should strive. As we will see in this chapter, Simḥah Zissel's demanding vision of the practice of musar emerged both from his profound pessimism about the obstacles that inevitably challenge human development and from his profound idealism about what should be expected from human beings.

## The Pursuit of the Ideal

Simḥah Zissel, like other traditional Jewish thinkers, has a "deontological" element to his moral theory: he is committed to following the rules set forth in the Torah and in rabbinic literature. But he clearly does not think of humanity's relationship with God as defined solely by rules. Like many earlier Jewish thinkers, Simḥah Zissel joins a deontological approach to proper behavior with a "virtue ethics" approach to proper behavior.[1]

Rosalind Hursthouse has characterized the deontological approach to morality as defining right action in the following way: "An action is right if and only if it is in accordance with a correct moral rule or principle"; a deontological moral theory will then seek to define correct moral rules and principles.[2] For Simḥah Zissel, correct rules and principles are defined by the Torah—which, as we have seen, is by and large grounded in "natural human reason."

A virtue ethics approach along Aristotelian lines, in Hursthouse's analysis, proceeds similarly: "An action is right if and only if it is what a virtuous agent would characteristically (i.e., acting in character) do in the circumstances." "A virtuous agent"—in Hursthouse's account, a *perfectly* virtuous agent—"is one who has, and exercises, certain character traits, namely, the virtues"; a theory of virtue ethics will then seek to define the virtues.[3] For Simḥah Zissel, these virtues are also defined by the Torah and by reason.

What is the relationship between rules and principles, on the one hand, and virtues, on the other hand? Simḥah Zissel describes how virtues support the rules and principles of the Torah, but he seldom *justifies* virtues in terms of the rules and principles that they support. On the other hand, he consistently justifies rules and principles in terms of virtues. Following Plato, Aristotle, and the tradition of medieval Jewish rationalism, Simḥah Zissel depicts the perfection of virtue as the ultimate goal of human life, and he sees law as aiming above all at inculcating virtue. The goodness of the rules and principles of the Torah can be seen precisely in the way they shape human beings to be virtuous.

As such, Simḥah Zissel privileges virtues over rules and principles. His moral theory is more of a virtue ethics theory than a deontological theory. In the final analysis, rules and principles are right to the extent that they are what a virtuous agent would follow in the circumstances. Of course, Simḥah Zissel assumes that following the explicit rules and principles of the Torah is at the heart of what a virtuous agent would do. But virtue requires more than following the Torah's explicit laws: it requires a range of other musar practices, and it requires supererogatory behavior that goes "beyond the line of the law" (*lifnim mi-shurat ha-din*). The pursuit of virtue must be guided by models of how a virtuous agent acts beyond the letter of the law.

### *Human Exemplars*

Following the tendency of classical rabbinic literature, Simḥah Zissel often finds moral exemplars within biblical narratives. Like many traditional rabbis, he tends to view biblical heroes as paradigms of excellence.

The patriarchs of the book of Genesis—Abraham, Isaac, and Jacob—are among those who serve as his models. Simḥah Zissel often quotes the rabbinic dictum that "a person is obligated to say, 'When will my deeds match the deeds of Abraham, Isaac, and Jacob?'" It is possible to reach the level of these three patriarchs, he writes, "if only one perfects his soul through character traits." As we have seen, Abraham is depicted as a paragon of philosophic rationalism who transformed his nature and developed deep qualities of lovingkindness. Abraham's son Isaac and his grandson Jacob are depicted as following in Abraham's footsteps.[4]

Simḥah Zissel thus explains that "matching the deeds of Abraham, Isaac, and Jacob" means that "just as they [philosophically] investigated through their understanding and were not drawn after the understandings of others, so too a person needs to be as if he was born today, and understand on his own how to obtain the principles of religion." And Simḥah Zissel takes seriously the rabbinic language that a person is "obligated" to aspire to match the deeds of Abraham, Isaac, and Jacob: "He is *obligated* to constantly prepare [with] effort to slowly, slowly change his evil nature, as did Abraham, Isaac, and Jacob," Simḥah Zissel emphasizes, "for the statement there says *obligated.*" A person is not morally guilty if he lacks the virtues of Abraham, Isaac, and Jacob, but he is morally guilty if he does not strive to emulate their virtues.[5]

Alongside the patriarchs, the matriarchs Sarah, Rebecca, Rachel, and Leah are held up as exemplars. Rebecca, for example, with her efforts to draw water for the camels belonging to Abraham's servant in Genesis 24, serves as Simḥah Zissel's model for the importance of engaging in small acts of lovingkindness.[6] Other figures from the narratives of Genesis are also idealized as paradigms of virtue—including Noah and Joseph, who are both presented as models of "sharing the burden."[7] And the hero of the later books of the Torah, Moses, is consistently singled out as the virtuous agent after whom all people should model their lives. Simḥah Zissel gives particular attention to Moses's disposition to share the burden of his fellows, and he sees Moses's compassionate love as grounded in the character trait that the Torah singles out as Moses's distinguishing virtue, humility—a trait that, as we have seen, does not always demand submissiveness.[8] Prophets, more generally, are not simply mediators of the divine will—which is how they are commonly depicted in biblical texts—but are also moral exemplars.[9]

It is not only prophets, patriarchs, and matriarchs, though, who are held up as virtuous agents to be emulated. Humbler biblical figures, such as the prostitute Raḥav, who aids Israel's spies in the book of Joshua and commits herself to God, and Pharaoh's daughter, who rescues and raises Moses, are also offered as models of virtue.[10] Though Simḥah Zissel follows the midrashic tradition that both Raḥav and Pharaoh's daughter join the Jewish people, it is worth noting that they are praised for deeds that they engage in before their conversions. Simḥah Zissel praises non-Jews as well as Jews as moral exemplars—as can also be seen, for example, with his praise for the Courland craftsmen discussed in chapter 1 or, above all, with his praise for the "the philosophers" discussed in chapter 3 of this book.

The sages of the Talmud—themselves sometimes presented as exemplars of philosophical wisdom—are also figures to be emulated. We have seen, for example, the model of Rabbi Joshua, who demands that reason be followed even when it conflicts with heavenly voices. Simḥah Zissel acknowledges that he and his students are far removed from Rabbi Joshua's ideal. But he often urges his students to model their lives on the lives of the sages: "a person who longs to have the crown of wisdom upon him should strive to habituate himself to desire that which the sages desire, for thus his character will model itself on the character of the sage, and it will slowly, slowly, come to the sage's level."[11]

The sages whom Simḥah Zissel recommends imitating are not only classical sages but also contemporary sages. As we have seen, he is cautious about some of his rabbinic contemporaries, but he does urge his students to model themselves after those with moral wisdom. So too, he describes his personal aspiration to emulate his own teachers, who included his father ("a man of peace, who loved peace and pursued peace—may the Blessed One send me His holy assistance, that I may walk in this way all the days of my life") and Israel Salanter (whose "ways were very dear in my eyes, and I wanted to imitate him, for my knowledge was poor, and his understanding and wisdom and reverence were broad").[12]

Simḥah Zissel no doubt wanted his students to regard him in a similar light. But he also stressed the importance of finding virtues to emulate in all people, even people with few commendable characteristics. Virtues can be found in every human being, he notes, pointing to Isaac's efforts to find good qualities in his wayward son, Esau. Unfortunately, Simḥah Zissel notes, many Jews don't follow the rabbis' counsel that one must "learn from every human being." Just as, he notes, a cobbler may pay attention to people's shoes but not notice other things about them, so too many observant Jews are trained to pay attention to other people's compliance with codes of Jewish law, but they fail to notice more subtle displays of virtue. Simḥah Zissel is eager to change this reality, encouraging his students to open their eyes to all instances of virtue and to seek to learn from them.[13]

Walking in the paths of virtuous exemplars is, in many ways, at the heart of moral education as Simḥah Zissel envisions it. But given the evil tendencies within human nature, it is clear that no human being can fully serve as a model for right action. Even the best people, as we have seen, struggle to maintain stability of character, easily reverting to viciousness. Even the greatest prophets need moral correction, which is why Moses needed to listen to Jethro's criticism. Dedicating oneself to following the examples of others has clear limits, and should be supplemented by efforts to focus one's eyes on the model of perfect virtue—God.

One should aspire to walk in the paths of the righteous, but one should ultimately aspire to walk in the paths of the divine. In the passage in which Simḥah Zissel describes his hope to walk in the paths of his teacher, Salanter, he goes on to exclaim "how much the more so . . . one should contemplate the goodness of the Blessed One and want to walk in His paths."[14] Indeed, one should dedicate every ounce of one's being to following the biblical command to "walk in God's ways," seeking to move ever closer to Perfection.

### *The Divine Exemplar*

Simḥah Zissel takes a standard Maimonidean approach to the question of how one can come to know God's ways. He begins with the premise that God is infinitely perfect, transcending anything that human beings can describe. When Israel, on crossing the sea of reeds, addresses God by asking "who is like You?" and then acknowledges God as "awesome in splendor" (Ex. 15:11), Simḥah Zissel sees them realizing, correctly, that "because of the magnitude of His perfection, and His infinite splendor, He is infinitely awesome."[15] Because God's perfection is beyond human comprehension, we cannot claim real positive knowledge of God: "It seems that the essence of knowing God is 'not knowing.' And he who is greater than his fellow in his situation and in knowledge, in what way is he greater? Insofar as he better understands his lack of knowledge, this is to his praise. . . . The honor of a human being who knows is only to recognize his 'not knowing.'"[16]

And yet, as Maimonides taught, it is possible to know God's "attributes." As Moses discovered in Exodus 33, a human being cannot see God's "face"—God's essence—but can see God's "back"—God's "goodness" or God's "ways," as the Torah also puts it (Ex. 33:13, 19, 23). Though these qualities are characterized by their perfect goodness, their perfect wisdom, and their perfect stability, human beings can still recognize these "ways" as virtues that are not unfamiliar and that we are obligated to emulate. When Moses asks to see God's ways, in Simḥah Zissel's reading, he is asking to behold virtues that human beings can emulate, so that they might draw closer to perfection and become more beloved by God. Simḥah Zissel's gloss on Exodus 33:13 is as follows: "Moses asked: 'Show me, please, your ways, that I may know you more, that I have more of a likeness to you, that you will love me more, that I may find more favor in your eyes.'"[17]

The "ways" that God does reveal are, as Simḥah Zissel puts it, ways of "showing infinite goodness to everyone."[18] But such infinite goodness takes form in concrete virtues and concrete acts that human beings can emulate. Simḥah Zissel generally describes God's primary virtues as virtues of compassionate love, and he regularly quotes the rabbinic understanding of emulating God's ways as, above all, a path of compassion: "'To walk in all His ways' (Deut. 11:22): 'The Lord, God, merciful and gracious' (Ex. 34:6). . . . As God is called merciful, so should you be merciful; as the Holy One, blessed be He, is called gracious, so too should you be gracious, as it is said, 'The Lord is gracious and full of compassion' (Ps. 145:8), and grants free gifts."[19] So too, Simḥah Zissel often cites the Talmudic text that describes God's virtues as taking expression through acts of lovingkindness shown to human beings in the narrative of the Torah. The commandment to "walk after the Lord your God" (Deut. 13:5) here requires "clothing the naked" (as God did for Adam and Eve), visiting the sick (as God visited Abraham), comforting mourners (as God did for Isaac), and burying the dead (as God did for Moses).[20] Here, God's love is expressed in concrete actions that are easy for human beings to emulate.

But Simḥah Zissel also views God as an exemplar when God performs actions that would seem quite impossible to emulate. For instance, Simḥah Zissel often describes how God's infinite goodness can be known from God's acts of creation. God brought the world into being in an incredible act of generosity and lovingkindness, such that "the world is built through lovingkindness" (Psalms 89:3).[21] Moreover, God continues to sustain the world at every moment, an idea reflected in the standard liturgy, which describes God's creation in the present tense: "every single hour and every single minute God gives life and health, for [the liturgy] does not say 'he made the great luminaries' but rather 'he makes the great luminaries' in the present tense."[22] God sustains creation and fills it with sufficient resources for all creatures on earth, which shows God's fundamental quality—"that He loves all creatures."[23] One can strive to emulate such infinite love, Simḥah Zissel suggests, by building communities grounded in lovingkindness. The building of communities directly parallels God's creation: "just as 'the world is built through lovingkindness,' it is by means of lovingkindness between people that the world, the political community, is sustained."[24]

And just as God's infinite goodness can be seen in creation, it can also be seen in the enduring presence of God's Torah. God not only sustains the physical world, but, through Torah, sustains the souls of human beings: "every single minute God shows lovingkindness by providing life, and also [by tending to] the welfare of the eternal soul."[25] God's loving care for human souls can be seen, above all, in God's giving of the Torah, which helped to sustain not only Israel's political needs but also its spiritual life. Human beings can emulate such concern through tending to not only the physical needs but also the spiritual needs of their neighbors.[26]

Just as one can learn God's ways from creation, one can learn God's ways from the text of the Torah—from its direct descriptions of divine attributes and, also, from meditating on its particular commandments. Simḥah Zissel explains the latter process in reference to a verse from Psalm 119, "I will speak of your commandments and I will see your paths" (Ps. 119:15). The verse teaches, in Simḥah Zissel's interpretation, "that King David, peace be upon him, understood the ways of God's governance from the laws of the Torah, meaning that, for example, he studied 'What is Interest?' [the section of the oral Torah concerning the prohibition against usury], [and] from this way he learned the ways of the Blessed Lord in His governance. And this is the meaning of 'I will see your paths'—the paths and the ways by which you govern your world."[27]

David—who is assumed in rabbinic Judaism to be not only the author of the Psalms but a scholar of the written and oral Torah—is imagined as studying God's ethical commandments and learning "God's ways" from his study of ethics. Simḥah Zissel sees the commandments as an expression of divine virtues, as they aim to inculcate virtues and perfect human souls. Studying and performing the commandments should, then, move a person closer to an understanding of divine perfection.

An obvious objection to this vision is that the Torah's laws and narratives may not always seem to depict God as infinitely loving; the events that happen in the created world might not always seem to reflect infinite divine love, either. But given his assumptions that God is perfectly loving and that the content of the Torah and the content of history follow God's will, Simḥah Zissel cannot help but view what would seem to be ostensibly bad as, in fact, good. Human suffering that might seem to be morally evil is, in general, understood to be a sign of divine love and justice. The infinite divine love that Simḥah Zissel seeks to emulate is by no means submissive to the wishes of the other; it may seek the good of others by withholding mercy, offering rebuke, and inflicting suffering. Simḥah Zissel therefore sees a place for emulating God not only through mercy but also through harshness: to "imitate the ways of the Blessed One," he writes, one must be "merciful in a place where one needs to show mercy and cruel in a place where one needs to show cruelty."[28]

Human wisdom is often unable to determine when to be merciful and when to be cruel. The ultimate goal of loving like God loves—bringing good to all creatures by perfectly balancing harshness and mercy—is very far off. And yet, Simḥah Zissel insists, it is a goal for which human beings must strive.

Though Simḥah Zissel understands the human soul as tending toward evil, he also understands that humanity's creation in the image of God means that human beings have the capacity to reflect divine perfection. Our own souls are designed to imitate the divine; because the divine image is imprinted on them, they bear a strong resemblance to God. As our virtue increases and becomes more stable, the correlation between the human and the divine increases: "with every bit more that consistency is found within [a person], his resemblance to the Blessed One will grow greater."[29] Simḥah Zissel also describes this process of becoming more like Perfection as a process of coming to know God or as a process of coming to love God. Though, as we have seen, full knowledge of God is impossible, "knowing God's greatness" as best we can means learning to "walk in His ways."[30] So too, loving God is a matter of walking in God's ways; the Torah's commandment to love God with all that one has requires dedicating one's life to seeking to follow the path of divine perfection.[31]

### *Striving Toward the Infinite*

The task of pursuing the divine ideal of moral perfection is an infinite task. Because the standard for truly right action is God's perfect virtue, there is no end to the work of musar. No matter how much effort is put into moral improvement, there will always be further to go. Simḥah Zissel therefore introduces a model of ethics whereby human beings must seek continual moral growth.

As I noted in chapter 3, Simḥah Zissel stresses that the greatest Jewish sages are generally called "the disciples of the sages" (*talmidei ḥakhamim*) rather than "the sages" because "for all of their days, they are like disciples who are learning." Like Socrates, who focused on his lack of knowledge and all that he still longed to know, the ideal sage is someone who realizes that he still falls short of the ideal and must grow further. As Simḥah Zissel puts it, one who is not growing continually is in fact "akin to one who is dead, who cannot feel." Only a person who is continually seeking God is spiritually "alive."[32] Simḥah Zissel emphasizes that moral education is ongoing, such that one should always have a teacher available to prod one toward further growth; after all, "a person does not see his obligation by himself," but needs to be challenged by another to grow in virtue.[33]

If the quest is truly unending, then it would seem that it would necessarily be unsatisfying. Perhaps arriving at the goal of perfection would be a source of joy, but can there really be joy when one is never able to reach the goal? Simḥah Zissel is sure to emphasize that there is joy in even modest attainments of virtue, so long as one is still on the journey toward greater virtue. In fact, orienting oneself toward God is a source of joy even when there is no success, so long as one maintains that orientation and continues to seek, as can be seen in Simḥah Zissel's reading of three lines from Psalm 105:

> "Happy are the hearts of those who seek the Lord.
>
> Seek out the Lord and His might!
>
> *Continually* seek His face!" (Ps. 105:3–4)
>
> The issue is that, for everyone who seeks, if he finds what he is seeking, he has joy; on the contrary, if he does not find it, he has sadness. But on the other hand, one who seeks the Lord, whether he finds or does not find, he has joy in any case. For "one who thought to fulfill a commandment and was forcibly prevented and did not do it, it is as if he did" (BT Kiddushin 40a).
>
> According to this, it would seem as if one does not need to arrive at the truth. But it would be unacceptable to think that the way of the Blessed Lord is that a person need not

> arrive at the truth. Therefore the psalm continues, "Seek out the Lord and His might"—know Him, and the power of His deeds, to arrive at the truth.
>
> But you should not imagine that you have arrived at the truth and that you do not need to seek further. Therefore the psalm continues on: "Seek His face *continually*"—for in all the days of your life, you will not have arrived at the end. You should have doubts: perhaps you have not arrived at the truth, and you must seek further.[34]

This passage begins by stressing that having the intention to seek God is worthy in and of itself; hence, the psalm teaches that "happy are the hearts of those who seek the Lord," even when they do not find God. But lest one be tempted to think that, then, one should not seek to actually arrive at the goal, Simḥah Zissel understands the psalm to stress that one must seek precisely this. Lest one think that it is possible to arrive at the goal, however, Simḥah Zissel understands the psalm to stress that one must never rest content. One must seek God continually. Even if you think that you have arrived at the truth, there is always further to go: you must continue to grow.

Is it really possible to continually grow? Aren't there limits as to how far the human soul can be stretched? At times, Simḥah Zissel describes how human reason can continue to grow far more than would seem possible:

> It is the nature of a rubber sack that although it may seem small, as if it would be filled with just a few items . . . to the extent that one increases the items in it, it will expand . . . and an eye of flesh will not be able to see empty space in it for anything else, but the one who goes on to increase what is placed in it can discern that, to the extent that he increases, it will expand further. So too human reason is said to have expansiveness by nature. The person who neglects making an effort to fill his soul with different forms of knowledge will not feel that he is lacking, and he will think that his soul is full. But one who exerts himself to add understanding and learning each day, his rubber sack will expand, and he himself will continually recognize and feel the lack in his reason, and how it is still not full, because when he tries adding more, he sees with his eyes that his sack will expand each time, and that it still is not full. But

> for the one who does not try to add more, it will seem to his eyes that his reason is full with all of the knowledge that can be found, and he will feel blessed in his heart that what he can see is all, and that there is no more. . . .
>
> In fact, the nature of the expansiveness of reason is far beyond the limits of the expansiveness of rubber, for each time that reason expands, this will help to prepare it for the next time, to expand with greater force and with greater ease, and so on, from level to level. And thus Scripture says: "[God] breathed into his nostrils the soul of life" (Gen. 2:7), and it is known that concerns of the Blessed Lord are not bound by time and place, and all His actions have not yet come to an end, and it is natural that when one blows into something, that thing expands, as the Blessed Lord has blown the soul of life, which continually expands.[35]

Though we doubt our capacities for continual expansion, Simḥah Zissel insists that our capacities are far more elastic than we assume. Indeed, God is constantly filling human beings with the capacity for greater and greater powers of reasoning (reason being "the soul of life"), which human effort can realize. In theory, our human capacities can grow greater and greater, bringing us to greater levels of virtue and so bringing us closer to God.[36]

At the same time, Simḥah Zissel acknowledges the limits to human growth: no matter how virtuous human beings may become, we are necessarily distant from the divine ideal. We are generally capable of being much better people than we think we can be—we typically think that we have filled our "sacks" when in fact they can continue to expand—but we are not capable of being divine. And so, in Simḥah Zissel's view, we are required to be much better people than we think we can be, but we are not required to be absolutely perfect. Simḥah Zissel generally qualifies his discussions of moral obligation by adding the qualification that humans are only required to be virtuous in accordance with their capacities.

Consider, for example, how Simḥah Zissel frames the goal of musar in the following passage:

> All of the labor and effort given to reverence and to traits of character is simply to arrive at knowing God *in accordance with ability of the person* [*ke-fi yekholet ha-adam*]. Therefore, one who is not engaged with them in accordance with the

> required labor will not reach the goal at all. To what can this be compared?—to one who needs to travel to a particular place and he walks and walks and as he approaches the place he stops walking—such a person has not arrived at the place. So too with knowing God's greatness—a person needs *to walk* in His ways.[37]

A person is required to be *walking* in God's ways—that is, to be moving in pursuit of the ideal, continually developing in virtue rather than standing still. But the goal is framed in terms of knowing God "in accordance with the ability of the person"; it is limited by human nature and by the capacities of the particular person. One is required to come to know God as best one can, but one is not required to do the impossible. Qualifications along these lines fill Simḥah Zissel's writings; he follows the precedent of Maimonides, who described the human being as obligated to imitate divine attributes "in accordance with his strength."[38]

Such an approach fits with Simḥah Zissel's vision of how divine commandments are not absolute ideals but are designed to fit the nature of human beings. Simḥah Zissel sees the Torah as the refraction of ideals into commandments that human beings can grasp; along these lines, he writes that "the Torah does not command the human being to fulfill the Torah with angelic strength, but with human strength."[39] Humans are not asked to do what is impossible for them to do. And so God judges people in accordance with what they can fairly be expected to do, "in accordance with the capability of the person."[40]

At the same time, Simḥah Zissel sees human beings as judged for failing to achieve what they are capable of achieving—and he emphasizes that they are capable of achieving a great deal. He is concerned about the various ways in which people fail to recognize their capabilities and therefore ask too little of themselves.

For one thing, Simḥah Zissel argues that Jewish legal norms are much more demanding than is commonly assumed. Most people assume that they obey the law prohibiting stealing, for example, but Simḥah Zissel follows the Talmudic assumption that "most people [sin] by stealing" (BT Bava Batra 165a).[41] Noting how people commonly cause damage to each other without even noticing, he seeks to build on Israel Salanter's project of innovatively applying standard rules (e.g., the prohibition on stealing) to contemporary circumstances, even when this leads him to indict people who had assumed that they were law-abiding Jews. The severity with which Salanter sought to enforce the laws against stealing is legendary—he is said to have been concerned with, among other things, those who held doors open and thus stole heat from buildings, as well as those who made noise in the night and so caused others to be robbed of their sleep.[42] Simḥah Zissel seeks to build on Salanter's efforts:

> Our master, teacher and rabbi of blessed memory [Israel Salanter] introduced many new laws, both monetary laws and laws concerning damages, which seemed strange in the eyes of many people, and even the greatest sages of the land who saw this were astonished by the wondrous innovations which had not been heard until now. This was because he illuminated the eyes of the Diaspora with his new contemplation and his new forms of knowledge, both with regards to the foundations of religion and with regards to the practice of religion and its commands, by reflecting deeply on the laws of damages—for instance, reflecting deeply on forbidden labors, and particularly on how Yom Kippur does not grant atonement until one has returned stolen goods or, with regards to character traits, until one has placated one's fellow.[43]

Simḥah Zissel points to the common view that atonement is not possible without paying for the damages one has caused. But his sense of what is required goes further: he also mentions the need to attend to the *character traits* that have caused harm to one's fellow. For Simḥah Zissel, placating a person whom one has harmed is legally required, and so attending to the character traits that have caused the damage is obligatory rather than supererogatory. As Simḥah Zissel often indicates, some level of inner virtue is a legal requirement of the Torah.

Beyond this, though, Simḥah Zissel emphasizes that people are generally obligated to go beyond legal standards, both when it comes to their behavior and when it comes to their inner lives. Even when one might say that these obligations are not "legal" obligations, one must still conclude that people are required to go "beyond the line of the law"—such that, in a sense, the law requires them to go beyond the law in accordance with their capacities.

Simḥah Zissel cites a famous conclusion of Naḥmanides: that while the Torah's laws technically permit a good deal of indulgent sexual intercourse and eating, the Torah's commandment to "be holy" (Leviticus 19:1) requires all people to separate themselves from self-indulgence even when it is not legally required. In Simḥah Zissel's view, the technical permission is really a test for human beings: God is testing human beings to ensure that they can choose to overcome their appetites. Simḥah Zissel assumes that human beings are generally able to do so to a significant degree—and so they are required to do so.[44]

Beyond this, individuals become obligated to reach for higher and higher standards as their capacities to meet such standards grow. The path of engaging in the work of musar, therefore, is a path by which one begins to discover more and more obligations. When one expands one's moral horizons, in Simḥah Zissel's model, one discovers more and more ways in which God's will might apply to one's life, such that one "expands" the dimensions of the Torah:

> One who is not immersed in musar reduces the size of the Torah, "the size of which is longer than the earth" (Job 11:9). It is so even for the greatest of the masters of musar, that the wisdom of musar arouses them to investigate laws between a person and God and laws between a person and his fellow, and they constantly have doubts, and they always suspect themselves to be prejudiced. . . . Musar obligates a person to always suspect himself of prejudice, so that he will automatically need to be many times more stringent, and the size of the Torah will grow very great for him, and therefore "his evil inclination will be greater," for he will have greater knowledge through his investigations and innovations, and the yoke of the kingdom of heaven will be placed upon him in a more difficult manner.[45]

Simḥah Zissel here builds on the Talmudic statement that "anyone who is greater than his fellow, his evil inclination is greater" (BT Sukkah 52a). In his understanding, those who are more advanced in musar are better able to identify evil tendencies within their souls, and they take on new obligations to combat those tendencies. It would seem that they also take on new levels of aspiration in accordance with their deeper knowledge about the soul, as they innovate new forms of law that they had not previously seen. The yoke of heaven becomes heavier on them: they realize that there is even more that they must do to sanctify God's name. Possibilities that might technically seem to be supererogatory now appear obligatory.

In taking on expanded obligations in accordance with one's ability, it is as if one is making a vow, binding oneself to new commitments.

This is one paradigm that Simḥah Zissel uses in explaining how people can come to take on greater and greater levels of obligation:

> With vows, we have found a clear path for how a person can take upon himself a prohibition in a matter that is not prohibited by the Torah. It is appropriate because it is the will of the Torah that one not be imprisoned within the prison of one's will. And so, after one has recognized that he must fence in his will, the person becomes obligated in accordance with his recognition, and this recognition becomes for him a recognition of the will of the Torah and the *halakhah*, so that it is forbidden by law.[46]

Biblical law authorizes people to take vows upon themselves, and Simḥah Zissel sees this institution as showing the importance of taking a greater level of obligations on oneself. He sees the Torah as seeking to free people from their desires—from "the prison of one's will"—and thus authorizing people to accept the additional obligations that bring them toward this goal. The biblical institution of the vow, in his view, shows that it is permissible to take on personalized legislation despite God's injunction that "you should not add to the word which I command you" (Deut. 4:2). In Simḥah Zissel's view, one who properly restricts himself with a vow is not really legislating additional laws but is instead recognizing what God demands of him.

To show precedent for this vision of obligation beyond the Torah's law, Simḥah Zissel also points to the following story from the Talmud (BT Bava Metzia 83a):

> Rabba bar Bar Hanan had porters who [negligently] broke his barrels of wine. He seized their garments [as collateral]. They spoke to Rav. Rav said to [Rabba bar Bar Hanan], "Give them their garments." [Rabba bar Bar Hanan] asked [Rav], "Is this the law?" "Even so [*In*]," [Rav] said: "that you may walk in the path of the good" (Prov. 2:20). He gave them their garments. They said, "We are poor, we have worked all day and are hungry; are we to get nothing?" [Rav] said, "Go and give them their wages." [Rabba bar Bar Hanan] asked, "Is this the law?" "Even so [*In*]," he replied: "You shall keep the path of the righteous." (Prov. 2:20).

The Torah's law concerning torts, here, would penalize the porters for their negligence. But, as Simḥah Zissel explains it, Rabba bar Bar

Hanan is capable of recognizing that he should go beyond the law in this way, in the fashion of a "saint": "Surely this is not 'law' but rather 'saintliness' [*ḥasidut*]. He asked if it was law, and how could he give his legal ruling in accordance with [the standard of] saintliness? Nonetheless, [Rav] showed him from the depths of the intention of the Torah, that if it is so that you can recognize saintliness, you are obligated in accordance with your recognition, and for you this is the law."[47] One is, in this model, obligated to imitate God in accordance with one's abilities; if one has the ability to follow the path of the "saint," then one is obligated to do so.

The idea that those with greater capacities should be held to higher standards appears throughout classical rabbinic literature. It is a paradigm common in a range of moral traditions, as Andrew Flescher has argued, but often neglected by moderns who have preferred less demanding moral theories.[48] It is an approach particularly well exemplified in Simḥah Zissel's writings. In his view, God asks people to perfect themselves to whatever degree they can, and the righteous people who can recognize very high moral standards are obligated to push themselves to meet those standards. Moses, as the most capable prophet who ever lived, had the strictest requirements placed on him. Whatever Moses's sin was when he sought to draw water from a stone in Numbers 20 (and Simḥah Zissel does not consistently commit himself to one explanation in particular), it is clear to Simḥah Zissel that Moses committed a minor sin unwittingly and yet was punished severely. Why was he punished so severely for a minor, unintentional sin? Moses was held to the highest possible standard because, as the Talmud puts it, "the Holy Blessed One is exacting with those who [most closely] surround him, even to a hair's breadth."[49]

In the end, though, Simḥah Zissel sees God as exacting with everyone. Though people are held to different standards depending on their capacities, all are required to do all that they can possibly do, even to a hair's breadth. God may not require His servants to be perfect, in this vision, but God requires them to be as perfect as they can be and to always strive for greater virtue.

## The Struggle for Moral Progress

Simḥah Zissel's vision of striving for the heights of moral perfection, however, is in tension with his belief that human beings are generally at a low moral level and that even minimal efforts at moral improvement are a real struggle. As we saw in chapter 2, Simḥah Zissel emphasizes the importance of understanding not only a vision of the human ideal but also a vision of the weaknesses of human nature. Human nature, in its untutored state, is in poor shape. Though the soul can be infinitely elastic in its pursuit of the good, for the most part it is deeply corrupt and resistant to any improvement.

Simḥah Zissel envisions the work of musar as a path for repairing human nature, but he sees even the smallest efforts to change bad character traits as incredibly difficult, requiring extraordinary effort. Human reason is very weak, the evil inclination is very strong, and human beings naturally resist even the most modest efforts at change. Not only is it difficult for human beings to grow toward the heights of perfection, but it is difficult for human beings to achieve much success at all in the realm of moral improvement.

### *The Problem of Stiff Necks*

The widespread vice that makes moral progress particularly difficult, in Simḥah Zissel's view, is the disposition to be "stiff-necked." A "stiff-necked" person resists *teshuvah*—"turning" toward God, repenting for sin—and is instead satisfied with his present condition. He refuses to "continue to grow and learn," and he does not heed the voices of those who offer critical advice on how to act—rather, he "hates the one who criticized him." As Simḥah Zissel notes, God implores Israel to distance themselves from such a posture in the book of Deuteronomy (10:16) with the commandment to "circumcise the foreskin of your hearts and not be stiff-necked anymore."[50]

Moreover, Simḥah Zissel points out, it is this vice that arouses God's anger following Israel's worship of the Golden Calf; God threatens to destroy Israel not because of their idolatry but because they are "a stiff-necked people" (Ex. 32:9):

> We should contemplate with understanding that [God] did not mention the fact of this great sin [with the calf], but He mentioned only that this was a stiff-necked people. The explanation of the matter is that [Israel] was not able to turn its neck to listen, meaning it was not able to turn from the habit to which it had been habituated. And, God forbid, on account of this it was far from repentance . . . for the character trait of stiffening against changing one's nature was worse than the great sin of the calf; were it not for this character trait, they would not have been fit to be destroyed.[51]

The people of Israel were so stiff-necked, in Simḥah Zissel's view, that future repentance seemed impossible; they were only saved from annihilation, in the end, by Moses's heroic efforts to persuade them to open up their hearts and to turn ever so slightly toward God.[52] While most people are not "hardened" to such an extent, Simḥah Zissel does think that most of us hate to accept criticism and to change our habits for the better. Not only do we resist growing toward the infinite heights of divine virtue, we resist repentance for sin and we tend to avoid any call to moral improvement.

*Troubles Within the Soul*

Even if, through great effort, one can overcome one's resistance to change, the task of harnessing the various faculties of the soul in pursuit of virtue is an exceptionally difficult task. And even those who make moral progress are often beset by unruly forces that lie deep within the human soul.

Simḥah Zissel depicts the soul as filled with chaos and inner warfare. Not only may reason wage war against the various "material" parts of the soul, but the material parts of the soul are themselves at war with one another. The "opposing material faculties" within the soul seek to "overcome one another" and "wage war against one another, constantly," leaving the soul in disarray.[53] Confronted with various material desires, most souls are "like the 'troubled sea' (Isaiah 57:20)—always raging and tempestuous," unable to achieve equanimity and often unable to achieve any positive goods.[54] Even a person with a reasonably well-ordered soul must deal with a fair amount of chaos—"many faculties, and the faculties in opposition to them, turning around, this way and that."[55] Amid the chaos that characterizes the human soul, any level of moral achievement is extremely difficult and requires extraordinary effort.

Gaining wisdom about the soul and improving its condition are especially difficult tasks because the chaotic forces in the soul are largely obscured from view. Like Israel Salanter, Simḥah Zissel sees many of the forces of the soul as operating at an unconscious level. Salanter, whom Hillel Goldberg has described as "an early psychologist of the unconscious," had identified both innate and learned appetites as below the level of consciousness.[56] Simḥah Zissel expands on these ideas, introducing his own distinctive language. He speaks of what later psychologists would call the "unconscious" by using the language of "disposition" (*hanaḥah*) and "rooting," "implanting" or "embedding" (*hashrashah*)—referring to that which is deeply implanted, rooted, and embedded within a person's soul, below the level of consciousness. Like Salanter, he discusses unconscious ideas and appetites that are inborn as well as those that are acquired.

The most formidable unconscious forces in the human soul, in Simḥah Zissel's view, are "where one has within one an implanting [*hashrashah*] from birth, from the womb."[57] Innate impulses to be cruel, for example, can rise up and foil any progress that one makes on the path of musar:

> One who wants to habituate himself in the character trait of beneficence, who engages in charity and acts of lovingkindness, who provides food and drink for the poor, he can deeply increase the beneficence within his heart . . . but nevertheless we know that even the best of them can revert to being reborn with a cruel nature. Why? Surely they immerse themselves greatly in acts of lovingkindness, but this is because of matter, the opposite of form, and human nature inclines more toward being "evil, all the time." Therefore, the initial disposition [*hanaḥah*] draws forth material urges, for cruelty and the like, which join together to strengthen the natural arousal of evil.[58]

In Simḥah Zissel's view, even when we have done much to develop habits of love, we easily revert to our "material" nature, with all of its evil tendencies. Though Simḥah Zissel implores his students to learn about these tendencies and to wage war against them, as we saw in chapter 2, he sees these unconscious forces as difficult to tame and as making moral development incredibly difficult.

Simḥah Zissel also sees the unconscious ideas and desires that take root during one's youth as exceptionally strong and difficult to change. What one encounters early in life generally serves as the foundation stone for the rest of one's life:

> We see [this] faculty within the human being: that he builds great buildings upon everything that is seated within the human heart. This is not only for a matter of appetite and will, but also for what is simply a matter of knowledge: simply because it is prior in time, all of the branches of knowledge that emerge for him afterward through his reasoning branch out from the root [*shoresh*] which is rooted within him, from the knowledge that was prior in

> time, and the root inclines reason to reason in accordance with the prior knowledge. . . . From this, the person of understanding can contemplate how there is an obligation upon the human being to be educated from his youth, for if mere knowledge affects us thus, what of the disposition [*hanaḥah*] of desire and appetite![59]

We become deeply habituated to the ideas and desires implanted in us from our youth, and these ideas and desires often corrupt our rationality. Thus, for example, Simḥah Zissel notes how the Israelites freed from Egypt had trouble freeing themselves from the idolatrous habits that had been "implanted within them" there. Even after they established a covenant with God, their long-repressed habits of idolatry rose back up when the temptation to worship the Golden Calf emerged.[60]

So too, destructive emotional habits developed in one's youth may rise up from the depths of the unconscious later in life. Simḥah Zissel illustrates this dynamic with reference to the biblical narrative of Joseph and his brothers, suggesting that the hatred that Joseph's brothers had learned in their youth remained deeply rooted within their souls. Even at the moment that they committed themselves to reconciliation with Joseph (Genesis 45), according to midrashic tradition, the brothers were suddenly confronted by the angry and vengeful passions of their youths and "sought to kill him." Despite the righteousness that they had developed, Simḥah Zissel notes, "what was first implanted within them was aroused." And if people of such righteousness are this susceptible, he concludes, then certainly the rest of us must be on guard: "all of the days of a person's life, a person needs to suspect himself of having savageness implanted within him from his youth, and especially a person who has not had an education [*ḥinukh*]."[61]

Simḥah Zissel trusts that education in the ways of moral discipline can help to combat deeply rooted savagery. And yet he often admits that the ideal of repairing the human soul and achieving stable virtue is generally beyond reach. Simḥah Zissel spent a good deal of his life focusing on the education of young men, hoping that he could root good habits within their souls and so save them from at least some of their morally destructive urges. But he clearly realized that, no matter how well a person is trained, human nature almost inevitably seems to give rise to evil, such that even moral consistency (let alone moral perfection) can seldom be fashioned out of its crooked timber.

*Torah "On One Foot": The Problem of Balance*

And even when we can make moral progress in one area of our lives, Simḥah Zissel points out, we often fail to attend to other sorts of obligations. Just as we may struggle with the many psychological impulses that compete for our attention, we struggle with the many important obligations competing for our attention. This problem may be especially acute for the Jewish people, given the multiplicity of commandments incumbent on them. In fact, Simḥah Zissel imagines that when the Talmud describes a potential convert as seeking a summation of the Torah "on one foot," the potential convert was pointing to this problem and asking for a basic principle by which to navigate the overwhelming variety of duties that the Torah imposed:

> The convert was a great sage. He saw that the religion of Israel has in it many details about which a person needs to be careful, and it is difficult for a person to be careful with and observant of every single detail in and of itself, for there are many details—and so if his thoughts are stuck on one matter, he can't succeed in paying attention to another matter. For example: if his thoughts are fixed on being careful with honoring his father and mother, his thoughts might not be able to focus on the commandment prohibiting coveting all that belongs to his neighbor, for the appetites of a person hunger for what his eye sees. Or, on the other hand, in his mental calculation to not covet what is not his—even as the heart has a desirous nature, in any case he would settle his mind and engage in calculations of justice, to break the desire of the heart, following the philosophers who would despise desire using their high and refined reason—behold, his reason would be fixed on this, and he would not succeed in impressing on his mind the greatness of the commandment to honor his father and mother. And [this would be a problem] especially given that there are 613 commandments, with innumerable general principles and specific applications.[62]

Simḥah Zissel goes on to note that the sage Hillel answered the query particularly well, articulating the unifying principle of love for one's neighbor as oneself. But Simḥah Zissel seems to remain anxious about the problem that the potential convert raised. To be sure, reason (and, especially, the virtue of practical wisdom) should ideally allow us to balance competing obligations, but he sees reason as very weak and as typically unable to handle such a task: "Truly, when a person focuses himself upon some matter, he is weakened in another matter. For example, one who immerses himself very strongly in the [study of] Torah, he becomes weak in the matter of loving and doing good for people. This is because our reason is too powerless to include all of the parts in balance. And therefore it is incumbent upon us to strengthen ourselves very much in improving our character traits, and may it go well for us."[63] The example here is striking, because Simḥah Zissel lived in a rabbinic culture that saw complete immersion in Torah study as the key to strengthening every aspect of one's life—if not by natural means, then because of the miraculous power of Torah study to transform moral character by itself. But Simḥah Zissel suggests that too much time spent in Torah study is in fact deleterious, distancing a person from other key obligations—above all, from the central obligation of "loving and doing good for people." While prominent Lithuanian rabbis such as Ḥayyim of Volozhin emphasized that Torah study alone can protect a person from sin,[64] Simḥah Zissel suggests that Torah study alone can lead directly to sin, because focusing exclusively on one activity inevitably leads to the neglect of others. Moral achievement is tenuous in part because moral success in one area may lead immediately to moral failure in another area.

One might view this situation as a cause for despair. But Simḥah Zissel insists on maintaining hope that human beings can overcome obstacles and, in fact, strive toward the divine ideal. When confronted with the persistence of evil drives within human beings, his response is to insist on educating the soul through the work of musar. When confronted with the variety of details in the Torah, his response is to urge Jews to focus on how ideals of love can unify all those details. When confronted with the difficulty of balancing competing obligations, he stresses that "it is incumbent upon us to strengthen ourselves very much in improving our character traits." To accept anything less, and so to refuse to make sincere efforts at overcoming one's vices, would be an instance of being "stiff-necked," of refusing to change.

## "No Remedy . . . Other than to Exert Oneself Very Greatly"

We saw in the first part of this chapter how Simḥah Zissel's acceptance of human inadequacy helped to temper the demandingness of his moral vision. Rather than simply describing people as obligated to be perfect, he described people as obligated to seek perfection in accordance with their capacities. But we can now see how Simḥah Zissel's acceptance of human inadequacy also increased his sense of how demanding the work of musar must be. Simḥah Zissel's sense of the difficulty of moral development led him to develop a model of slow, arduous musar work and to reject all promises of shortcuts to moral improvement.

This approach is significantly different from the dominant view among Lithuanian rabbis of Simḥah Zissel's era, who emphasized a direct path to moral transformation that did not involve the work of musar. In the view of the Lithuanian rabbinic elite, the study of Talmud was a direct, supernatural path to perfection—or, in some versions, simply engaging in the study of Talmud (with no ulterior motives) could itself constitute perfection.[65] Ḥayyim of Volozhin noted the inferiority of those who put great effort into the work of cultivating reverence and humility; the superior path, he made clear, was simply studying Talmud ("being occupied with Torah"), which guarantees moral transformation "by itself":

> Truly, for a person who is focused on being occupied with Torah for its own sake . . . for reverence for the Blessed One to be fixed in his heart, he does not need the great labor and effort and lengthy time spent immersed in books regarding reverence needed by those who are not focused on being occupied with Torah. For the holy Torah, by itself, drapes reverence for God upon a person's face, with little time and little effort spent on this, for this is the path and the [supernatural] remedy [*segulah*] of the holy Torah, as they say: "All who occupy themselves with Torah for its own sake . . . it clothes him with humility and reverence" (Mishnah Avot 6:1). And the first section of the midrash on Proverbs [teaches]: ". . . If a person learns Torah, and sits and occupies himself with it as necessary, then behold: he has in his hand [both] wisdom and moral discipline [*musar*]."[66]

The study of Talmud is here envisioned as a *segulah*—a supernatural remedy for the soul, providing a shortcut to moral transformation. Those who are not Talmud scholars may indeed need to spend time with "books regarding reverence"—that is, musar literature—but a scholar need not devote much time or energy to focusing on his moral development. The preferred path here is to spend "little time and little effort" actively cultivating virtue, and instead to fully devote oneself to the study of Talmud.

Simḥah Zissel, by contrast, emphasized the necessity of devoting much effort and much time to the cultivation of virtue. He did not see complete immersion in Talmud study as having miraculous power; on the contrary, as we have seen, he saw such immersion as potentially distancing people from other central obligations such as acting with lovingkindness toward others. Ḥayyim of Volozhin, like other Mitnagdim (the Lithuanian rabbinic elite), was far more optimistic about the powers of Torah study.

From another perspective, though, the Mitnagdim may be viewed as extremely pessimistic in comparison with Simḥah Zissel. As Allan Nadler has argued, the Mitnagdim sought to "dissuade the Jews from striving too brazenly" in their attempts to know God.[67] They saw human beings as deeply sinful, afflicted by the metaphysical evil described in Kabbalistic language as the *sitra aḥra*, the "other side." They were deeply pessimistic about what human initiative could accomplish; the divine grace available to those who immersed themselves in the study of Torah was the only real path by which the evil inclination and its "spirit of impurity" could be defeated. The Musar movement was far more optimistic, arguing that if they worked at it very hard, human beings could take the initiative to act in the world in ways that could lead them to rule over their evil inclinations and strive toward moral excellence.

As Immanuel Etkes has argued, Israel Salanter was influenced by the naturalistic understandings of the human soul common in the thought of the European Enlightenment, especially as expressed through the musar writings of the Haskalah author Menaḥem Mendel Lefin. Lefin presented a thoroughly naturalistic portrait of the soul, describing it as an entity that could be controlled by human efforts; he broke with the tendency of Kabbalah-influenced musar writings to describe the soul as controlled by the metaphysical forces of the *sitra aḥra*.[68] Salanter adopted this nonmetaphysical vision to a significant degree, following Lefin by stressing the need for individual human effort to achieve moral change. He did not abandon the more metaphysical view entirely: his writings also discuss the "impure spirit" within the human being, which cannot be repaired through natural means but only through the miraculous healing power of Talmud study. Nonetheless, Salanter indicates that such miraculous help is only available for a person who has fully exerted himself and achieved an extremely high level by his own efforts, through the painstaking work of musar.[69]

Simḥah Zissel's approach follows along these lines, though his naturalism is a bit more pronounced. As we saw in chapter 3,

Simḥah Zissel does acknowledge the possibility of supernatural help in the work of musar—"if a person does absolutely all that is in his power to do, and he immerses himself in effort and work until the point where nothing more is possible." But he sees "miraculous providence" as extremely rare, such that "the Torah commands doing all that is possible by means of nature, and not relying on miracles at all." One must "exert oneself" to hear God's word, he notes, and "we should not depend upon the miracle that his ears will be opened by Heaven, especially because it is incumbent upon a person to open up his [own] ears."[70]

To be sure, a natural sort of divine "grace" appears to be available to everyone to the degree that they exert themselves; as we have seen, Simḥah Zissel views every occurrence in the natural world as a miraculous, divine gift. Thus one can ordinarily speak of divine providence as occurring in proportion to a person's exertions, but not more than this.[71] God is by no means absent here; God guides people through every aspect of reasoning and fighting against the evil inclination, and God's infinite love sustains them through what we typically call "natural" means. Truly supernatural aid, however, seems extremely unlikely.

For the Mitnagdim, the acceptance of the reality of human frailty led to pessimism about human initiative and hope for miraculous grace; for Simḥah Zissel, by contrast, the acceptance of the reality of human frailty should lead to attempts to redouble one's efforts. One passage that makes this point begins with a meditation on the heroic efforts of the greatest of philosophers, Abraham, in subjugating his appetites to his reason. Abraham's accomplishment was incredible, Simḥah Zissel argues, not only because of the specific difficulties resulting from Abraham's childhood, but also because of how weak human reason is and how easily it is overpowered by bodily appetites:

> It is like the matter that we have described with this image: that a small barrier can block one off from the sun, even though the sun is a million times larger than the sphere of the earth. Nonetheless, because of its great distance, even the smallest barrier can block out and darken such a great light. This is all the more so with the light of reason, which is more distant from the body than the sun is from the earth—for the sun and the earth are of one kind, both being material . . . but reason and the body are not of the same kind at all. And because of this great distance, who knows how small a power granted to the body can block out

> the sun of reason's light? Therefore, [Abraham] saw that he had to crush and afflict his afflicted body. . . . and he set his heart to make himself like an ox under the yoke, to receive upon himself the yoke of the kingdom of heaven, to bind his senses and his movements so that he would be like a field cultivated for strong reason, to endure harsh and bitter afflictions for the filthy body. . . . And how very much it is incumbent upon us to accept the yoke of the kingdom of heaven. But *because of our many sins*, we are totally unable to receive upon ourselves the yoke of the kingdom of the Blessed One as is required; therefore, we have taken it upon ourselves (though without making a vow or agreement) [to set aside] one day out of every ten days on which we may do better in receiving upon ourselves the yoke of the kingdom of heaven.[72]

There is, here, a deep sense of the magnitude of human sinfulness and human weakness. Simḥah Zissel sees divine reason as trapped within a "filthy," sinful body, which can blot out its light with even the slightest desire; to subdue the body, as Abraham did, requires great effort and great bodily suffering. Simḥah Zissel confesses that he and his students are unable to meet this level of achievement "because of our many sins," but the response to the reality of sinfulness is not to seek grace; it is, rather, to pledge to increase one's efforts in the work of musar. The specific initiative proposed here is to dedicate every tenth day to a variety of special exercises and meditations. What is significant to note here is that the response to sin is to try harder—for, as Simḥah Zissel writes in another discussion of Abraham's journey, "there is no remedy for a human being other than to exert oneself very greatly."[73]

In nearly every one of his discourses and letters, Simḥah Zissel points out the effort (*hishtadlut*) and exertion (*yegiah*) involved in musar work, whether the effort required to overcome basic obstacles or the effort required to reach the heights of virtue. He is consistently concerned that people think it is "easy" to be a good person. When speaking of developing foresight, for example, he emphasizes "the effort required for this—so that one should not think that this is an easy thing to achieve."[74] When it comes to developing empathy, doing what comes "naturally" is not good enough: one must rather "*make an effort* to feel the nature of his fellow's pain."[75] To fulfill the obligation to "see oneself as if one came out from Egypt" requires far more effort than anyone realizes: "for this, one needs exertion and study—and yet who is there who exerts themselves for this?"[76]

In particular, Simḥah Zissel notes his contemporaries' skepticism about the need to engage in the effort of what Simḥah Zissel, following Salanter, calls "*hitpa'alut*"—being emotionally "engaged," "excited," or "exercised." Exciting one's emotions, appetites, and imagination is required by Simḥah Zissel's moral theory, as he sees virtue requiring the engagement of all parts of the soul; virtue cannot be developed merely through cognition, but only through great efforts to change one's whole self. Simḥah Zissel acknowledges that his contemporaries considered such efforts to be excessive. "Why should I immerse myself in developing habits and devising stratagems?" he reported them asking. "Surely I [already] believe that it is forbidden to be arrogant . . . and if so why become emotionally exercised—do I not [already] believe this?"[77] For Simḥah Zissel, though, having correct beliefs about the sinfulness of arrogance is insufficient; the necessary and difficult task is the work of engaging one's emotions and embedding such beliefs deeply within one's soul.

## The Slow Pace of Change

Such work, Simḥah Zissel emphasizes throughout his writings, will inevitably require great patience and perseverance. While some teachers connected with the Musar movement idealized sudden moral transformations, Simḥah Zissel emphasized that the development of virtue is a slow process. The Aristotelian idea taken up by Maimonides that "a sudden transition from one opposite to another is impossible," as "man, according to his nature, is not capable of abandoning suddenly all to which he was accustomed,"[78] is a firm principle in Simḥah Zissel's writings.

Simḥah Zissel assumes that human character is generally stable, as we are habituated to certain patterns of thought, emotion, and behavior. Change can happen when new patterns are introduced, but these new patterns must interact with human beings as they are, with all of their weaknesses. Simḥah Zissel assumes (as did Maimonides) that moral change requires accommodating human flaws and working with them, guiding a person to adopt incrementally better thoughts, emotions, and behaviors over a period of time. Though human reason must seek to harness the irrational parts of the soul, the work of educating such forces is very hard and, not surprisingly, takes a very long time.

It is not that one should be gentle in accommodating one's bodily appetites; properly subduing one's appetites often requires physical pain, as when Abraham "had to crush and afflict his afflicted body" and "endure harsh and bitter afflictions." In one metaphor that Simḥah Zissel uses, a rider must recognize that a wild horse is dangerous, and use great force to harness it. But he also must avoid abusing the horse if he wants to be able to ride it. So too, one must use force in harnessing one's bodily appetites—but not abuse them.[79] And crucial to treating the appetites properly, even if one must use great force, is to take one's time in educating them. As Simḥah Zissel writes, a person must "prepare himself to labor in breaking his appetites and character traits, using tremendous force—for a great force *and a long time* are required if he wants to bend a firm tree which has already been bent to one side and which is [now] to be bent the other way."[80] One must use tremendous force to break one's bad appetites and character traits, but Simḥah Zissel indicates that one's force will not produce a *sudden* change; rather, "a long time" is required. The image of a tree being bent from one side to another seems to indicate that a sudden yank is not going to solve the problem. Given that it has been bent in one direction for so many years, the tree could not withstand being pulled too quickly to the other direction. It must, rather, be bent slowly over a long time.

Simḥah Zissel mentions the slow process of moral change in many of his discourses.[81] Repentance in itself is a matter of "slowly, slowly changing [one's] deeds and changing [one's] nature."[82] A person must "slowly, slowly give his reason dominion over his heart—that is, always to habituate himself, little by little, in breaking or subduing the will."[83] "One is obligated to constantly prepare [with] effort to slowly, slowly change his evil nature, as did Abraham, Isaac, and Jacob."[84] One must develop compassionate love for others and thus "slowly, slowly distance oneself from self-love."[85]

Moral improvement happens incrementally—and so too does moral degeneration. A vice can begin as "a small speck born within" a person, Simḥah Zissel notes, but that vice may then grow "slowly, slowly"—as in the case of Abraham's nephew Lot, who slowly developed a destructive love of wealth over the course of time.[86] Just as people will not transform into saints overnight, they will not transform into sinners overnight.

As we have seen, Simḥah Zissel imagines that virtue may never be fully established, because even the best people can revert to viciousness at times. But he also posits that people are generally habituated to certain ways of behavior and so have a general stability of character. When the best people engage in an unjust act, this shows that virtue is not fully established in their souls, but it will not change the fact that their characters are generally virtuous. If they engage in additional unjust acts, however, their characters may slowly begin to change for the worse. If habits of acting justly are to wither away, they will wither away slowly. So too, one cannot expect persons of low moral character to have a sudden conversion to the moral life; they must slowly, slowly train themselves to develop the wide array of habits that make for virtue—habits of desiring, feeling, imagining, reasoning, and acting in certain ways.[87]

Many Jewish thinkers have had a very different model of moral transformation, assuming that it is possible for one's character to be radically transformed overnight, as it were. The conviction that such a transformation is possible may depend on assumptions that character can be changed through a miraculous act of divine grace, grace that may be triggered by the proper human performance of a certain action—such as the act of studying Torah, or alternatively, through certain words of prayer.

Simḥah Zissel notes that some Jews hope for the latter possibility during the holiday of Rosh Hashanah, for example, when they declare God's kingship and assume that their sins will be erased on account of their declaration. In Simḥah Zissel's generally naturalistic model of human psychology, such transformations are not possible. Enthroning God as king, he writes, "requires very much preparation"—and so "could it be that one could change one's nature in one hour on Rosh Hashanah during the hour that one recites [the prayers of] Kingship? Can one transform his will from bad to good in an hour?" Rather, to enthrone God as King, one must labor over the course of the entire year leading up to Rosh Hashanah, cultivating the lovingkindness befitting subjects of God's kingship: "There is an obligation . . . to occupy ourselves *during the entire year* with the positive commandment of 'You shall love your fellow as yourself' (Lev. 19:18), and through this there will be unity among the servants of the Blessed Lord, and [God's] Kingship will come into our hands well. . . . We must accept upon ourselves the work of loving people and of unity, and through this one's path will slowly, slowly improve."[88] Establishing God as one's king takes time and effort; it is only accomplished through transforming one's character in the only way that it is possible—climbing up the ladder of virtue one rung at a time.

Even without positing God's supernatural intervention, of course, one could still imagine the possibility of a rapid transformation of character. As Simḥah Zissel points out, one might imagine sudden repentance motivated by a momentary fear. But, in truth, such change does not last: "Sometimes, an awakening will occur to a person at the moment when he is sick (God forbid)—and, afterward, he returns to his foolishness."[89] Lasting moral change requires working with the faculties of one's soul and slowly habituating them to moral goodness over a long period. Virtues cannot be struck deeply in a person's soul without such work.

Of course, one might also deny that human beings need to be so accommodating to their baser appetites. One might assume that one can simply demand sudden change and overpower those appetites rather than nurturing resistance to them over time. One might reject Maimonides's assumption that "man, according to his nature, is not capable of abandoning suddenly all to which he was accustomed."

Indeed, some within the Musar movement did just this. In the period after Simḥah Zissel's death, some leading figures in the Musar movement rejected Simḥah Zissel's stress on needing to engage in a slow and gradual process of moral change. The clearest rejection of Simḥah Zissel's view came from Yosef Yoizel Horowitz (1848–1919), the founder of the Novaredok yeshiva, who was perhaps the most influential figure in the Musar movement in the generation after Simḥah Zissel. Horowitz is said to have studied with Simḥah Zissel in Kelm for a short time, but he took a path that was far more ascetic and that, as David Fishman has suggested, borrowed the uncompromising tenor of radical revolutionary politics. As Fishman describes it, the vision of Novaredok was that "there can be no concessions or compromises with the *yetzer hara* [evil inclination], because concessions, no matter how small or temporary, will merely serve to strengthen its power. The *yetzer hara* cannot be harnessed or transformed; it can only be defeated."[90]

Horowitz had no interest in Simḥah Zissel's model of "slowly, slowly" working to harness and transform the evil inclination. On the contrary, he stressed that moral change needed to be sudden and total, and offer no accommodations to one's present moral state. As Fishman has noted, this attitude was well expressed by Horowitz in a parable:

> If someone has a *treyf* [non-kosher] kitchen and wants to repent and make it kosher, he might say "how can I repent all at once and break all my dishes? It will cost a great deal of money! I'll do it gradually. I'll break one dish, and replace it with a kosher one; later I'll replace a second dish, later a third, and later a fourth, until it is completed." Such a person would be considered a fool. For as soon as the [first] kosher dish mixes with the rest, it is all *treyf.* He can live as long as Methuselah—breaking one dish and replacing

> it, breaking one dish and replacing it—they will be *treyf* forever. If he wants to repent he must break all the dishes at once, and buy entirely new ones.[91]

The path that Horowitz regards as foolish is precisely the path that Simḥah Zissel advocated: breaking one character trait at a time in order to gradually bend one's will toward moral goodness.

Simḥah Zissel joined Horowitz and all other thinkers associated with the Musar movement in seeing the soul as dominated by the evil inclination. To use William James's typologies, we would say that the Musar movement clearly saw human beings as fundamentally "sick" rather than "healthy," given its awareness of evil and its stress on the need to be "born again" as a radically new person. But, as James pointed out, those who experience spiritual change can also be divided into those who experience a "crisis"—a sudden transformation—and those who change through "lysis"—a gradual process.[92] Simḥah Zissel joined the company of those who advocated healing sick souls through a gradual process, whereas Horowitz joined those who sought to heal such souls through a sudden transformation. While Simḥah Zissel thought that the extreme difficulty of moral transformation demanded a gradual and compromising approach, Horowitz was certain that such difficulty meant that there was no room for compromise.

Simḥah Zissel, to be sure, can be accused of creating an overly demanding model of ethics. He demanded that people change themselves entirely, modeling themselves on an ideal of perfect virtue and battling against every untoward impulse within the soul. But within the context of the Musar movement, he was a moderate. His lofty ideals were tempered by his realism about what human beings can withstand. As we saw above, he demands that human beings push themselves beyond ordinary standards to do all that they are capable of doing, but he thinks that people should be judged in accordance with their ability rather than according to an impossible standard of excellence. As we have now seen, Simḥah Zissel demands that human beings seek to overcome their many flaws in every way possible, but he assumes that human flaws should be accommodated rather than simply obliterated. There is a sort of optimism here—that people are capable of working with their flaws and devising stratagems whereby they may be controlled and transformed over time.

On the other hand, there is also a deep pessimism in Simḥah Zissel's thought, as he joined his colleagues in the Musar movement in seeing the soul as fundamentally sick. He lacked the sort of confidence associated with the spirit of the Enlightenment and expressed by many modern Jews, such as Joseph Soloveitchik in his condemnation of the Musar movement in his book *Halakhic Man.* Suggesting that the efforts encouraged by the Musar movement might be necessary for sick souls, but that most people in fact have healthy souls, Soloveitchik offered the following message, which he imagined coming from the mouth of Ḥayyim of Volozhin in response to a suggestion to engage in musar-style meditation on "the day of one's death":

> If a person is sick we prescribe castor oil for him. However, it is certain that if a healthy person ingests castor oil he will become very sick. If that vile wretch (the evil impulse) meets you, and if you are sound in spirit and soul, if your consciousness and character are still whole and intact, occupy yourself with the Torah, drag him to the study house (see Sukkah 52b; Kiddushin 30b). This is the most effective and tried remedy in man's ongoing battle with his evil impulse. However, if you are spiritually sick, if a fit of madness has seized hold of you, if some psychic anomaly has put forth its diseased tendrils in your inner world, then you must use more powerful drugs, those that are designed for the very ill—the remembrance of the day of death. We in Volozhin, thank God, are healthy in spirit and body, are whole in our Torah; there is no need here of castor oil. If the scholars of Kelm and Kovno feel compelled to drink bitter drugs—let them drink to their heart's content, but let them not invite others to dine with them.[93]

This passage does not in fact embody Volozhin's critique of the focus on musar work, which we saw above; as Allan Nadler has pointed out, Ḥayyim of Volozhin joined the Musar movement in viewing human beings as having very sick souls, and he was in fact far more pessimistic about human initiative than Simḥah Zissel.[94] But this passage from Soloveitchik represents the modern confidence typical of many influenced by the Haskalah—a sort of confidence that Simḥah Zissel did not share. Simḥah Zissel was certain that, indeed, human beings did need to engage in all sorts of efforts, taking "bitter drugs"—not to suddenly shock their souls, but to slowly, slowly push their sick souls toward greater health and, insofar as it was possible, toward emulating God's perfection.

# 5

# Learning to Love

Simḥah Zissel often describes God's primary virtues as qualities of compassionate love, qualities generally indicated by the Hebrew words *ahavah* (love) and *ḥesed* (lovingkindness). Human exemplars, those who best walk in God's ways, are also distinguished above all by these virtues which, at their best, are described as the quality of "sharing the burden of one's fellow," *nosei be-ol im ḥaveiro.*

Simḥah Zissel, however, is not a systematic writer, and he never devises a formal hierarchy of the virtues. In fact, in his discourses he singles out a variety of virtues as embodying "the general principle of the Torah" or as being "the crown of the virtues." But these virtues each seem to culminate in compassionate love for other human beings.

Thus, for example, Simḥah Zissel often describes love and reverence for God as the purpose of the Torah; but he also indicates that such virtues are best expressed in love for others. For example, he argues that following the central biblical commandment to "love one's fellow as oneself" (Lev. 19:18) means emulating all of God's virtues—which is the same thing as drawing close to God in love:

> "'Love your fellow as yourself' is the great principle of the Torah"—because it includes all obligations towards one's fellow and it includes all of the virtues with which God governs His world (as is explained in *The Palm Tree of Deborah*); and also love of Israel *is* love of God, remarkably, and so this is the great principle, with all of the Torah contained in this.[1]

The idea that loving one's fellow as oneself is "the great principle of the Torah" is brought in the Jerusalem Talmud and in various midrashic collections in the name of Rabbi Akiva.[2] Here, Simḥah Zissel interprets Rabbi Akiva as suggesting that loving one's fellow is the ultimate expression of loving God.

As we have seen, Simḥah Zissel also describes equanimity as "the crown of the virtues" and as constituting "the purpose of all creation." But Simḥah Zissel seems to think of equanimity as an instrumental virtue: it is necessary for acquiring other virtues rather than being an end in itself. Above all, possessing equanimity means clearing away the "grit" that prevents one from loving one's fellow, for "it is not possible to love one's fellow as oneself until one has removed all of the material impurities from one's soul."[3]

In other places, humility is ranked as the highest of virtues. Simḥah Zissel notes that the Torah singles out Moses as the greatest of prophets and that it sees Moses's distinguishing characteristic as his humility (Num. 12:3); Simḥah Zissel explains here that "humility encompasses all of the character traits."[4] But he also depicts humility as especially significant because "humility leads to mercy" and ultimately to the highest levels of love. Thus Simḥah Zissel describes Moses as distinguished by his humility but above all by his disposition to compassionately "share his fellow's burden."[5] Proper humility necessarily leads to such love.

One other virtue that might be understood as the greatest of virtues in Simḥah Zissel's thought is the virtue of practical wisdom. As we have seen, Simḥah Zissel admires Shammai, one of the great rabbis of the first century BCE, for pointing to the centrality of practical wisdom when confronted with the challenge of explaining the Torah "on one foot." But Simḥah Zissel tends to present practical wisdom as an instrumental rather than an ultimate virtue. And he offers even more praise for Hillel, Shammai's counterpart who answered the same challenge by pointing to an ultimate ideal of love toward which all human action should be oriented. He commends Hillel for helping his questioner by teaching him "the foundation of the religion, that upon which it was built, so that he could meditate at all times upon the foundation of the religion, and then the details would be strengthened accordingly."[6]

The actual words that Hillel offers, as the Talmud records them, are: "Do not do to your fellow what is hateful to you." Is merely refraining from hateful action really the foundational principle that unifies all aspects of the moral life? What of emulating God's positive expressions of lovingkindness? As we will see, Simḥah Zissel suggests that Hillel's words actually mandate positive expressions of love as well. As Simḥah Zissel explains, Hillel teaches the prospective convert that "the prime foundation in a person's life is that he instill in his heart true love of human beings [*ahavat adam*], whatever religion they may be, because the entire political community is a partnership"; this true love should create a community in which everyone is engaged in acts of care for one another, with "everyone making preparations for each other."[7] In this vision, all of the details of the Torah can be unified under the banner of positive love that extends to all people. Every detail of the Torah should contribute to instilling such love in the hearts of those who observe it. Therefore Simḥah Zissel concludes that loving one's fellow as oneself is "the foundation of character traits and the great principle of the Torah—that is, for fulfilling the Torah."[8]

## Love as a Virtue

Not all Jewish thinkers have understood Hillel to be offering such an expansive conception of the virtue of love as standing at the center of Judaism, nor have all Jewish thinkers followed Rabbi Akiva's idea that the command to "love your fellow as yourself" is *the* all-encompassing principle of the Torah. In fact, Akiva's formulation does not use a direct article, and so he might simply be teaching that "love your fellow as yourself" is *a* great principle of the Torah rather than *the* all-encompassing principle of the Torah.[9] In any case, Akiva's view seems to be challenged by one of his contemporaries, Ben Azzai, who is quoted by the Talmud (in seeming dissent to Akiva) as offering an alternative "great principle of the Torah": "This is the book of the generations of Adam: When God created man, He made him in His own image" (Gen. 5:1).[10]

Even if one understands the commandment to "love your fellow as yourself" to be absolutely central to God's will, it is not obvious that the command ordains cultivating love as a virtue. A legally-oriented thinker might view the commandment as focused not on the virtue of love but on particular behaviors mandated by the commandment in Leviticus. Rabbinic tradition, after all, specifies a number of requirements directly mandated by that commandment, including obligations to attend to the sick, to comfort mourners, to bury the dead, to provide for and rejoice with the bride and groom, and to escort travelers to ensure their safety.[11] Simḥah Zissel values such particular requirements greatly, and he sees many other particular sorts of behaviors as mandated by the Torah's commandment to love—indeed, as we have seen, every detail of the Torah seems to be linked to that commandment. That various deeds are specified by tradition means that observing the commandment is never merely a matter of subjective judgment; certain deeds are legally required by God's commandment to love. But, for Simḥah Zissel, the commandment to love requires more than specific outward behaviors.

In Simḥah Zissel's view, God's central demand is for each individual to strive to cultivate love as a virtue. As a virtue, love must involve the emotions—crucially, it should involve intense empathy—but it is more than merely an emotion. Emotions may be distorted and ephemeral, whereas love should be a firm and rational virtue, guided by reasoned, autonomous choices. It should become a person's second nature, etched deeply into one's character in accordance with reason's clarifying light. One should be guided by this disposition to love at all times, Simḥah Zissel argues; even when one is unable to act, one should show loving concern for all of one's neighbors, such that one is responding to the commandment to love "tens of thousands of times in every single moment."[12] But love should ideally find expression in action, in accordance with the dictates of practical wisdom.

As much as Simḥah Zissel valued contemplative activity, he made it clear to his students that they should not be like "the philosophers" who valued contemplation of goodness over acts of goodness; nor should they be like typical yeshiva students who learned to privilege the study of Talmud over the performance of good deeds. Simḥah Zissel wanted his own students to follow a different model, characterized not only by inner concern but by outward expressions of love. One should "think continually of the positive commandment that 'you should love your fellow as yourself,'" Simḥah Zissel instructed his students, and also actually "seek out opportunities for showing lovingkindness to people."[13] As Simḥah Zissel's student Reuven Dov Dessler noted in his records of the proceedings of one of the musar groups at the Talmud Torah, it was resolved that one must "arouse within himself the desire for *activities* of lovingkindness, and endeavor not to let even one day pass without showing lovingkindness that is *actually in action*, whether great or small, whether through [one's] body, money, or speech."[14]

## Love as Partnership

Even simple displays of honesty, respect, and concern for the common good, Simḥah Zissel argues, are acts of love with profound social consequences. This, in his analysis, was part of what Hillel was indicating when he summarized the Torah as forbidding "doing to your fellow what is hateful to you." Such a formulation clearly forbids destructive behavior, but it also serves as a translation of the Torah's commandment to "love your fellow as yourself"—meaning, as Simḥah Zissel puts it, "do good for your fellow as you would do for yourself." Eager to show the positive dimensions of love despite Hillel's negative formulation, Simḥah Zissel sees Hillel as warning against evil as part of his vision of creating a loving and mutually supportive community. Not doing what is hateful is necessary to "guard the partnership in which they do good for you in accordance with your doing good for them"; it is the foundation of a good society characterized by its mutual beneficence.[15]

But "guarding the partnership," Simḥah Zissel goes on to note, requires more than simply refraining from harm. To guard against socially destructive behavior, Hillel surely knew, a person is required to engage in socially constructive behavior. One must move beyond self-interest and seek the well-being of others, expressing the virtue of love.

The examples of love that Simḥah Zissel offers, in his discussion of Hillel's words, include the Talmudic example (BT Berakhot 17a) of Rabbi Yoḥanan ben Zakkai, who had an unparalleled commitment to extending words of greeting and good will to everyone he saw, "even the idolater in the marketplace." He did so, Simḥah Zissel argues, out of love, "in order to habituate himself to the love of God's creatures [*ahavat ha-beriyyot*]." Small acts of wishing people well, here, cultivate the virtue of love, contributing to a sense of fellowship and respectful concern for the well-being of others.

So too, engaging in commerce may cultivate love. Simḥah Zissel sees commercial dealings as fraught with moral danger, because pursuing one's livelihood easily leads to pride, greed, dishonesty, and a lack of concern for other people. But he imagines that buying and selling in the marketplace can be transformed into an activity that promotes a sense of partnership and a spirit of caring for others. He reflects on the example of the Talmudic sage Ben Zoma who, on seeing a great crowd, praises God "who has created all these to serve me" (BT Berakhot 58a). As Ben Zoma explains, he is grateful to be able to purchase ready-made food and clothing, depending on the labors of others rather than having to create such things by himself. His gratitude for everyone "serving him" could be taken as an expression of self-centeredness, but Simḥah Zissel reads it as an expression of love for the political community on which he depends:

> The prime foundation in a person's life is that he instill in his heart true love of human beings, whatever religion they may be, because the entire political community is a

> partnership. This person makes shoes for his fellow, and his fellow sews clothing for him; this one builds a house for his fellow, and his fellow plants a vineyard for him; this one makes food for his fellow, and his fellow prepares a drink for him. Partners, if they want to succeed, must each do his work for his fellow faithfully, for if one makes shoes for his fellow fraudulently, his fellow will reciprocate accordingly with clothing made fraudulently, and so everyone will act this way. Therefore, if you want the work that you need to be good, you should do good work for what your fellow needs, as this will be reciprocal. And therefore Ben Zoma wanted to instill in his heart love of human beings, whether Jewish or not, and he said: "all were created to serve me," and if so they are my partners, and they prepare for me what I need, and I also prepare for them, with love, what they need.
>
> And in this way one will become habituated to always think that everyone is making preparations for each other—in order that love of God's creatures (whether Jewish or not) can be implanted in his heart. . . . If you deal with them faithfully, they will also deal with you faithfully. If you prepare your hearts to love your fellows, they will also prepare their hearts to love you.[16]

The economic and social cooperation that Ben Zoma finds to be such a blessing could be understood as emerging from the individual pursuit of self-interest, but Simḥah Zissel sees love at work. Engaging in constructive work, and so providing goods that contribute to the well-being of others, can inculcate and express profound lovingkindness. Honest business dealing can help to build loving bonds of trust and civic unity. A businessman can come to see himself as dependent on his customers but also as concerned to provide for their well-being; his customers, like Ben Zoma, come to see themselves as dependent on him while also concerned to provide for him. Political communities are sustained, in Simḥah Zissel's view, not by mere self-interest but by a sense of loving, mutual concern—loving one's fellows as oneself.[17] This, Simḥah Zissel thinks, is what Hillel meant when he posited that refraining from "what is hateful" is the basis of the Torah. Refraining from what is hateful and instead seeking the other's good, coming to see oneself as a partner rather than a competitor, means seeing the other "as oneself"—as a moral equal, on the same level as oneself—and loving the other accordingly.

Simḥah Zissel emphasized the sense of fellowship created through love with particular force during the month preceding Rosh Hashanah, the holiday marked by its proclamation of God's kingship. For God to reign, Simḥah Zissel instructed his students, God's subjects must be united by bonds of love; hence a sign posted on the door of his school during this month proclaimed the necessity of focusing on the commandment to "love one's fellow as oneself." In working at cultivating a sense of partnership, Simḥah Zissel taught, human beings should strive toward an ideal of love and unity rarely known in human history but experienced by Israel while fleeing from Egypt. The daily liturgy describes Israel "all together" (*yaḥad kulam*) at the moment of exodus, and Simḥah Zissel recommended meditating on this ideal moment of partnership "every day during prayer" as part of one's effort to inculcate the virtue of love within one's soul.[18]

This liturgical passage offers Simḥah Zissel an image of the community of Israel united by the bonds of love. But while appreciating the love that unites Israel and the special obligations of Jews to love one another, the emphasis in Simḥah Zissel's teachings is often on love of humanity and love of all of God's creatures. As we have seen, his paradigmatic examples of love include Yoḥanan ben Zakkai's good will toward idolaters and Ben Zoma's appreciation of the partnership of all of his fellow citizens, whether Jewish or not. The Talmud does not describe these examples in terms of love and, indeed, while premodern Jewish texts speak of obligations to care for those who are not Jewish, they often reserve the language of love for those within the more intimate covenant of Israel.[19] Simḥah Zissel, however, was among the early modern Jewish thinkers who sought to broaden the reach of love, inculcating a sense of partnership between the people of Israel and all with whom they might interact. He thus concludes his discussion of Hillel's message with the thesis that the Torah is aiming at "instilling love in a person's heart from his youth, love of human beings whether Jewish or not—for all are partners."[20]

## The Reach of Love

Simḥah Zissel was not the first traditionalist rabbi in modern Europe to speak of love as the proper attitude toward a Jew's non-Jewish neighbors. Those who had touched on this theme included Simḥah Zissel's ancestral relative, Rabbi Jacob Emden, and those who devoted greater energy to a universalist understanding of love included Samson Raphael Hirsch, the leader of German neo-Orthodoxy whom Simḥah Zissel much admired.[21] Simḥah Zissel may have been strengthened by these examples, and he may well have been encouraged by the general tenor of Enlightenment thought, with its characteristic emphasis on the equality of all human beings.

Simḥah Zissel's efforts to extend the boundaries of love would also seem to have emerged naturally from his own focus on emulating divine love. Though God's love may be known through God's particular concern for Israel, it is clear to Simḥah Zissel that God's perfect love must be universal love, extending to all that exists in the world—certainly to non-Jews as well as to Jews. For Simḥah Zissel, God's perfect love extends beyond human beings as well, to all of creation:

> The [fundamental] quality of God is that He loves all creatures; were it not so, they could not exist in the world. And we find that loving God's creatures is closeness to the Blessed One. . . . Our sages, in their holy way, have taught us (BT Sotah 14a): how can a person draw close to the Blessed One? By cleaving to His attributes. And there are no character traits of the Blessed Lord more apparent to us than love of His creatures. "You open up your hand and satisfy the desire of all that lives" (Psalms 145:16)—we see that every single creature receives pleasure and satisfaction for its desire, and this is simply God's love for His creatures. And consequently we find that the prohibition on causing suffering to animals comes from the Torah.[22]

The natural world is sustained by God's infinite love, and human beings are called on to emulate that love to the degree that they can by caring for all living beings. The paradigmatic way for human beings to emulate God's universal love, in this passage, is through following God's demand in the Torah to prevent the suffering of animals.

Simḥah Zissel sees human beings, who possess the capacity for morality and reason, as generally meriting greater love than animals. But human beings can forfeit their value and become like animals, as we have seen. The wicked human being who acts like an animal, failing to use his reason and control his irrational "animal soul," is no longer part of the human species but is "an animal in the form of a human being."[23] In fact, animals are on a higher level than the person who acts like an animal: “the animal is better than him, for it fulfils its purpose,” whereas he does not.[24]

But even wicked human beings who rank below animals in their status are described by Simḥah Zissel as deserving compassionate love. Simḥah Zissel reasons that “the Torah has compassion for animals, and so (learning from this) we should have compassion for [evildoers] as we do for animals.”[25] He also derives the obligation to love the most wicked of people from traditions about God’s behavior with the wicked, such as from the midrash in which God silences the angels who were celebrating while Pharaoh’s army drowned in the Sea of Reeds: “the works of my hands are drowning in the sea, and you are singing?” (BT Sanhedrin 39b). So too, Simḥah Zissel teaches, God shared the plans for the destruction of Sodom to Abraham in order that Abraham would see God’s compassion for the wicked and seek to emulate it by praying on their behalf. God taught Abraham, Simḥah Zissel posits, that it is God’s nature to seek traces of goodness even in the wicked; this is in contrast to “the nature of the human being who, faced with his enemy, will turn his eye away from the goodness that is in him, and not see it at all.” Abraham learned “to have mercy for the wicked and to seek their goodness”—that is, even when they are deserving of punishment, never to deny the value which makes them worthy of love, and never to give up on seeking that value.[26]

Love for the wicked does not, however, require forgoing their proper punishment. In Simḥah Zissel’s view, love should not always lead to mercy, and just punishment is often the properly loving response. The biblical assertion that God’s “lovingkindness is infinite” suggests to Simḥah Zissel that “even [God’s] punishment is lovingkindness.” Israel’s exile, for example, was designed to convince Israel to repent and draw closer to God, and even while promising exile, God kept Israel’s virtues in mind, remembering their potential for renewed “love” and “kindness” (Jeremiah 2:2).[27] While the punishments carried out by God seek to help those who are being punished, though, Simḥah Zissel notes that most human beings themselves sin by failing to show proper concern for the sinner and his dignity. Instead, they “are overcome by their hatred, tormenting him to death rather than giving him life.”[28]

It is not entirely clear, then, how Simḥah Zissel sees lovingkindness at work when God decrees death on sinners who are so wicked that they are unable to repent—such as the inhabitants of Sodom, Pharaoh’s army, or the Midianites. He may see a decree of death as a sign of kindness, insofar as death itself would offer sinners their only hope for atonement. Or he may see lovingkindness as less directed at the sinners and more directed at the potential victims who would now be shielded from the sinners' further crimes.[29] In any case, though, Simḥah Zissel views such death sentences as last-resort options; he sees the ideal model in Abraham's efforts to avert the destruction of Sodom by seeking goodness among its inhabitants.

The obligation to find goodness in all people—even in the wicked—is, in Simḥah Zissel's view, a core part of the obligations of love in which Abraham instructed his descendants. Love, in this view, is best strengthened through recognizing the goodness of the other. Thus Abraham's son Isaac, in Simḥah Zissel's reading, sought to find goodness even in his wayward son Esau, and "he loved him in accordance with the value of the good that he found in him."[30] Simḥah Zissel urged his own students to follow in this Abrahamic tradition, seeking out the good in all people. "One should endeavor to sometimes consider the positive commandment 'to love your fellow as yourself' in the manner of always looking for the virtue of one's fellow," he instructed, "for from this one will come to love one's fellow."[31] "Place before your eyes the good that your fellow has shown you, and the virtues of your fellow and not his vices, and, in this way, love every person."[32] "Endeavor to always find the virtue of one's fellow, seeking to learn from him and to comprehend that 'the sage learns from all people,' and thus love for God's creatures will be increased within."[33]

Focusing on the virtues of one's fellows, however, does not mean that one should ignore the vices of one's fellows. Quite the contrary—Simḥah Zissel understands offering criticism, and so helping others to improve their moral stature, as one of the highest manifestations of love. The Torah's commandment to "reprove your fellow" (Leviticus 19:17) comes in the verse immediately preceding the command to "love your fellow as yourself," and Simḥah Zissel follows a long Jewish tradition in understanding appropriate criticism to be a sign of deep love for others. Indeed, as he puts it, building on a statement by Jacob Emden, "the love of a loved one does not seem trustworthy to me if it does not seek out my blemishes—that is, criticize my faults."[34]

Harsh rebuke may, at times, be an ideal expression of love; Simḥah Zissel's models of loving reproof include the rebuke of Queen Esther by Mordecai (at Esther 4:13) and the unforgiving words of the prophet Samuel to King Saul (at I Samuel 15). Mordecai and Samuel treated their fellows like bitter enemies "for the moment," in Simḥah Zissel's understanding, as was required by the circumstances. But uncontrolled anger is never appropriate; anger must always be controlled by reason, as Simḥah Zissel assumes it was in these circumstances.[35]

Accordingly, caution is required before criticizing another person. One should ideally be persistent in one's criticism, but one should use one's wisdom and only continue to criticize if the recipient makes it clear at the outset that he or she is open to change.[36] And one must ensure that one's criticism comes from a place of reasoned, loving concern, recognizing the other person's virtues even while pointing out areas for improvement. Sometimes, Simḥah Zissel suggests, the best way to offer reproof is in fact not to mention a person's weaknesses but "to tell him of his fine virtues, and from this he will understand [the need] to repair his flaws by himself." Simḥah Zissel explains that this strategy will be most effective with people who are already on a high moral level, who are aware of the high standards by which they will be judged, and who are aware of their own weaknesses. One should encourage such people to think of their "loftiness of the soul [*hitromemut ha-nefesh*]" and how "lessening virtue would not be suitable for one on such a high level." For such people who are already aware of their flaws, merely focusing on those flaws may simply lead them to despair.[37]

Simḥah Zissel's various concerns regarding reproof build on classical rabbinic concerns.[38] He endeavors to find a model of how one might offer reproof well, motivated by love, guided by practical wisdom rather than self-interest. Simḥah Zissel considers it morally unacceptable to retreat from offering reproof that can help others, but he is also concerned that people offering reproof are often motivated by "self-love." Too often, he indicates, our attempts to help others by criticizing them are colored by our own self-interest and our desires for self-aggrandizement. Introspection and self-criticism must therefore always precede our efforts to criticize, he writes, following the Talmud's injunction to "clean yourself up first, before you clean others up."[39] As one of Simḥah Zissel's students summarized his teacher's approach: "one must use one's reason and understanding to distance oneself as much as one can, to the greatest degree, from self-love, and one's labor must simply be to spread the truth and glorify it, without the hope of any pleasure at all."[40]

## Loving One's Fellow and Loving Oneself

Just as the central virtue in Simḥah Zissel's writings is the virtue of loving one's fellow, which is closely linked with the proper service of God and with humility, the central vice is "self-love" (*ahavat atzmo*), which is closely linked with idolatry and with pride. Simḥah Zissel's concerns about self-love are very much present in his discussions of reproof—he is concerned both with how self-love keeps us from listening to reproof and also with how self-love keeps us from offering reproof effectively. On the one hand, "the person who loves himself does not give himself over to the advice" offered by others; on the other hand, one offering advice must "distance oneself as much as one can, to the greatest degree, from self-love."[41] But self-love infects every other area of human striving as well.

When Simḥah Zissel refers to the vice of self-love, he generally means the disposition to prioritize one's own interests over God's interests, seeking goods for oneself (typically wealth, prestige, or other sources of personal pleasure) rather than seeking goods that are "truly," objectively needed in the world. Moving beyond such self-love means seeking what is truly needed—in other words, what God demands: "in accordance with the diminution of one's self-love, there will grow love of the truth, which is 'the seal of God.'"[42] As a rejection of God in favor of the self, self-love is depicted by Simḥah Zissel as idol-worship: "it is essential to root out the idolatry that is within a person, as 'there should not be an idol within you'—namely, self-love, which is actual idolatry."[43]

Simḥah Zissel characterizes self-loving "idolaters" as those who care only "for themselves," living carefree lives so long as their own needs are met, "making every day into a holiday"; such people should expand their vision and consider "the needs of God"—the good of their greater community.[44] But Simḥah Zissel suggests that all people are afflicted by the vice of self-love, himself included. In one introspective passage, he reflects on how easily he remembers kindnesses done to him but has trouble remembering the good deeds that people do for others. "Why do I not thank someone who has done good for another?" he asks. "Surely it is because of self-love, that one feels what is good for oneself and not what is good for another. There is a wonderful lesson in musar here: how far the human being is from loving his fellow."[45]

The ideal of love here is to do away with our familiar, natural preoccupation with our own interests and to place the needs of others before our eyes. Given our natural disposition to privilege ourselves, we are prone to think that we love our fellows when in fact we are oriented toward our own worldly interests. Mishnah Avot 5:19 contrasts the lasting love of Jonathan for David, "love that does not depend upon something," with the short-lived love of Amnon for Tamar, "love that depends upon something." The latter form of love, in Simḥah Zissel's understanding, seeks self-gratification and is not the true other-directed love that God demands. In fact, it does not merit being called "love": "'love' should not, in fact, be ascribed to this [case] except for as a metaphor." In Simḥah Zissel's view, we are naturally disposed to this false form of love, which is actually a form of "self-love." But we can train ourselves to recognize that, in fact, love that seeks self-gratification is not true love at all.[46]

In condemning "self-love," however, Simḥah Zissel is not condemning all forms of regard for oneself. He in fact argues that overcoming "self-love" and cultivating love for others is a sign of true care for oneself. "Concern for one's fellow *is* concern for oneself," he writes, and this seems to be true for Simḥah Zissel both insofar as love for others heals one's own soul and also insofar as it creates a cooperative social climate in which other people reciprocate with love.[47] "Self-love," by contrast, not only harms others but also "destroys the self."[48] Engaging in "self-love," then, shows insufficient concern for oneself—or, one might say, insufficient love for oneself. Indeed, elsewhere in his writings Simḥah Zissel argues that the common, "foolish" conception of "self-love"—seeking to gratify the self with worldly goods—is not true self-love. It is the person who seeks to walk in God's ways, directing himself toward others, who is truly "the person who loves himself."[49] As he notes in another passage, those who distance themselves from momentary, worldly pleasures but pursue activities leading to eternal spiritual pleasures are clearly showing better care for themselves:

> The world thinks that wicked people are those who love themselves and therefore busy themselves in the pleasures of the world, whereas righteous people have no self-love at all and therefore have no business with this world. But it is on the contrary: those who love this world do not recognize [true] self-love at all. And this is like what Aristotle wrote . . . [about how] every thing is loved in accordance with the value of the thing. . . And so, in this case, one who loves this world cannot have love for himself beyond the good that this world gives him, and in fact this world is "like a passing shadow" (Ps. 144:4); as we have explained, it is like a moment. . . . On the other hand, love of the world to come is without limit, and therefore one who [truly] loves himself does so without limit.[50]

As we saw in chapter 2, Simḥah Zissel hesitates to encourage people to seek out spiritual pleasures—he sees the philosophers as erring by seeking personal happiness when "their goal is their self-love."[51] But he clearly believes that the disinterested pursuit of moral excellence is extremely good for people, and so such a pursuit is certainly a sign of a proper sort of self-love.

And while, in this vision, caring for things of this world would seem to have little value, elsewhere Simḥah Zissel indicates that overcoming false, worldly "self-love" does not demand a total disregard for one's own legitimate physical needs. In condemning worldly self-love, Simḥah Zissel appears to condemn our tendency to seek more than we need rather than condemning all care for the body. As we saw in chapter 1, Simḥah Zissel urged his students to care not only for their souls, but also for their bodies. This theme is borne out in his writings, which teach that treating one's body with respect shows respect for the soul, especially insofar as it allows one to have the equanimity that the soul requires. More generally, Simḥah Zissel writes of how the Torah forbids disregard for one's physical well-being, such that we are called to treat our bodies with compassion.[52] As I emphasized in chapter 2, Simḥah Zissel is convinced that spiritual values can only be realized through the physical world, "the world of action"; proper lovingkindness, then, must involve physical deeds of lovingkindness, attending to legitimate physical needs. And while in general we should turn our attention away from our own needs and toward the needs of others, our own bodies have legitimate needs as well.

There are, then, legitimate forms of "self-love" that can be distinguished from the disposition to self-centeredness that Simḥah Zissel harshly condemns. Just as he seeks to find goodness in wicked people, he finds good aspects in what is generally a wicked disposition.[53] Simḥah Zissel thinks that one can show appropriate love for oneself through concern for one's soul and for one's physical needs.

Moreover, he argues that the *manner* in which we naturally show such concern for ourselves should serve as a model for how we love others. We tend to provide for ourselves, Simḥah Zissel points out, not out of a sense of duty, but naturally, easily, and spontaneously. People are already accustomed to give to their children as they give to themselves, he points out, and we should train ourselves to give to others in the same way:

> We are warned to slowly, slowly accustom ourselves to the character trait of generosity to such an extent that one gives charity in the way that one gives to one's children, to whom one does not give because of the commandment of charity

> but in the way that one puts food in one's own mouth: a person finds joy whenever he is able to please his family with clothes and food and drink. A person needs to accustom oneself to the character trait of generosity in this way, to such an extent that he finds joy in helping and providing for the poor, as if they are truly part of his family. . . .
>
> And this is as the matter of "loving your fellow as yourself" . . . . One should love one's fellow as one loves oneself, for a person does not love himself to fulfill the commandment of loving God's creatures, but rather loves himself *naturally*. . . . Thus the warning is given to a person that he should accustom himself to the character trait of loving God's creatures, slowly, slowly, until he *naturally* loves the other, and *naturally* rejoices in the good of the other, just as he *naturally* rejoices in his own good and the good of his children, rather than to fulfill a commandment, for then his love would not be complete. His love will only be complete if he loves *naturally*. And this is the goal of the commandment and the desire of the Blessed One in commanding "loving your fellow as yourself," and in this way one will come to resemble the Blessed One.[54]

Thus, in Simḥah Zissel's understanding, "loving your fellow as yourself" as God desires, and in the way that God Himself loves, means loving others in the same sort of natural way that we love ourselves. Ideally, love of others should be inculcated as a virtue within the soul so that it flows forth joyfully, without reference to duty. Simḥah Zissel offers a novel interpretation of the phrase "as oneself," which he sees as teaching us to move beyond a sense of duty and to find a more natural way to love others.[55] Our self-love, then, has a certain dignity insofar as it should serve as the model for our care of others.

Hence, when Simḥah Zissel summarizes his approach to the commandment to "love one's fellow as oneself," he lists two complementary interpretations. On the one hand, "as oneself" is an adjectival phrase, explaining the nature of the other whom we love: "he is like you"—that is to say, he is your moral equal, such that the concern for yourself which you are permitted to have should not eclipse your concern for him. On the other hand, the phrase "as oneself" is an adverbial phrase, explaining how loving others may be grounded in love of oneself: "love of others should be like self-love [*ahavat atzmo*], which is the quintessential love [*ahavah atzmit*]."[56]

With his appreciation of self-love, Simḥah Zissel lacked the drive for complete self-effacement that characterized some other figures in the Musar movement and that was especially prominent in the history of Kabbalistic musar literature. Thus, for example, one of the musar texts that Simḥah Zissel treasured most greatly, Moses Cordovero's *The Palm Tree of Deborah*, advised that "a person should not find any value in himself at all, but rather he should think of himself as nothing [*ayin*]" and "make himself into an actual nothing [*ayin mammash*]." Cordovero stressed self-annihilation because he did not think that embodied, individuated human existence in this world has much value.[57]

Simḥah Zissel had a more positive estimation of the value of being embodied as an individual in this "world of action." As much as he saw the body as evil, he also saw individual physical embodiment in the world as a reality that must be respected. Simḥah Zissel saw physicality as loathsome in many respects—but he also thought that rationality could not be fully expressed in this world in any way other than through physical deeds. He saw embodied human nature as deeply evil—but he knew that to possess any strength in the physical world, reason must harness and work with our evil inclinations. He saw self-love as the most pernicious bodily vice of all—but he suggested that our instinct toward self-love can be harnessed for good, because in fact we should care for our own legitimate needs. As such, our own individual bodies and souls deserve our love. Annihilating them is not the ideal, as it is for Cordovero.

Simḥah Zissel's ideal of appropriate self-love is, accordingly, the sort of ideal that would not be found in Kabbalistic musar literature along the lines of *The Palm Tree of Deborah.* It instead adopts a language found in the more worldly musar literature produced by the Haskalah. This language is, notably, found in at least one piece of Haskalah musar literature that Simḥah Zissel undoubtedly read, the book *Moral Accounting* by Menaḥem Mendel Lefin, which had been reprinted in Lithuania by Israel Salanter. Lefin, like Simḥah Zissel, described "self-love" as a given of human nature that could be used for good if properly trained.[58] Simḥah Zissel agreed with this Haskalah notion that "self-love" can be good, that it is a part of our nature that can be harnessed rather than simply being annihilated.

## Moses and the Burden of His Fellows

But while his vision of self-love may have made Simḥah Zissel sound more like a moderate *Maskil* than a follower of Cordovero,

Simḥah Zissel hardly embraced another common "moderate Haskalah" idea regarding loving one's fellow as one loves oneself. That idea is expressed in Naftali Herz Wessely's commentary on Leviticus 19:18, in which he concludes that "as oneself" should *only* be understood adjectivally—"he is equal to you, he is like you, for he is also in the image of God, and he is a human being as you are." In Wessely's understanding, one should recognize one's kinship with other human beings, and thus refrain from doing what is hateful to one's fellow (as Hillel taught), but one should not pretend that it is possible to do the impossible, to actually give one's fellow the same treatment that one gives to oneself: "If this were so, one would need to grieve over the sorrow of his fellow just as for his own sorrow, and he would not live his life, as there is no moment in which one would not see or hear of the sorrow of someone in Israel. And so too, with the idea that the good that one would need to do for one's fellow should be all that one does for oneself, this is also an absurd idea."[59]

Wessely takes a realistic approach that is grounded in earlier Jewish perspectives such as that of Naḥmanides; he suggests that it would be impossible to set aside one's own self-centeredness, to grieve for everyone's losses the same way that one would grieve for one's own. Simḥah Zissel might acknowledge the impossibility of such a stance but, as we have seen, he insists that human beings should strive toward the impossible, seeking to emulate the idea of perfect divine goodness. As Simḥah Zissel sees it, God does grieve for every loss and seeks the good of all creation, acting in accordance with an objective standard, not in accordance with the self-interest of individuals, and human beings must strive for this ideal as best we can. Simḥah Zissel would have seen Wessely's view as encouraging too much self-love. We may be entitled to have some self-concern, in Simḥah Zissel's view, but we must strive to have equal concern for everyone else to the degree that it is possible.

Simḥah Zissel is demanding that human beings seek to radically recalibrate their vision. We naturally see the world from our own perspectives, attending to what we desire to see, motivated by self-love to focus on our own interests. But our self-love gives us a false picture of the world—"self-love is the epitome of falsehood," as Simḥah Zissel explains—as we fail to see the world and all of its needs from a true, objective perspective. It is to counter this failure of vision, Simḥah Zissel suggests, that the sages urge us to turn away from our own desires and to "share the burden of one's fellow." It is by means of "sharing the burden of one's fellow" that one might "slowly, slowly distance oneself from self-love . . . and approach the truth and merit acquiring Torah."[60]

"Sharing the burden of one's fellow" is the phrase that Simḥah Zissel uses to characterize the highest form of the virtue of love. The phrase comes from a list of the forty-eight virtues necessary for acquiring Torah in Avot, the Mishnah's classical anthology of moral wisdom.[61] It is not singled out there for particular attention, and it is a phrase that receives little attention in the history of Jewish thought until Simḥah Zissel labels it as the highest level of virtue demanded by the Torah. He uses the phrase to refer to the disposition to see the needs of others, to empathically identify with those in need, and to respond compassionately. Empathic identification, for Simḥah Zissel, is not always a matter of responding to suffering, as the obligation to "share the burden" also directs us to rejoice along with those who have joy.[62] But Simḥah Zissel sees suffering (both physical and spiritual) as ubiquitous, and so his discussions of "sharing the burden" focus on compassionately responding to it.

The virtue of "sharing the burden of one's fellow" was exemplified, Simḥah Zissel teaches, in the life of Moses. As I noted at the start of this chapter, the Torah takes humility to be Moses's exemplary virtue, but Simḥah Zissel sees proper humility as a matter of turning away from pride and "self-love," such that one can "feel the pain of his fellow and share his fellow's burden." Possessing such virtue was what made Moses fit to receive the Torah.[63]

Simḥah Zissel tells the story of Moses coming to this point as a story of Moses changing the way he saw the world. The Torah tells that Moses, living as a prince in Pharaoh's palace, "grew up . . . and saw their sufferings," the physical sufferings of the people of Israel (Exodus 2:11). Rashi's classic commentary on the verse understands that Moses "focused his eyes and his heart to suffer on their account." Simḥah Zissel builds on this: focusing his eyes, he explains, means that Moses meditated on their suffering, refusing to let his vision turn from it; focusing his heart means that "he brought this into his heart, so that his heart would feel their pain as if he himself was in this pain." Turning away from his life of privilege in Pharaoh's palace, Moses fills his mind with images of the suffering of others, and meditates on them: "he habituated himself to seeing these mental images to such an extent that he felt their pain as if he himself was in such pain, and so he came to be sharing their burden."[64] Moses's love, here, is not just a feeling, but it becomes a way of seeing, a fixed virtue, a habit of the heart formed through meditating with deep empathy on the sufferings of others.

Such virtue demands action; seeing the suffering of others before his eyes compels Moses to respond. His initial effort is to rescue a Jewish slave being beaten by his Egyptian taskmaster. As Simḥah Zissel notes, Moses's intervention shows that he has moved from concern about the people in general to concern about particular individuals who are suffering: "the Torah tells that he shared the burden not only of the many but also of the individual." Simḥah Zissel goes on to describe Moses as having developed "brotherly love" (*ahavat aḥim*), because Moses sees the slave as "one of his brothers" (Ex. 2:11) and feels his brother's pain deeply in his own heart.[65]

Moses's ensuing act of "brotherly love" is, then, to kill the task-master—an act not typically described as an act of "love." Simḥah Zissel clearly believes that this killing is justified—presumably following the midrashic traditions that Moses is preventing an attempted murder and that he conferred with the angels before killing the taskmaster—but Moses is generally described as pursuing justice, not love per se.[66] Simḥah Zissel is, here, continuing to insist that proper justice should be viewed as an expression of love: in this example, the just killing of a taskmaster is an expression of loving compassion for this particular slave and perhaps also for the rest of the Jewish people who are suffering grave injustices. From Simḥah Zissel's perspective, Moses is sensitizing himself to the needs of others, identifying with their suffering, and responding with practical wisdom and compassion.

In this first episode, love is expressed in solidarity with his kinsman against Egyptian taskmasters, but as the Torah proceeds to describe, Moses then expands his concern to include Jews afflicted by other Jews, seeking to intervene when he sees "two Hebrew men fighting" (Ex. 2:13). In this case, too, "he shared the burden of the one being oppressed . . . and he sought to save him from the hand of his oppressor."[67]

Simḥah Zissel points out that, in these examples, Moses's compassion is facilitated by the fact that he is in his homeland, protected by his authority as a prince in Pharaoh's palace. What is remarkable, he notes, is that Moses continues to deepen his compassion by pursuing justice for those outside his community after he flees Egypt for Midian:

> Not only in his own land, in his homeland, where he was dwelling in peace and tranquility, but even in a foreign land, in Midian, where he was a stranger in a foreign land, fleeing from Pharaoh and from death, reeling from and troubled by his own sorrow—despite all of this, when he

> saw what the shepherds there were doing to the daughters of Midian, "driving them away" (Ex. 2:17) unlawfully, "Moses rose up and saved them" (Ex. 2:17). Even in the land where he was a stranger, even fleeing from death, even there he hated unjust gain (meaning "injustice," as Naḥmanides of blessed memory explained regarding Exodus 18:21)—even there, Moses rose up and saved them. And Scripture goes on to tell that not only did he save the daughters of the priest of Midian from their oppressors, but he also "watered their flocks" (Ex. 2:17).[68]

At that moment Moses could easily have been consumed by his own interest, Simḥah Zissel suggests; but when he comes across the shepherds assaulting Jethro's daughters at a well, he is moved by empathy to respond. He extends his compassion beyond his own community of Israel, showing his love for strangers in a strange land; and he shows extra kindness, Simḥah Zissel remarks, by not only preventing injury but by seeking to help the victims draw water for their sheep.

Moses may also be demonstrating his care for animal life here; indeed, as he proceeds to take over the shepherding of Jethro's flocks, Simḥah Zissel notes that he goes on to devote himself to compassion for animals. Simḥah Zissel points out the great value of engaging in the work of shepherding; Moses was, he explains, like Jacob and David, a shepherd whose work taught him to overcome "self-love" and to share the burden borne by his flocks:

> In accordance with what has been explained above regarding the lofty matter of sharing the burden of one's fellow, we can understand why the great [leaders] of Israel chose to be shepherds. First, they chose lowly work, making a living in a humble manner. Second: humility leads to mercy, because pride is self-love and nothing else, and one who is proud does not feel the pain of his fellow and does not share his fellow's burden. Therefore, they habituated themselves in the work of shepherding and in having mercy on the flock, leading them gently and compassionately, as befit their fine manner. And when their nature was imbued with mercy for creatures who do not have reason, all the more were they inclined to be merciful with rational beings and the chosen people. They were educated to lead the chosen people and to walk in the ways of God.[69]

The lack of honor afforded to shepherds is part of what helps to shape the souls of Jacob, David, and Moses; the key effect of their work is that it trains them to be more compassionate human beings who will be fit to be the leaders of the people of Israel. In another passage, Simḥah Zissel makes no mention of the humbling nature of being a shepherd, but focuses on the task of "sharing the burden" of animals: "Our forefathers—our father Jacob, peace be upon him, and David, and also our teacher Moses the shepherd, peace be upon him—concerned themselves with livestock as shepherds for this reason: they wanted to habituate themselves even to share the burdens of animals—all the more so to share the burdens of people of their generation."[70]

Sharing the burden is, at its best, directed toward those with the greatest value and the greatest potential—human beings created in God's image. Morally capable human beings possess greater moral value than animals, in Simḥah Zissel's view, yet animals still possess real moral status, being beloved in God's eyes. The status of nonrational animals is roughly analogous to the status of the nonrational human body, which is inferior to the rational soul but still possesses value and should be treated with compassion. The analogy is imperfect insofar as Simḥah Zissel sometimes sees animals as possessing a higher status than mere human bodies, especially since he sees animals as having an intuitive spiritual relationship with their creator, "surrendering themselves to be servants of God."[71]

In any case, Simḥah Zissel describes Moses, David, and Jacob's care for animals as focused on responding to physical needs with compassion. In the case of Moses, Simḥah Zissel quotes the midrash that describes how Moses's compassion for his flock proves his worthiness to lead the people of Israel:

> Our sages have said that when Moses our teacher, peace be upon him, was shepherding the flock of Jethro, a lamb escaped. He ran after it until the lamb reached a pool of water where it stopped to drink. When Moses arrived there, he said: "I had not known that you had run away because of thirst. You must be tired." He placed it on his shoulder and walked back. God said: "You have shown mercy in guiding your flock in this way. By your life—you should shepherd my flock, Israel."[72]

Moses here develops the ability to empathize with the suffering of his lamb and to respond with kindness. His act of compassion is a small act, and Simḥah Zissel notes that actions like these have little value in most people's eyes—"these are the simple things that people scorn," as "they are considered foolish in people's eyes."[73] But these are actions that, according to the midrash, God values; indeed, God views Moses's act of compassion for his sheep as exemplifying the trait of compassion.

All of the acts of compassion that lead up to Moses's selection by God come in response to physical suffering—the physical suffering of the slaves who are beaten in Egypt, the physical suffering of Jethro's daughters who are assaulted, and the physical suffering of the lamb who is in need of water. Simḥah Zissel sees the relief of the soul's suffering as more important than the relief of the suffering of the body, but caring for the body is also important. One can only serve God through the spirit if one cares for one's body. And so while Simḥah Zissel sees Moses's ultimate achievement as providing for Israel's spiritual needs by teaching them the Torah, he sees Moses's efforts to relieve physical suffering as the essential prerequisite to this task:

> The opening statement regarding the life of Moses our teacher, peace be upon him, was that "he saw their sufferings," and in line with the commentary of Rashi this means that he was ready to be the agent who would do good for the bodies of the people of Israel, bringing them out from the physical hardships of Egypt so that they could serve God at "this mountain" (Ex. 3:12), Mount Sinai. The Torah therefore proclaims that he was the person fit to be the agent for Israel because he had this character trait of "sharing the burden of his fellow," which points to the value of the body and of the soul.[74]

In Simḥah Zissel's view, Moses understands the importance of responding to both the physical and the spiritual needs of his people. He is following God's model of love for Israel: Moses's "deep-seated love [*ahavat nefesh*] for them joined love for their bodies with love for their souls, just as the love of the Blessed One for His chosen people is for their bodies and for their souls."[75] Moses, the greatest of all prophets, develops an understanding of God's compassion for all parts of the created world.

The depths of Moses's compassion can be seen insofar as he not only empathizes with Israel, with Midianites, and with animals, but also in that he empathizes with the divine as much as any human being can. When he encounters God in a burning bush, Moses realizes the degree to which God suffers when others suffer:

> After [telling the stories of Moses's early life], the Torah tells that God appeared to Moses in the bush, to say, as it were, "I am also suffering along with them," and also to proclaim that Moses had become accustomed from his youth to walk in God's ways. So it is written: "you should walk in His ways" (Deut. 28:9)—"just as I am merciful and gracious," etc., "so too you should be merciful and gracious," etc. And: "if [a poor person] cries out to me, I will hear, for I am gracious" (Ex. 22:26).[76]

Simḥah Zissel here alludes to a midrash that describes God as suffering when Israel suffers; according to the midrash, God chooses to speak from amid painful thorns to symbolically demonstrate God's pain. Simḥah Zissel suggests that Moses has trained himself from his youth to follow God's path of identifying with the pain of others; it is not surprising, then, that he can also identify with the pain of the divine. God, the ultimate exemplar of sharing the burden, identifies with Israel's suffering as slaves; we might understand that Moses, in empathizing with God's pain, can now be seen as empathizing with Israel not for subjective reasons but because it is objectively required by God. Moses learns to perceive what is needed in the world through God's eyes, insofar as this is possible. "Sharing the burden," compassionately opening one's eyes to the needs of others, culminates with opening one's eyes to God's needs and "walking in God's ways" by emulating God's empathic concern. Moses achieves this level of emulating God and therefore is fit to receive the Torah, which Simḥah Zissel sees as the ultimate expression of God's empathic love—God's ultimate response to human physical and spiritual needs.[77]

## Love and the Practice of Musar

Not only is God a model of compassion, but God is pictured by Simḥah Zissel as modeling the sorts of spiritual exercises used by human beings to build their empathy. Exodus 24 depicts a vision of "brickwork" under God's feet, which one midrashic tradition understands as showing that while Israel was enslaved in Egypt, making bricks, God joined them in slavery. Simḥah Zissel expands on this, suggesting that, as it were, God placed a reminder of Israel's enslavement in the divine field of vision, to remind God to continually empathize with Israel. "It is not, God forbid, that God needs a physical likeness to remember"—but, rather, this image is designed to give human beings a model for how we should cultivate empathy for those who suffer. The vision of the brickwork before God is designed to teach that human beings need to cultivate "mental images" so that we can continually place the suffering of others before our eyes.[78]

God here models the same sort of visualization exercise that Moses performed in Pharaoh's palace when he "habituated himself to seeing these mental images" of Israel's suffering "to such an extent that he felt their pain as if he himself was in such pain." For Simḥah Zissel, engaging in this sort of meditation is essential. Love depends on empathy, and empathy depends on creating mental images in one's mind: "it is only possible to feel another person's pain and to share his burden with him by utilizing significant mental images, so that with all the pain and suffering and injury which happen to another person, it is as if it happened to oneself." Wicked people, by contrast, are those who are "far from [developing] mental images of their fellows, and who therefore do not feel the pain of their fellows."[79]

Simḥah Zissel describes such people as being like "beasts," lacking the human capacity for moral empathy.[80] But he suggests that all people naturally tend toward this sort of animal level. We lack the natural ability to keep in mind the suffering of others for whom we are obligated to care. In Simḥah Zissel's view, we do have a natural inclination to feel the pain of people who are suffering right before us, but once they are out of sight, our empathy wanes. It is the job of reason, harnessing our emotions and our imagination, to focus our attention on suffering even when it is not before our eyes, fixing images of the suffering of others in our minds so that it is as if we are suffering as well. The following text, though it may have been written by one of Simḥah Zissel's students rather than by his own hand, does well in capturing Simḥah Zissel's sense of the limits of our natural capacities for "sharing the burden":

> Anyone whose understanding is through the senses, without the labor of reason, knows every matter only at the time that the senses are engaged, and when the senses move on from the matter, one no longer knows it and will therefore remember the general but not the specific matter. With a *natural* character trait like mercy for a poor person, mercy is naturally only through the senses, and one will only have mercy for the time that the poor person is in front

> of him, and when he moves on he will not remember the poor person and he will not use this character trait. The *rational* character trait, on the other hand, will know and bring itself into the details and will always remember, so that [the person] will not depart from memory. Even if the poor person has already moved on, this force has placed a mental image of all of the details of the poor person's suffering before him.[81]

Our "natural" compassion is all too ephemeral, but when compassion is guided by reason, we are directed to impress the details of others' suffering on our memories. Proper love for one's fellow requires employing reason in this way, allowing us to take a person's needs seriously even when the person is not physically present. Such compassion must be nurtured through musar, through disciplined efforts at cultivating it.

But even in the moment of being approached by a person in need, when that person is present, one needs to engage in the work of visualization. The natural capacity for compassion that we do have is easily challenged, especially when it comes to sharing our wealth. The commandment to freely lend to "the poor that is with you" (Ex. 22:24), for example, is easily ignored unless we do the work of imagining ourselves in the place of the poor person who is asking us for a loan. Rashi's classic commentary on the commandment sees its stress on the poor person being "*with* you" as teaching that you must "see yourself as if you are the poor person." Simḥah Zissel takes this to mean that one must make an effort to visualize oneself in poverty, actively considering how one would like to be treated:

> Scripture is giving advice to a person, that he should not refrain from lending, for it is human nature to refrain from doing so. And so Scripture says: see yourself as if you are the poor person, and see whether it would be good for you if the lender refrained from lending; now, therefore, you should not refrain from lending. Our words should be explicated to emphasize that Scripture commands bringing the matter into one's sense-experience so that it is as if you were the poor person, so that then giving the loan will be easy for you.[82]

This sort of visualization exercise is at the heart of loving one's fellow as oneself: one must treat the other as one would want to be treated in the same circumstances, and this requires empathy—using one's imagination to put oneself in the other's place. As always, abstract theories are insufficient to motivate embodied human beings, who are best motivated by things that are made accessible to our senses. Though sense perceptions are naturally allied with evil, they can be harnessed for the good, helping to encourage proper care for others.

How does one go about realizing what it is like to stand in someone else's place? How reliable can a person's attempt to enter into someone else's experience be? Simḥah Zissel indicates that developing proper empathy requires actually joining someone else in their pain to whatever degree is possible. One can best "share the burden of one's fellow" in one's mind, developing a mental image of another person's suffering, when one actually seeks to take up some of their burden for oneself:

> Among the character traits by which Torah is acquired, [our sages] included "sharing the burden of one's fellow," and we have not known its meaning well, but we can understand when we see a wagon driver steering a full wagon, when his horse does not want to go forward, and he beats it and beats it. If the wagon driver were himself to try to pull the burden with all his might, like a horse, then he would not be so cruel to the horse. But because he is not pulling along with the horse, he does not have a mental image which demands compassion for the horse, which is continually pulling with all its might. And this is what [our sages] hinted at: if you want to feel the pain of your fellow, stand next to him and pull his burden along with him, and then you will feel your fellow's pain.[83]

To develop a mental image of his horse's experience, the wagon driver must actually tug on the load that he expects his horse to pull. Simḥah Zissel extends this model to other realms as well: a political leader, for example, should empathize with members of the public by taking on some of their suffering. Thus Joseph, for example, while serving as vizier of Egypt during the years of scarcity, felt obligated to deprive himself so that he could identify with the suffering of the community—"so that he would share the burden of his fellow."[84]

In addition to cultivating empathy for the living, Simḥah Zissel also notes the importance of cultivating empathy for the dead by imagining the suffering that inevitably occurs after death. As all people sin to some degree during their lifetimes, all people experience some painful process of spiritual purification after their deaths. "Sharing the burden of the dead" is, therefore, one of the primary purposes of mourning. Mourners can take on some of the suffering of the deceased: the Torah's laws of mourning impose privations on the mourners, allowing them to experience some hint of the suffering that the dead experience. The mourner "shares the burden of the dead," Simḥah Zissel explains, and this act of empathy actually reduces the burden that the deceased must bear, "making it easier for the dead."[85]

Simḥah Zissel explains that a mourner's encounter with death also has another, more general function: it awakens the mourner's soul and inspires repentance. Not only is the pain of mourning a direct sign of compassion for the dead, but the contemplation of death should inspire mourners to reflect on their moral state and to increase their lovingkindness toward all of God's creatures. An awareness of the imminence of death itself can be gained through mourning, in line with the teaching of Ecclesiastes that "it is better to go to a house of mourning than to go to a house of feasting" (Ecc. 7:2). Simḥah Zissel suggests that mourning makes the reality of death tangible, providing firm "mental images" that remind a person of the reality of one's actual death and the fate that awaits one after death. Keeping this in mind can help one focus on the state of one's life and the need for self-improvement.[86]

Simḥah Zissel sees a suggestion of this notion in a Talmudic story regarding a pious man who, after being scolded by his wife, went to spend the night in a cemetery.[87] He follows the understanding of this story that he learned from Israel Salanter, according to whom the husband became irrationally angry at his wife and went to the graveyard to quell his anger: "he stumbled with anger. . . . Therefore, he went to spend the night in the cemetery, in order to bring the remembrance of the day of death into sense-experience." As Simḥah Zissel's friend Isaac Blazer explained when reporting the same teaching, the direct confrontation with "the final end of the body" deepened the man's humility, helping him to respond to his wife with greater kindness. Doing what it takes to become aware of one's mortality—even spending the night at a cemetery, if that is what it takes—is essential for cultivating one's character and nurturing proper relationships with others.[88]

One should meditate on what will happen to one's body after death, in Simḥah Zissel's view, but all the more so one should one meditate on what will happen to one's soul. He sees people as inclined to engage in immoral behavior because they do not foresee the punishments in store for such behavior; therefore, he sees people as required to improve their foresight by imprinting clear images of rewards and punishments before their eyes.[89] Contemplating the consequences of one's deeds in this manner is, for Simḥah Zissel, at the heart of the practice of musar. But other practices of visualization, such as the empathic visualizations discussed above, are also important; moreover, visualization exercises should supplement many other forms of musar practice, including the practices explicitly commanded by the Torah and whatever other practices might help to bring moral discipline to the human being. What particularly characterizes all of these forms of practice is a clear sense that intellectual knowledge is insufficient, because our material selves can only be persuaded through concrete forms; Simḥah Zissel's continued insistence is that "it is not possible for a person to understand any rational matter completely except through bringing it into sense-experience."[90] Proper love cannot develop merely through knowledge, but by engaging one's entire being, so that one's body, appetites, emotions, perceptions, and imaginative abilities are all directed toward walking in God's ways.

## Love and Worldly Occupations

Some of the practices of musar that Simḥah Zissel advocates are solitary and contemplative, requiring a certain level of withdrawal from social life. Simḥah Zissel himself reportedly spent a good deal of time in contemplative solitude, both before and after he took over the leadership of the Talmud Torah.[91] He believed that retreating from the rest of the world could help with the repair of character traits; in one address to his students, for example, he admiringly cited the precedent of a rabbi who, "when he saw that he was too much immersed in worldly matters," withdrew from the world. "He prepared a special room for himself and, slowly, slowly, he became unfamiliar to his friends, until he sat as a recluse."[92] But such a retreat appears to have been temporary, and Simḥah Zissel nowhere endorses an ideal of spending much of one's life in solitude.

That ideal of prolonged solitude was in fact a significant ideal among rabbinic scholars in nineteenth-century Lithuania, especially inspired by the behavior of the Vilna Gaon, who had spent much of his life in such a fashion. As Immanuel Etkes has written, the Gaon insisted on the virtues of withdrawing from contact with society altogether: "He was convinced that contact with the world, especially social contact, was replete with obstacles and impediments. Therefore ascetic withdrawal serves as a safe haven for anyone who tends to be drawn after his appetites. Further, ascetic withdrawal can serve as preventive medicine for anyone who wishes to avoid entanglement in difficult trials. In the spirit of this view, the Gaon recommended to his family that they have as little social contact as possible, even for the sake of performing a commandment."[93]

Simḥah Zissel certainly agreed that social contact was filled with moral dangers. But he had little tolerance for the Vilna Gaon's ideal of a life lived outside of a community altogether. In this, he followed Israel Salanter, who reportedly rejected the possibility of becoming a saintly recluse when he considered his obligations to the community.[94] Simḥah Zissel seems to have seen withdrawal from the community as a valuable temporary remedy but as morally unacceptable when too prolonged. For the Vilna Gaon, virtuous "withdrawal" (*perishut*) meant withdrawal from social life; for Simḥah Zissel, virtuous "withdrawal" generally meant withdrawal from worldly pleasures, not withdrawal from social life altogether.

Indeed, Simḥah Zissel often stressed that engagement with others is at the heart of the moral life. Studying with others, offering and accepting loving reproof from one's neighbors, and engaging in other acts of lovingkindness are among the practices that he most valued; he also showed an appreciation of economic and political activities. When he perceived his students as committing themselves to the path of withdrawal in the style of the Vilna Gaon, he railed against them. His attitude can be seen from the following letter regarding the choice of one of his students to become a recluse in Jaffa, in the land of Israel, where some disciples of the Gaon had settled. The letter, written to another student who had contact with the aspiring recluse, presents Simḥah Zissel's argument that life cannot be lived in solitude:

> From your letter to me today, I have seen that our friend has traveled to Jaffa to study there as a recluse. I have hurried, without delay, to write today so that you may answer him in my name, for he is acting wrongly—very, very much so. . . . You should know that it would not be possible to do such a strange thing, acting without refined equanimity, unless one lacked the feeling for "sharing the burden of one's fellow". . . . One who does not have a sense for this character trait, he is truly uncivilized [*eino min ha-yishuv mammash*]. So should one understand.

All philosophers describe the human being as "political"—meaning that the world cannot be sustained except by means of everybody [acting in cooperation]. And why was it created in this way? Could not the Creator have created a world in which people did not need each other? But [God created the world this way] in order to show that a person needs to be concerned for the healing of his fellow's soul just as his own, because a person only can sense worldly things and not heavenly things, and therefore the world was created such that he would be concerned for his fellow, and this is in fact being concerned about himself. Similarly, one who works the earth is concerned to prepare bread for people, and this is a preparation for himself [as well], since he will profit from this, and will come to have other human needs (for clothing, etc.) fulfilled. So too the merchant travels to far-off places to prepare clothing for people, and this is a preparation for himself. So too with all of the goods of the world—as is explained above. One who contemplates this will understand that it is all the more so with heavenly things—how very much more so is concern for one's fellow in fact concern for oneself.

This comes from God's kindness, as God seeks what is good for the human being without end and wants to provide one with it, such that one will have a portion of all the good that is in the world. God created ways to heal the body in this manner, and one should also understand the healing of the soul in this way—it comes about when one is concerned for one's fellow. One who is not concerned for his fellow is not concerned for himself, as we have explained.

And, in accordance with this, how beautiful and pleasant is the explanation of [the Talmudic statement that] "anyone who lacks moral decency [*derekh eretz*] is not part of civilization" (BT Kiddushin 40b). For if one does not recognize the essence of creation, that the human being is created in such a way that concern for one's fellow is in fact concern for oneself—if so, he does not know and does not recognize civilization. And it is forbidden for such a person to live with other people, for he would be dangerous to people. So teaches the sage [Jacob Emden] in *Migdol Oz* regarding moral decency: "Anyone who lacks moral decency is considered by everyone to simply be an animal, or one of

> the beasts of the wilderness, about whom it is said, 'Man is born as a wild ass' (Job 11:12)."
>
> Let us consider that had our patriarch Abraham not been concerned with the dissemination of the idea of God, what would there be for us? We would lose our place both in this world and in the world to come! And had our teacher Moses not sacrificed himself in order to ascend to heaven and receive the Torah (as our sages taught), from where would we have received Torah? And how would we know the laws of civilized behavior (as in *Tractate Derekh Eretz*)? From the existence of civilization in the world we can understand that a person needs to be concerned for the healing of his fellow's body, and all the more so for his soul—the soul by means of which even the foul body can live in connection with eternity when its materiality is purified.
>
> . . . .You have written, my friend (with, I beg your forgiveness, words of folly) that you envy our friend who has gone to Jaffa to study as a recluse. I do not envy him at all, though I have pity on him, for he has done a thing without reflection . . .[95]

Simḥah Zissel begins his letter by condemning the student who seeks to isolate himself and who therefore fails to fulfill the central duties of "sharing the burden of one's fellow." Human beings are instead required to live in a political community. As Simḥah Zissel sees it, God has set up the world in such a way that, to benefit both physically and spiritually, one must rely on other people. Physical growth is not possible without trade and reliance on the work of others, nor would spiritual growth be possible without the insights of others (such as, paradigmatically, Abraham and Moses). Failing to engage in loving partnership with others is, in Simḥah Zissel's view, a sign of irrationality and sinfulness.

Would it also be a sin, then, to retreat in a group from the broader society and only focus on the needs of a small group? That is, seemingly, precisely what Simḥah Zissel did in forming the small community of the Talmud Torah which was, especially in Grobin, a total institution very much removed from the rest of the public. But Simḥah Zissel seems to have hoped that, while retreating from the public, he could shape students who would go on to serve the public, whether as businessmen or as community rabbis—both lines of work scorned by traditional Lithuanian rabbis, who idealized a life of greater solitude and Talmud study. Israel Salanter acknowledged the dignity of both of these forms of work, however,[96] and Simḥah Zissel went further than his teacher in his attacks on those who denied the dignity of commerce and public leadership.

*Love Through Commerce*

A number of Simḥah Zissel's closest disciples, including his son Naḥum Ze'ev Ziv, became businessmen, and Simḥah Zissel had many positive things to say about such work. As I suggested earlier in this chapter, Simḥah Zissel saw honest commercial activity as potentially fostering a deep sense of partnership and lovingkindness within a society. In one striking passage he goes even further, suggesting that retreating from the economic realm is in fact a sin:

> The human being is naturally political, meaning that the world was created so that we would be partners with each other, serving one another—we have discussed at length how before prayer, one therefore needs to accept upon himself the commandment "to love one's fellow as oneself"—and, therefore, when one learns a trade, one can intend to show lovingkindness to people with it. Then the activity is good in its essence, reflecting God's attributes, and the activity becomes eternal. And so the philosopher Aristotle, when he investigated human conduct in light of the goal of happiness, said: the conduct of ascetics who go off to the forests and deserts is not good. Although the virtue of those who practice "withdrawal" is good in moderation, when one [both] receives benefits from others and provides benefits to others, those who unwittingly benefit from others to satisfy their few needs but who do not benefit others are found to be "cheating the laborer of his wages" (Malachi 3:5). And we find that the Torah verifies this for us. Our sages taught: the Torah begins with lovingkindness and ends with lovingkindness" (BT Sotah 14a). And they included among the forty-eight virtues "sharing the burden of one's fellow" (Mishnah Avot 6:6), which is the essence of the way of God, that one abstain from the world for oneself but benefit others. And thus our sages taught: "one who does not teach his son a trade" (BT Kiddushin 29a)—he does not benefit others, and so he is "cheating the laborer of his wages" and so it is "as if he had taught him to be a bandit."[97]

The Talmudic statement referenced at the end of this passage teaches that, if one does not teach one's son a trade, it is as if he had taught him to be a bandit, and the conventional explanation for this requirement is that his son will have to resort to crime if he does not have a marketable skill.[98] But Simḥah Zissel sees trade as not only keeping people from evil but also expressing lovingkindness by contributing to the public good. As for one who does not contribute to the public good in this way and yet reaps the benefits of those who do—this, for Simḥah Zissel, is robbery.

Simḥah Zissel is by no means confident that commerce will promote love; on the contrary, he admits that "business is a great danger for a human being."[99] As I noted earlier in this chapter, Simḥah Zissel believes that business activity typically encourages pride, greed, dishonesty, and a lack of concern for other people. But Simḥah Zissel refuses to follow the mainstream view among Lithuanian rabbis—also affirmed by some figures within the Musar movement, especially within the Novaredok school—that saw business as inevitably sinful. He instead builds on a long-standing rabbinic tradition, affirmed by Maimonides, which sees work as a positive social good. And he goes further than earlier sources by depicting reclusiveness as sinful and by insisting not only that commerce is good but that it is linked with the highest possible virtues.[100]

### *Love Through Politics*

A similar dynamic is at work when it comes to more explicitly political activity. Simḥah Zissel warns against political involvement, which he sees as exceedingly corrupting, such that "the early sages fled from political power" and even Moses initially refused God's call to take on a position of community leadership.[101] But Moses did eventually accept God's call, and both Israel Salanter and Simḥah Zissel similarly seem to have overcome their own reluctance to be involved in the public realm; Salanter also acquiesced to his students taking on the most explicitly political role available to an observant Jew: the position of a community rabbi.[102] Simḥah Zissel did not take on such a public position, and his critics saw him as an overly private and reticent figure.[103] But Simḥah Zissel saw himself as taking responsibility for "the needs of the public" in his own idiosyncratic way, eventually focusing on training a small number of future leaders at his school who would themselves "share the burdens of their fellows without taking pleasure for themselves at all."[104] He hoped that many of his students would "share the burden" either through their teaching or more explicitly political roles as community rabbis. Even when he kept his students secluded in the Talmud Torah behind high walls, he seems to have hoped that they would later take on positions of leadership within the wider community.

Simḥah Zissel sees rabbinic leaders as serving a political function, quoting a Talmudic passage in which God declares that rabbis are comparable to "kings." As Simḥah Zissel explains, "the disciples of the sages of the early generations were trained in the character trait of sharing the burden of one's fellow, to set the world upon its foundation, and this is a matter of kingship." They did not just deal with abstract wisdom or concerns of private faith but with "external things"—above all, with social problems. The greatest of rabbis, like a king, "shares the burden of his fellows, providing for the maintenance of the world, and this is the crown of the virtues."[105]

Simḥah Zissel's praise of political leaders is not just limited to rabbis, though. He also idealizes the way that the heroes of the Torah served as governmental leaders with considerable coercive authority—such as Moses and Joseph, both discussed above. He also depicts David and Solomon as ideal kings, motivated by love rather than by honor:

> This is why the great ones of Israel, King David (peace be upon him) and King Solomon (peace be upon him), wanted to be kings. I had not always understood this—were these saints pursuing honor? [But] indeed it is as a king that a person is truly able to come to the highest of the virtues, for he can habituate himself to "sustain the land through justice" (Prov. 29:4), and he has the power to expand wisdom and to promote it through schools and [to be involved in] all forms of the repair of the world [*tikkun ha-olam*]—all of this is in the monarch's power. This is the intent of the Tosefta, that "a king is occupied all his days with the public's needs" . . . with all forms of repairing the world; and there is no form of "sharing the burden of one's fellow" that is greater than this, and so this is the crown of the virtues. Therefore David and his son Solomon greatly desired kingship in order to share the burden of the entire world. And behold this is the essence of walking in God's ways, to set the world in its proper place. Therefore one who sits in judgment becomes a partner with the Holy and Blessed One in the work of creation.[106]

Using political authority to "share the burden of one's fellow" is here depicted as the highest possible level of love and as "the essence of walking in God's ways." Those who can best emulate God, the loving king of the universe, are flesh-and-blood kings, who have the power to provide not only for human physical needs but also for spiritual needs, through schools, for example. Simḥah Zissel offers here a highly optimistic view of what political authority can accomplish, though he is aware that politics can be deeply corrupting and he is surely aware that most kings are hardly paragons of lovingkindness. It is hard to imagine that he would have had such high praise for the czars with whom he was familiar, but he plainly believes that kings have great potential to transform the nature of the world by sharing the burdens of their subjects. And certainly when a king does indeed "share the burden," Simḥah Zissel would seem to demand total submission:

> We are commanded regarding the honor of a king, for he has a high level of this virtue of sharing the burden of one's fellow—and thus we are commanded that "the rebel against the kingdom deserves death" (Joshua 1:18). This is because kingship rests upon "sharing the burden of one's fellow" in an amazing way: for the monarchy keeps a watchful eye upon every burden, [so that it may] rescue the oppressed from the hand of his oppressor, as "a king sustains the land through justice" (Prov. 29:4), and there is no [example of] sharing the burden of one's fellow greater than this.[107]

This sort of devotion seems applicable toward kings who do act with justice and lovingkindness, but elsewhere Simḥah Zissel offers praise even for more flawed kings who nonetheless provide security for their subjects. Government "serves to restrain violent people with a strong hand, and to provide protection from violence and injustice," Simḥah Zissel writes, and "even with kings who were not accustomed in lovingkindness, [the sages] nonetheless honored them because of the general matter that the kingdom is built upon lovingkindness for the world through sustaining the world and its settlement." Hence the rabbinic injunction to pray "for the peace of the kingdom" (Mishnah Avot 3).[108] Simḥah Zissel's praise for state power seems to stem from his conviction that human beings are inclined toward evil and in need of restraint: "human nature is evil, aiming to cast an evil eye on one's fellow, and were it not for fear of the kingdom, how very many people would be slain in every single city, and, God forbid, the world would be destroyed."[109] The provision of law and order that prevents evildoing is itself a fundamental expression of lovingkindness.

Even as he admires the assertion of state power, though, Simḥah Zissel points to the limits of that power. "Human power only has dominion over visible [conduct], and not over conscience," he points out, "for Scripture teaches 'the hidden things belong to God' (Deut. 2:28), and human power cannot rule over conscience." An implication of this reality, he goes on to note, is that political leaders themselves cannot be coerced into being properly moral leaders; they must rather "find ways to strengthen the conscience that is within the heart, through principles of love and uprightness."[110] They are, in other words, in need of musar.

Simḥah Zissel sees the practice of musar as essential for politics, and he dreams of public life guided by those who, like Moses, Joseph, David, or Solomon, learn to "share the burden of their fellows." Simḥah Zissel certainly cautioned that public life was dangerous, but he also hoped for his students to be public leaders. Unlike other Lithuanian rabbis who shunned the realm of politics, including those within the Musar movement who viewed it as "too worldly," Simḥah Zissel emphasized that politics was the arena in which the highest forms of virtue could potentially be expressed.[111]

### *Love and the Family*

Simḥah Zissel shared the common traditionalist concern about the dangers of being too immersed in the worldly realm of commerce and politics, but he seemed to believe that these dangers could be neutralized by people dedicated to the work of musar, and that in fact both business life and political life could potentially express tremendous love. In addition to advocating "withdrawal" from these areas, there was one other realm from which Lithuanian traditionalists advocated detachment: the realm of family life. The greatest hero of Lithuanian rabbinic culture, the Vilna Gaon, even lauded those who could ignore the basic needs of their family. As the Gaon's commentary on Proverbs put it, "True heroes are men of noble heart with the fullest trust in God, constantly doing *mitzvot* and meditating on the Torah day and night even though their home be without bread and clothing and their families cry out: 'Bring us something to support and sustain us, some livelihood!' But he pays no attention at all to them nor heeds their voice . . . for he has denied all love except that of the Lord and His Torah."[112]

The Vilna Gaon seemed to put this ideal into practice to a significant degree; he withdrew to a private room, dedicated himself to full-time study, and seldom even inquired after his family's welfare. He appears to have had little interest in supporting the efforts of his wife to make a meager living and keep their family from illness or starvation. As Immanuel Etkes has noted, the Vilna Gaon's model was not accepted in its full severity by most Lithuanian traditionalists, but it was held up as an ideal, and it influenced the character of family relations in scholarly circles, including within the Musar movement.[113]

Simḥah Zissel seems to have shown more concern for family life. Not only do his many letters to his son, Naḥum Ze'ev, often express a deep concern for his son's welfare, but his disciples told stories about Simḥah Zissel's exemplary devotion to the rest of his family. He is reported to have invited his wife and daughters to his musar sermons, for example, and a number of stories focus on his appreciation for his wife. As I mentioned in chapter 1, he was admired for the way that he showed his gratitude for his wife's Sabbath preparations; another story tells of how, after leaving his home and setting out on the road, he insisted on going back home because he had forgotten to properly say goodbye to his wife as he always did. Then again, although while he lived in Kelm he seems to have returned home to his wife every Sabbath, there were seemingly long periods during his tenure in Grobin when he seldom saw her. Refusing to take a salary for his work, he also provided no financial support for the family, leaving his family's home cold in the winter, with a leaky roof, and with little food on the table, although his wife is said to have supported this decision. Other stories depict a deeper level of disengagement from his family, though—such as a story of how he refused to budge from his office until he had completed his weekly study regimen, even when he had heard a report of his son being injured.[114]

And on the whole, Simḥah Zissel's writings, despite their focus on loving care for one's fellow, show relatively little interest in questions regarding care for one's family—especially female members of one's family. Though his writings display interest in his son's education, he followed the cultural norm of showing little concern for his daughters' education. He did not have much to say about the obligations of spouses to one another. Like many other traditionalist rabbis, he did not give much attention to the standard Jewish legal requirements mandating that husbands attend to their wives' needs. With the exception of the one passage mentioned above regarding a pious man who felt anger toward his wife, he did not grapple with obligations to one's wife that would go beyond the law. When he speaks of the importance of finding a friend with whom to take counsel on one's moral state, he does not recommend seeking out one's wife—though this was precisely what some modern musar literature produced by the Haskalah movement suggested.[115]

Simḥah Zissel offered no advice of this sort; indeed, he seems to have spent relatively little time with his wife, and his teachings were directed at men who followed, or would grow up to follow, the same pattern. Immanuel Etkes has pointed out that, in general, there is a silence within Musar movement writing regarding spousal relationships (as well as familial relationships more generally), and he has noted that many Musar movement leaders spent significant time away from their homes. "That behavior is particularly surprising in that Salanter and his disciples emphasized and deepened the demand for morality in human relations," Etkes has written. "Did that imply alienation from one's wife?"[116] Perhaps so. Simḥah Zissel, I suspect, while he lauds great female prophetesses and biblical heroes (as well as the Talmudic female hero, Beruriah) in his writings, had relatively little interest in real-life women, and he probably saw women as inferior and as (potentially erotic) distractions from the male world in which he was most comfortable. In this respect, Simḥah Zissel did not seem to stand out from the larger culture of which he was a part.

## Practical Wisdom Revisited

For all that Simḥah Zissel emphasized the need to emulate God's empathic love for all creatures, it is not clear that he thought a great deal about how this might apply to the respective treatment of women and men. To what degree did Simḥah Zissel reflect on other questions of how to apply universal love to the world, given the wide range of creatures who would seem to be deserving of such love? We might note, for example, Simḥah Zissel's teachings that animals deserve considerable love but that human beings generally deserve more attention—but he does not sort through the practical implications of his concern of animals. He is also clear that Jews should be concerned for non-Jews, while showing some sort of special concern for Jews—but it is not clear how the covenantal relationship within the Jewish community should influence moral decision-making. He is clear that one should be concerned with physical suffering while being even more concerned with spiritual suffering—but here, too, he offers little guidance for how a human being should divide his attention when faced with opportunities to relieve both forms of suffering.

The virtue of practical wisdom would seem to be the essential virtue for figuring out how to divide one's resources based on one's circumstances. This virtue, we saw in chapter 3, must be acquired through experience over the course of a long time. Simḥah Zissel does share some bits of acquired wisdom regarding questions of how to allot one's resources—he advises, for example, that one must be sensitive even to minor manifestations of pain (for example, the pain that convalescent patients might continue to feel even when they seem to be on the road to recovery[117]) and so he might caution against a consequentialism that would be blind to such cases. But his writings do not lay out general theories to guide action, nor does he deal with questions of practical ethics involving priorities of care. And he does not turn to the literature of the Jewish legal tradition, which has often confronted such cases; the focus of his writings is on basic virtues and principles and how to acquire and learn them, but seldom on the questions of how to apply them in the inevitable cases in which there are many conflicting demands.

One area in which Simḥah Zissel does offer strong advice, though, is in urging his students to distinguish between people's wants and their legitimate needs. An overly close identification with another person can lead to uncritical endorsement of their perceptions and desires, however wrong they may be. Indiscriminate empathy can cause a person to identify with another person's will and to endorse it without critically assessing it. Simḥah Zissel addresses this concern in arguing that love must be guided by reasoned consideration and a sense of "justice." In one striking passage, he contrasts true lovingkindness (*ḥesed*) with mere "mercy" (*raḥamim*). Mercy seeks "to fulfill the wishes of a person's heart, even if it may be to his detriment," as in the case of a mother who refuses to discipline her badly behaved child. Lovingkindness, in contrast to this, "seeks the good of one's fellow even if it is not what he wants." In explaining this, Simḥah Zissel considers the obligation to support beggars who come to one's door, which is generally a firm obligation and a sign of love. If, however, one has clear evidence that the beggar is capable of working but simply does not want to, and if one examines oneself to ensure that one is not motivated by one's own stinginess, then one may refuse to give him money but instead encourage him to find work. And, of course, love often requires reproving one's fellows, or even punishing one's fellows, rather than simply endorsing their wishes. True lovingkindness refuses to "surrender to the other regarding everything"; it instead requires justice, which reasons about what is properly due to others.[118]

Attempts to look beyond a person's desires and uncover "what they really need," though, are also fraught with moral difficulties. Because we cannot fully comprehend another person's inner life, attempts to empathically understand the needs of other people are easily skewed by our own mistaken projections. We may be certain that people's spiritual lives are in bad shape, for example, because we are certain that they have mistaken ideas about God and the nature of the universe; we may assume that their souls are suffering and seek to show compassion for them accordingly. It is easy to see how such compassion might in fact reveal a mistaken and condescending certainty about what in fact ails another person's soul.[119]

Simḥah Zissel was no doubt guilty at times of such misplaced sympathy. His students reported, for example, that when Simḥah Zissel heard the news of the death of the pro-Haskalah newspaper publisher Alexander Zederbaum, a critic of the Musar movement, he was devastated to imagine the punishment in store for him, and he urged his students to "share the burden" of this heretic through their compassion for his soul. An alternative model of "sharing the burden" would, of course, involve putting oneself in the place of the critic, seeking to find value in his criticism rather than assuming his wickedness. Other students reported Simḥah Zissel taking a similar attitude toward non-Jews who had failed to acknowledge the superiority of the Jewish tradition during their lifetimes. Here too, they recalled Simḥah Zissel "sharing the burden" with his sympathy for the soul of a non-Jew who had failed to convert to Judaism.[120] An alternative model of sharing the burden would involve sympathy for the dignity of other traditions rather than rash assumptions about the superiority of the path of the Torah.

But if at times Simḥah Zissel displayed the common human tendency to condemn enemies or people of other backgrounds, his own writings provide the resources to guard against these tendencies. Simḥah Zissel's writings do urge that sympathy for one's fellows is best accomplished if one actually stands next to them and seeks to understand their perspectives. His writings urge his students to be skeptical about their own assumptions, to welcome criticism, and to seek goodness even in those who appear to be wicked. He specifically urges learning from non-Jews, at times noting their superior insights or behavior, and he seems to have accepted certain insights of the Haskalah even while he viewed it as a dire threat. Moreover, he warns that efforts to show love to others by offering reproof are often colored by our own self-love, such that caution and introspection must always accompany our efforts to help others.

It would be no surprise if at times Simḥah Zissel struggled to implement his own ideals. Being deeply critical of oneself and sympathizing with others in just the right way is obviously hard work. Indeed, every aspect of love that we have seen in this chapter would seem to require significant labor to achieve. Overcoming our natural self-centeredness and loving our fellows as ourselves out of deep empathy is an obviously difficult task, especially if we share Simḥah Zissel's observation about the difficulties of maintaining any level of virtue within the human soul.

Given this situation, Simḥah Zissel teaches that the ideal of "sharing the burden" must be approached slowly; progress toward the ideal requires a lifetime of musar, of patient and disciplined work. Still he insists that we should strive toward an ideal of empathic love, which can be planted deeply in our souls so that we do not need to be motivated by thoughts of duty but can respond "naturally" to the needs of others. Through disciplined work on ourselves, through changing the way we see and respond to the world, we can strive toward an ideal of "sharing the burden of one's fellow," to respond to the needs of others as readily as we respond to our own needs. In sharing their burdens, in this model, we can love our fellows as ourselves—seeing them as like ourselves and caring for them as we care for ourselves.

# Conclusion

After Simḥah Zissel's death in 1898, the leadership of the Talmud Torah in Kelm passed to his younger brother, Rabbi Aryeh Leib Broida (d. 1928). A few years later, Aryeh Leib and much of the rest of Simḥah Zissel's family began the process of moving to the land of Israel; included in the group was Aryeh Leib's son (and Simḥah Zissel's son-in-law), Rabbi Tzevi Hirsch Broida (1865–1913). But while part of the family settled in Jerusalem, the students in Kelm implored Tzevi Hirsch to remain in Kelm and to take up the leadership of the yeshiva. Tzevi Hirsch did so, leading the yeshiva until his death in 1913. During the latter years, he was assisted by Simḥah Zissel's own son, Rabbi Naḥum Ze'ev Ziv (1857–1916), who returned to Kelm after years of working as a businessman in Königsberg; after Tzevi Hirsch's death, Naḥum Ze'ev took over the Talmud Torah until his own death in 1916. He was succeeded by Simḥah Zissel's disciple Rabbi Reuven Dov Dessler (1863–1935), and Dessler was succeeded by Rabbi Daniel Moshowitz (1880–1941). In July 1941, the Nazi army arrived in Kelm and murdered all of the Jewish inhabitants of the town, including Moshowitz and his students at the Talmud Torah.[1]

Simḥah Zissel's successors at the Talmud Torah embraced many of its founder's teachings. They influenced the wider Jewish world in varying degrees; among the most influential was Reuven Dov Dessler, especially given Dessler's influence on his own son Eliyahu Eliezer Dessler (1892–1953), a student of the Kelm Talmud Torah who went on to become a major figure within twentieth-century ultra-Orthodoxy. Many of Eliyahu Dessler's teachings regarding the centrality of loving-kindness echo the teachings of Simḥah Zissel, though his influential vision of rabbinic authority, discussed in chapter 3, is in tension with Simḥah Zissel's teachings. A similar dynamic was at work with another of Simḥah Zissel's influential students, Yeruḥam HaLevi Levovitz (1873–1936), who later became the spiritual supervisor at the Mir yeshiva in Poland. Though he studied with Simḥah Zissel for only a short time, he was especially influenced by his teacher's vision of "sharing the burden of one's fellow." But he joined Dessler in downplaying the role of autonomous human reasoning.[2]

The student of Simḥah Zissel's whose influence was perhaps most substantial and through whom Simḥah Zissel had the greatest influence was Rabbi Natan Tzevi Finkel, discussed in chapter 1 as the creator of a rival musar yeshiva and a critic of the Grobin Talmud Torah who nonetheless sent his best students to study with Simḥah Zissel for periods of time. Finkel's Slobodka yeshiva also resembled Simḥah Zissel's Talmud Torahs in a number of respects: it approved of bourgeois European manners and dress, it attempted to watch over the lives of its students to the greatest degree that it could, and it devoted significant attention to the work of musar.[3] Though the Slobodka yeshiva devoted more time to formal Talmud instruction than Simḥah Zissel's institutions did, in its early days Slobodka devoted less time to Talmud instruction than many other yeshivas. Musar study was less prominent than in Kelm, but nonetheless students in the 1880s and 1890s devoted time to meditating on regular musar sermons delivered by Finkel and to chanting moral maxims, sometimes amid tears.[4] Shaul Stampfer has argued that at Slobodka, "Talmud was considered less important than *musar* study—even though more time was devoted to the study of Talmud."[5] The model of musar education developed by Simḥah Zissel appears to have had significant weight at Finkel's Slobodka yeshiva.

Finkel's efforts to break with his teacher and emphasize the study of Talmud, moreover, need not be seen as a rejection of Simḥah Zissel's legacy. Finkel's efforts to fit within more established frameworks allowed him to attract a wide array of students to Slobodka who would never have attended an institution like Simḥah Zissel's Talmud Torah, and these efforts allowed Simḥah Zissel's teachings to reach a wide audience, far beyond the insular environment of the Talmud Torah in Kelm and Grobin. As Yeḥiel Ya'akov Weinberg put it, Finkel was able to spread musar teachings precisely because he developed a Talmud-centered vision of musar, with "no mixing with non-Jewish wisdom, and no inquiring into what is beyond the domain of our Torah." Rather, "thanks to his wonderful integration of Torah and musar, the musar method was accepted in the whole Talmudic world, and it was elevated to be a part of the education of every Torah scholar."[6]

And Finkel did seek to reach great Talmud scholars, allegedly saying that his audience was very different from Simḥah Zissel's: "he wanted to educate householders, and I want to shape great scholars [*gedolim*]."[7] But these scholars would not be ordinary Talmud scholars, as Finkel sought to teach them the importance of musar and to connect them with the legacy of Kelm. Finkel actively sought to connect his students with Simḥah Zissel, brought Simḥah Zissel's other students to help lead the Slobodka yeshiva, and continued to send his students to the Kelm Talmud Torah after Simḥah Zissel's death. As Shlomo Tikochinski has argued, Simḥah Zissel and his Talmud Torah appear to have been widely admired in Slobodka:

> R. Finkel and his students saw R. Simḥah Zissel as the "guardian of musar," they were accustomed to evaluate [themselves] against his Talmud Torah, and they thus contributed to strengthening its status in the interwar period. Moreover, during all of his years at Slobodka, R. Finkel always had by his side one or more Kelm students who assisted in the work of supervising and guiding students. . . . [Moreover, Finkel] sending his senior students to Kelm to complete their studies sent the message to all that "the real thing" in the realm of musar was to be found there. So too, employing Kelm students as supervisors in his yeshiva sent the message that it was fitting to learn from—and take pleasure in the light of—those whose musar was from the original source [i.e., from Kelm]. His criticisms of integrating general studies [into the curriculum] at Grobin, of the interest in "external wisdoms," and on the distancing of "scholarship," were humbly expressed in a whisper, and only among close associates, whereas in the open he showed solidarity with and open appreciation of Kelm.[8]

Still, the criticisms that were whispered against Simḥah Zissel, discussed in chapter 1, were of no small consequence. The Slobodka yeshiva passed along many aspects of Simḥah Zissel's teachings, but they did little to emphasize some of his most characteristic teachings that I have emphasized in this book. Among the teachings that they did not promote are those that engaged with the role of philosophy and non-Jewish wisdom, or that indicated the limits of Talmud study and pointed to the importance of emotions and the imagination in other settings, or that stressed the difficulty of moral development.

Finkel built on Simḥah Zissel's vision of the potential moral greatness of the human being, but he did not emphasize the evils of human nature and the difficulties of moral progress in the same way that his teacher did. He saw rapid moral change as possible, as Simḥah Zissel did not, and he saw the study of Talmud as extremely effective in creating that change, such that, in the words of Yeḥiel Ya'akov Weinberg, musar teachers should require not only "no mixing with non-Jewish wisdom, and no inquiring into what is beyond the domain of our Torah," but rather, above all, an unwavering dedication to the study of Talmud.[9] Compared to that of his teacher, Finkel's approach was more appealing to many Lithuanian Jews, especially those traditionalists who were attracted to the modern, optimistic views of human nature advanced by the Haskalah but who were also dedicated to the supremacy of Talmud study.[10]

Even with Finkel's renewed emphasis on Talmud study, though, his teachings were hardly popular within the mainstream of the Lithuanian yeshiva world. Finkel also continued to emphasize musar in ways that left many of his students unhappy; many of them had come to Slobodka to study with its scholarly Talmud faculty, not to study musar at all. As Shaul Stampfer has noted, "They came in order to study, confident that Talmud study for its own sake was all that was necessary in life. Those who came to a yeshiva considered themselves gifted students, and it was not easy for them to accept the idea that an education in musar made one a better person than an education in Talmud. It was usually the best students who rejected musar since it threatened their status."[11]

In 1897, student protests against musar broke out at Slobodka, and about three-quarters of the students abandoned Finkel and opted to join a new yeshiva in Slobodka where musar was not taught. Similar protests broke out at the Telz yeshiva, where Simḥah Zissel's student Rabbi Leib Ḥasman had been teaching musar. Even though the Slobodka and Telz yeshivas emphasized the importance of Talmud study to a degree that Simḥah Zissel did not, their attention to musar was not acceptable to the vast majority of Lithuanian yeshiva students.[12]

The most successful institution created by the Musar movement was an institution that rejected the importance of Talmud study to a far greater degree—the Novaredok yeshiva founded by Rabbi Yosef Yoizel Horowitz. Horowitz studied with Simḥah Zissel for a brief period, and he followed Simḥah Zissel in some respects, especially in his skepticism regarding Talmud study and his emphasis on the work of musar. Horowitz, too, helped disseminate Simḥah Zissel's teachings, publishing some of them in his yeshiva's journals.[13]

But Horowitz's approach was in many respects opposed to Simḥah Zissel's. Though the two teachers agreed on the difficulty of moral change, Simḥah Zissel emphasized the slow process of change and the need to cooperate with the evil inclination, whereas Horowitz castigated any such efforts at cooperation and urged "breaking" the evil inclination through extreme asceticism. Deeply pessimistic about the human ability to avoid sin while engaging with the broader world, Horowitz also condemned the worlds of commerce and of politics, and he was utterly horrified by the incursion of general studies into yeshivas. He joined Natan Tzevi Finkel in criticizing Simḥah Zissel for quoting non-Jewish sources and introducing general studies,[14] but he went far beyond Finkel in rejecting all aspects of the Haskalah, including its ideas of decorum. Horowitz advocated revolting against social norms, including those regarding hygiene, dress, and manners, urging his students to humiliate themselves in public and thereby break their pride. As David Fishman has argued, Horowitz's uncompromising radicalism and his calls for revolt were deeply attractive to young Jews living in a wider milieu where radical ideologies filled the air. Horowitz's yeshiva, despite being scorned by most Jews, thus attracted a large number of students during the first part of the twentieth century. It developed into a successful network of seventy yeshivas and roughly 3,000 students. While Finkel's optimism appealed to traditionalist Jews attracted to the confident spirit of modernity but firmly committed to the value of Talmud study, Horowitz's radical pessimism appealed to traditionalist Jews attracted to the revolutionary spirit of the age.[15]

Simḥah Zissel's more balanced approach, however, also continued to be welcomed among traditionalists. In fact, his name was often invoked by those who developed non-Hasidic Haredi (ultra-Orthodox) Judaism in the twentieth century. Not only Finkel but other students of Simḥah Zissel's, such as Yeruḥam Levovitz and Elyah Lopian (1876–1970), as well as later students of the Talmud Torah such as Eliyahu Eliezer Dessler, were important figures in the development of ultra-Orthodox ideology, and these rabbis often pointed their own students back to the "saintly" teacher who inspired them. Levovitz, strikingly, taught his students to treat Simḥah Zissel's teachings as "Torah from Sinai"; he recalled that when he had listened to Simḥah Zissel at the Talmud Torah, "it seemed . . . as if we were standing at Mount Sinai and hearing the voice of the Lord."[16] Levovitz claimed that in fact all of his own teaching was only "like a commentary on the articles of the holy Elder [Simḥah Zissel] of blessed memory."[17]

Testimonies such as these have no doubt helped Simḥah Zissel's writings to be welcomed in contemporary ultra-Orthodoxy, including by the heirs of the Lithuanian traditionalists who once opposed Simḥah Zissel's efforts. Simḥah Zissel's writings have been published and republished in Haredi communities in recent years, and many of the core concerns of those writings are core concerns shared by Haredi Jews of all sorts.[18] In particular, his commitment to stringency, his pessimism about human progress, his strident defense of divine power, and his faith in the perfection of the Torah have made Simḥah Zissel a welcome voice in contemporary ultra-Orthodoxy. Even his advocacy for yeshivas to dedicate some time to musar study is tolerated by much of the contemporary Haredi mainstream; many mainstream yeshivas have come to allot some limited time for musar in their schedules. To be sure, most of these yeshivas have given far less attention to musar than Simḥah Zissel saw as ideal, but the compromise that they have made has helped to make Simḥah Zissel a more popular figure today.

Other aspects of Simḥah Zissel's legacy have been far less appreciated by today's ultra-Orthodoxy. In particular, his embrace of general studies, which was frowned upon by traditionalists in his own day, is no more appreciated today. Indeed, as I noted in chapter 1, the contemporary Haredi publisher of Simḥah Zissel's writings had to edit them to erase the memory of the general studies program at his Talmud Torah.

And, as I discussed in chapter 3, Eliyahu Dessler also linked Simḥah Zissel with the key Haredi doctrine of *da'at Torah,* which demands submission to the decisions of learned authorities. But Simḥah Zissel's rationalism and his focus on human fallibility stand in tension with this sort of authoritarianism.

As Tamar Ross has argued, the later leaders of the Musar movement who played key roles in the development of ultra-Orthodoxy rejected the sort of rationalism that Simḥah Zissel taught. Yeruḥam Levovitz, for example, did not simply follow his teacher on these questions, but came to regard independent human reasoning as a blasphemous challenge to divine authority. Eliyahu Eliezer Dessler similarly glorified the submission to norms that defy human reason.[19] Simḥah Zissel, by contrast, gloried in the idea that God's will was accessible to natural, human reason—such that even the philosophers could access the divine to a considerable extent. If ultra-Orthodoxy is to challenge its tendencies to oppose rationalist philosophy and valorize rabbinic authority, Simḥah Zissel's perspective is an important perspective for it to recover.

Simḥah Zissel's appreciation of human reasoning and his support for a general studies curriculum would seem to make him an especially relevant figure for contemporary modern Orthodoxy. Indeed, his support for general studies has been noted approvingly by a number of modern Orthodox figures. For example, Jacob J. Schacter of Yeshiva University, modern Orthodoxy's flagship institution, has criticized the ultra-Orthodox tendency to cover up this aspect of the history of the Kelm Talmud Torah.[20] Jacob Agus, considering the legacy of the Musar movement in 1950s America, depicted the Talmud Torah not as an ultra-Orthodox institution but as a forerunner to Yeshiva University, as he pointed out that both engaged general studies alongside Talmud study.[21]

But, as we saw in chapter 4, the Kelm Talmud Torah was condemned by Joseph Soloveitchik, the influential leader of Yeshiva University and of modern Orthodoxy. Soloveitchik only admired Musar movement figures who radiated a proper sense of joy and confidence and a firmer commitment to the supremacy of Talmud study; Soloveitchik thus exempted Natan Tzevi Finkel and Yeruḥam Levovitz of Mir from his condemnation. But their teacher, Simḥah Zissel, was implicated when Soloveitchik condemned those—like "the scholars of Kelm and Kovno"—who were "spiritually sick" and felt the need to "drink bitter drugs" to combat their illness. The activity of halakhically-focused Talmud study was more or less sufficient, in Soloveitchik's view, to ensure that the human inclination to evil could be controlled. Soloveitchik considered Simḥah Zissel and his colleagues to be wasting their time by engaging in introspection: "one must not waste time on spiritual self-appraisal, on probing introspections, and on the picking away at the 'sense' of sin," he wrote. [22] Nor was the thought of figures like Simḥah Zissel compatible with Soloveitchik's sense that God's demands could always be expressed in mathematically precise laws, nor his sense that emotions are not particularly relevant for ethical reasoning.

It is important, I think, for contemporary Orthodoxy to consider the counterarguments to these claims, and for this purpose Simḥah Zissel's writings serve as a good resource. In particular, there is much to appreciate in Simḥah Zissel's claims that practices of introspection are often essential for nurturing spiritual health—and in Simḥah Zissel's open-mindedness in considering how many forms of behavior can shape moral virtue, often depending on the individual. Simḥah Zissel recommended using "all possible stratagems"; particular practices of musar that he endorsed included performing specific ritual actions, performing various deeds of lovingkindness, meditating in various ways, and conferring with others and following their specific prescriptions. In addition to the practices specifically mandated by the Torah, other practices for helping us to walk in God's ways are, in this vision, also mandatory, and Simḥah Zissel endorsed thinking broadly about the wide range of behaviors that might encourage progress toward that end. Jews who are dedicated to the particular commandments of the Torah are often reluctant to think so broadly about other forms of practice that may be obligatory; Simḥah Zissel's teachings can encourage Jews to think more openly about such forms. We should recognize that one's moral obligations cannot be fulfilled by simply checking off a list of the discrete commandments listed in the Torah.[23]

So too, Simḥah Zissel's sense of the importance of practical wisdom in moral decision-making offers an important challenge to the tendency of contemporary Orthodox authorities (within both modern Orthodoxy and ultra-Orthodoxy) to think that all moral norms can be codified in fixed rules. In Soloveitchik's view, for example, "the Halakhah declares that any religiosity which does not lead to determinate actions, firm and clear-cut measures, chiseled and delimited laws and statutes will prove sterile."[24] In contrast to this, Simḥah Zissel preserved an older, virtue ethics approach. The virtues that he taught do not always shed great clarity on particular moral situations, which may be frustrating to those seeking clear guidelines. But particular moral rules cannot cover all situations, and so Simḥah Zissel's invitation to reason about how to apply virtues to particular situations is a welcome alternative to the rule-based reasoning that dominates much of today's observant Judaism.

Simḥah Zissel can also provide an important counterweight to those who, like Soloveitchik, tend to disparage the importance of emotional engagement for ethical reasoning. For Simḥah Zissel, intense emotional engagement is essential for reasoning—so long as, crucially, one's emotions are under the control of one's reason. As we have seen, Simḥah Zissel does not think that reason can function without engaging the other forces within the human soul. He views human appetites as pernicious, but he insists that reason must generally work with them, rather than simply trying to "break" them. He sees the human imagination as generally aligned with evil tendencies, but as being especially key for proper morality. We have seen how the imagination is especially important for visualizing the consequences of one's actions, and also for empathically visualizing the suffering of others. Even the drives to engage in commerce and politics can be harnessed by reason to best realize God's goal, and even the instinct to "self-love," which Simḥah Zissel sees as the greatest of vices, can be a virtue. Simḥah Zissel stresses the need to cooperate with potentially vicious parts of the human soul, accepting that our material natures can be tutored by reason rather than simply annihilated. While modern Jews have sometimes depicted "reasoning" as a process that takes place without the cooperation of emotions, appetites, and the imagination, Simḥah Zissel's more accommodating view of what "reasoning" should look like is a welcome corrective.

Simḥah Zissel's vision of how reasoning should culminate in acts of loving concern also offers an important corrective to those who would see intellectual contemplation as the supreme good—a perspective shared by some medieval philosophers and some modern

Talmudists, among others. Many of his contemporaries in Lithuania viewed Simḥah Zissel as denigrating the honor of traditional forms of Talmud study, and indeed he was challenging models of overintellectualized study that were detached from action. His vision of how study must translate into action, and especially acts of love, provides an important challenge to those with a more intellectual orientation. So too, his vision of how love is more than a feeling, but a virtue that must be developed over time, provides an important challenge to those with a less demanding vision of what love entails.

Simḥah Zissel does well, I think, to see love as a virtue with emotional and intellectual aspects that can be cultivated—with difficulty—through a range of activities. And he does well to stress that this virtue must culminate in compassionate action. For those of us who fail to see the suffering around us, Simḥah Zissel can remind us that the world is filled with suffering and that compassion in response to such suffering is the ultimate form of love. Simḥah Zissel is also an important example of a traditionalist Jewish thinker who sees all human beings and creatures as deserving love—including those outside the Jewish community, including evildoers, and including animals. He also offers the important insight that love does not always endorse the activities of the beloved but that it ideally offers reproof and that it always meets the requirements of justice.

I have my doubts, though, as to whether Simḥah Zissel did a terribly good job in guiding his students on how they might put such love into practice. Like most figures in the Musar movement, Simḥah Zissel developed his theories within an insular yeshiva environment—and his yeshivas were even more insular than most. While he preached loving-kindness for the broader world, including in the political sphere and beyond the Jewish world, his students were generally more focused on the social unit of yeshiva communities than on the world beyond their walls. While some students did become businessmen or community rabbis, it is not clear that Simḥah Zissel or his disciples achieved a high degree of broad social concern. Above all, as I suggested in chapter 5, Simḥah Zissel advocated empathy toward everyone, but it seems that he did not make substantial efforts to understand the perspectives of those whom he viewed as most misguided. And, like other men in his culture, he seems to have paid little attention to the perspectives of women.

Simḥah Zissel also erred, I think, in developing an overly demanding vision of morality that allowed little room for joy. Soloveitchik was wrong, I think, to critique the Musar movement for its focus on introspection, but he was right to worry that "picking away at the 'sense' of sin" can be psychically damaging—leaving little room, as Soloveitchik put it, for "a powerful sense of the holiness and joy of life."[25] While Simḥah Zissel did have a sense of "the joy of life," as we saw in chapter 2, he sometimes seems to have gone too far in encouraging guilt and shame. He sometimes seems too eager to condemn students for seemingly minor, errant passions; although his students may indeed have been capable of controlling such passions, Simḥah Zissel may have sometimes set the bar too high. And while his appreciation of the potential moral goodness of base appetites might indicate a willingness to accommodate human weaknesses, his unwillingness to accommodate weakness can be seen in his insistence on transforming such appetites, despite the virtual impossibility of doing so.[26]

It would be no surprise if Simḥah Zissel placed tremendous pressure on his students to strive toward perfection and to feel deeply ashamed of any imperfections. His expelled student Israel Elyashev certainly recalled the immense pressure in the Talmud Torah to uncover one's own sins; Elyashev recalled an atmosphere in which even momentary failures to concentrate in prayer were a cause for grave concern.[27] Outside critics also saw the Talmud Torah as filling its students with too much regret, worry, and despair, and these emotions may well have been counterproductive, damaging the equanimity that Simḥah Zissel so prized. Simḥah Zissel may have also had insufficient appreciation for the importance of rest, recreation, and laughter. Like many other sincere pietists, Simḥah Zissel may have lacked the ability to laugh at, or even respect, the limitations of human nature.[28]

And yet Simḥah Zissel did himself caution that moral standards should not ignore the limitations of human nature; if he erred by being too demanding, it was in part because he failed to heed his own warnings. As I suggested in chapter 4, Simḥah Zissel's writings often emphasize that human beings are required not to be perfect, but to emulate God *as best they can*, and to slowly work toward the ideal. His teachings often demonstrate his willingness to compromise, rather than demanding perfection: to take an example from chapter 2, Simḥah Zissel views it as less than ideal when human beings are motivated by promises of rewards and punishments, and yet he saw it as necessary to appeal to them, given the weaknesses of human nature. He certainly could have been more demanding, rather than acquiescing to such weaknesses. Nor was Simḥah Zissel oblivious to the need to care for the self, as we saw in chapter 5, and he showed some understanding of how praise may sometimes be a more effective teacher than criticism.

And even if Simḥah Zissel did devise overly demanding standards, we should find much to admire in his dissatisfaction with a culture marked by great self-assurance. Lithuanian yeshiva culture was confident that, possessing the Talmud, it did not need the work of musar—a sentiment later echoed by Joseph Soloveitchik. Simḥah Zissel was right to criticize this confidence by pointing to the ways in which deeper moral growth was necessary, and his demanding ethic is also a fitting rejoinder to much of today's culture. Observant Jewish culture today is marked by its own self-assurances about the sufficiency of meeting minimal legal requirements, and similar trends are present in the wider culture in which, as Andrew Flescher has put it, "people do less, or as much as, but rarely more than they perceive to be expected of them."[29] As Flescher has noted, we admire moral saints who dedicate their lives to sharing others' burdens to an extraordinary degree, but we often consider ourselves exempt from going "beyond the letter of the law" as they do. Simḥah Zissel would rightly point out that our evil inclinations are, in these cases, probably making excuses for us. People throughout the world are indeed in need of much attention and care, and we have little justification for hiding our faces at a time of need. Overcoming our penchant for self-centeredness and cultivating broad empathy is difficult, slow work, as Simḥah Zissel pointed out, but we are obligated to do this work as best we can. There are many burdens to share in the world, and we should do what we can to help to share them.

The highly self-critical and demanding vision of love and musar practice found in Simḥah Zissel's writings surely goes against the grain of much of contemporary culture, especially in North America. And yet there has been a revival of interest in the Musar movement in America over the past decade. Some of this has been a countercultural reaction against the general tenor of American culture, but there are also aspects of the Musar movement's legacy that are deeply appealing to many Americans. Many Americans are attracted to ethically focused models of Judaism, to models of practice that can be tailored to individual situations, and to focusing on the inner life.[30]

Simḥah Zissel may well be a figure of particular interest to many contemporary Jews, especially insofar as his ethical vision is reasonably well developed. A Jewish thinker focused on love may be particularly appealing in American culture, where love is often viewed as the supreme value, even though Simḥah Zissel's vision of love may be far more demanding than most. But the appeal of such a demanding vision is part of what has drawn the interest of many. One of the leading teachers of musar in contemporary America, Rabbi Ira Stone, was drawn to the thought of the Musar movement in large part by the attractions of Simḥah Zissel's demanding vision of love, a vision that Stone has characterized as resembling that of Emmanuel Levinas.[31] I was introduced to Simḥah Zissel and the Musar movement by Stone, and my own interest in musar was also encouraged by an attraction to Simḥah Zissel's vision of loving one's neighbor as oneself and his acknowledgement of the difficulties of cultivating such love.

Strikingly, much of the contemporary interest in the Musar movement has been among non-Orthodox Jews who are not committed to the inerrancy of the written and oral Torahs. Such views would horrify Simḥah Zissel and the other leaders of the Musar movement who were deeply committed to defending the perfection of the Torah. But a non-Orthodox skepticism is in fact a helpful corrective to another major weakness in Simḥah Zissel's moral vision. Simḥah Zissel is a proud advocate of guiding behavior in accordance with moral virtues, but of course he cannot tolerate allowing one of those virtues to challenge any norm that he sees as mandated by the Torah. He stresses the moral importance of offering and embracing criticism, but he refuses to criticize any view that he understands the Torah to be advocating. So for example, as we saw in chapter 2, when Simḥah Zissel considers God's commandment to slaughter the nonvirginal women and male children of Midian, he is obligated to defend Moses's desire to carry out the commandment; indeed, he sees Moses as being rational, just, and appropriately humble in submitting to God's will. Simḥah Zissel would not permit himself to question the dogma that God's will was indeed correctly recorded in the Torah.

Simḥah Zissel is, of course, driven to uproot false assumptions implanted in people's hearts. He applauds Socrates's mission to question certainties, and he applauds the Talmudic rabbis who refused to trust even heavenly voices if they did not demonstrate their rationality. But he cannot question his own assumptions regarding the perfection of the Torah. As we saw in chapter 3, he asserts that the norms of the Torah are obviously rational, but his arguments in defense of his faith are severely lacking. A better model of musar, I think, would be willing to question such pious assumptions about the perfection of traditionally authoritative sources.

Of course, a less orthodox incarnation of the Musar movement might not do any better; non-Orthodox Jews can certainly be overly credulous in other ways. But the skeptical questions that Orthodoxy is reluctant to ask can be tremendously helpful in the task of musar. The virtue of love that Simḥah Zissel teaches is occasionally distorted because it is not willing to hear those questions, such that Simḥah

Zissel cheers on the destruction of the Midianites rather than considering whether the Torah recorded God's commandment correctly. It would be better to encourage the humility to critically examine our own commitments, and the wisdom to critically examine authoritative sources. The obligation to critically consider our moral norms, an obligation that Simḥah Zissel urges us to take so seriously, would seem to demand no less.

# Notes

## Introduction

1. Baruch Spinoza, *Theological-Political Treatise,* 2nd ed., trans. Samuel Shirley (Indianapolis: Hackett, 2001), especially chapters 3–5.

2. *The Book of Direction to the Duties of the Heart,* trans. Menahem Mansoor (Oxford, UK: Littman Library of Jewish Civilization, 2004), 92.

3. See Hava Tirosh-Samuelson, *Happiness in Premodern Judaism: Virtue, Knowledge, and Well-Being* (Cincinnati: Hebrew Union College Press, 2003). On the genre of musar literature, see Joseph Dan, *Sifrut Ha-Musar Ve-Ha-Derush* [Hebrew Ethical and Homiletical Literature] (Jerusalem: Keter, 1975); Isaiah Tishby, *Mivḥar Sifrut Ha-Musar* [Hebrew Ethical Literature: Selected Texts] (Tel Aviv: M. Newman, 1970); Alan Mittleman, *A Short History of Jewish Ethics: Conduct and Character in the Context of Covenant* (Chichester: Wiley-Blackwell, 2012). Among the classics of the musar literature available in English translation, in addition to Baḥya's work, are Shelomo Ibn Gabirol, *The Improvement of the Moral Qualities,* trans. Stephen Samuel Wise (New York: Columbia University Press, 1902); Moses Maimonides, *Ethical Writings of Maimonides,* trans. Raymond L. Weiss and Charles E. Butterworth (New York: New York University Press, 1975); Jonah ben Abraham Gerondi, *The Gates of Repentance,* trans. Yaakov Feldman (Northvale, NJ: Jason Aronson, 1999); Seymour J. Cohen, trans., *Orchot Tzaddikim: The Ways of the Righteous* (New York: Ktav, 1982); Moses Cordovero, *The Palm Tree of Deborah,* trans. Louis Jacobs (London: Vallentine, 1960); Moshe Hayyim Luzzatto, *Mesillat Yesharim: The Path of the Just,* 3rd ed., trans. Shraga Silverstein (Jerusalem: Feldheim, 1990).

4. On the Haskalah, see Harris Bor, "Enlightenment Values, Jewish Ethics: The Haskalah's Transformation of the Traditional Musar Genre," in *New Perspectives on the Haskalah,* ed. Shmuel Feiner and David Sorkin (Oxford, UK: Littman Library of Jewish Civilization, 2001), 48–63. On the conflict between Mitnagdim and Hasidim regarding musar literature, see Immanuel Etkes, *Rabbi Israel Salanter and the Mussar Movement: Seeking the Torah of Truth,* trans. Jonathan Chipman (Philadelphia: Jewish Publication Society, 1993), 17–56.

5. Etkes, *Rabbi Israel Salanter*, esp. 102–9, 211, 234–37; Hillel Goldberg, *Israel Salanter: Text, Structure, Idea: The Ethics and Theology of an Early Psychologist of the Unconscious* (New York: Ktav, 1982), esp. 25, 32–36, 46, 78–79.

6. See Etkes, *Rabbi Israel Salanter*, 117–152. Regarding the Musar movement as part of what can be called "Orthodoxy," see 8–9.

7. Ibid., 79–114.

8. It is not clear that Salanter knew that Lefin was a *maskil*. Lefin's text, indeed, had been accepted by other traditionalists in Lithuania, such as Salanter's teacher Yosef Zundel; see ibid., 118–19.

9. Ibid., 145–49, 177, 351n1. Salanter was probably also concerned that students at the seminary did not spend sufficient time focused on the text of the Talmud; see 221–22.

10. Ibid., 213–15, 229–38.

11. On the institution of the dormitory as an innovation in traditionalist circles, see Shaul Stampfer, *Families, Rabbis and Education: Traditional Jewish Society in Eastern Europe* (Oxford: Littman Library of Jewish Civilization, 2010), 211–228. Stampfer sees the innovation as beginning with Simḥah Zissel Ziv, the subject of this book, but Simḥah Zissel may well have been building on a model established by his teacher.

12. See the complete list in Dov Katz, *Tenu'at Ha-Musar*, 2nd ed., vol. 1 (Tel-Aviv: Beitan Ha-Sefer, 1952), 171.

13. See, e.g., Ya'akov Mark, *Be-Meḥitzatam Shel Gedolei Ha-Dor*, trans. Shemu'el Ḥagai (Jerusalem: Gevil, 1958), 219; David Zaretsky, *Torat Ha-Musar* (Tel-Aviv: Moriah, 1959), 19; Dov Katz, *Tenu'at Ha-Musar*, 2nd ed., vol. 2 (Tel-Aviv: Avraham Tzioni, 1954), 27.

14. Zamet (also spelled Zamut) was the Yiddish name for the area of northwestern Lithuania known as Samogitia or Zemaitija. Regarding Simḥah Zissel's name, note that "Simḥah Mordekhai Ziskind" was his personal name; "Zissel" is a diminutive Yiddish form of "Ziskind."

15. See Katz, *Tenu'at Ha-Musar*, 2:28–29; Mark, *Be-Meḥitzatam*, 219. Simḥah Zissel's father was descended from Rabbi Avraham Broda (d. 1717), chief rabbi of Metz and of Frankfurt, and author of *Eshel Avraham;* his mother was the descendent of Ḥakham Tzevi Ashkenazi (1660–1718), chief rabbi in Hamburg, Wandsbeck, and Amsterdam, and author of *Ḥakham Tzevi*. On the support for the Haskalah among Orthodox Jews in nineteenth-century Russia, see Joseph Salmon, "Enlightened Rabbis as Reformers in Russian Jewish Society," in *New Perspectives on the Haskalah*, ed. Shmuel Feiner and David Sorkin (Oxford, UK: Littman Library of Jewish Civilization, 2001), 166–83.

16. Katz, *Tenu'at Ha-Musar*, 2:30.

17. For a discussion of the state of Simḥah Zissel's writings, see Geoffrey Claussen, "Rabbi Simḥah Zissel Ziv: The Moral Vision of a 19th Century Musar Master" (PhD thesis, Jewish Theological Seminary of America, 2011), 5–9.

18. In seeing philosophical significance in Simḥah Zissel's writings, I am following the lead of Tamar Ross, "Ha-Maḥshavah Ha-Iyunit Be-Khitve Mamshikhav Shel Rav Yisra'el Salanter Bitnu'at Ha-Musar" [Moral Philosophy

in the Writings of Rabbi Salanter's Disciples in the Musar Movement] (PhD thesis, Hebrew University, 1986).

## Chapter One

1. Katz, *Tenu'at Ha-Musar,* 2:30, 60–61, 64. See also Etkes, *Rabbi Israel Salanter,* 182–83, 190–91.

2. Katz, *Tenu'at Ha-Musar,* 2:64. Regarding Simḥah Zissel's reticence, see Eliezer E. Friedman, "Toledot Ba'alei Ha-Musar [Part 2]," *Ha-Melitz,* May 29, 1897, 7. In turning down a rabbinic position, Simḥah Zissel followed the example of his teacher, Salanter, and the approach favored by many other pietists, although Salanter eventually supported his students taking such positions. See Etkes, *Rabbi Israel Salanter,* 59–60, 73, 288.

3. Immanuel Etkes, "Marriage and Torah Study among the Lomdim in Lithuania in the Nineteenth Century," in *The Jewish Family: Metaphor and Memory,* ed. David Charles Kraemer (New York: Oxford University Press, 1989), 153–178.

4. Mark, *Be-Meḥitzatam,* 219; Katz, *Tenu'at Ha-Musar,* 2:61–62; Eliezer E. Friedman, "Toledot Ba'alei Ha-Musar," *Ha-Melitz,* May 25, 1897, 7; Eliezer E. Friedman, *Sefer Ha-Zikhronot* (Tel Aviv: Aḥdut, 1925), 78.

5. See Etkes, *Rabbi Israel Salanter,* 197.

6. Friedman, *Sefer Ha-Zikhronot,* 81; Friedman, "Toledot Ba'alei Ha-Musar [Part 2]," 6. On the correlation between Talmudic skills and social status, see Stampfer, *Families, Rabbis and Education,* 147, 163–64.

7. Friedman, "Toledot Ba'alei Ha-Musar [Part 2]," 6.

8. Friedman, *Sefer Ha-Zikhronot,* 78; Friedman, "Toledot Ba'alei Ha-Musar [Part 2]," 6; Katz, *Tenu'at Ha-Musar,* 2:127–29; *Kitvei Ha-Sabba Ve-Talmidav Mi-Kelm,* vol. 2 (Benei Berak: Siftei Ḥakhamim, Va'ad Le-Hafatzat Torah U-Musar, 1997), 566; Simḥah Zissel Ziv, *Sefer Ḥokhmah U-Musar (ḤuM),* vol. 1 (New York, 1957), 91.

9. The date of the establishment of the institution under Simḥah Zissel's leadership is not clear. See Claussen, "Rabbi Simḥah Zissel Ziv," 33n68.

10. See Steven G. Rappaport, "Jewish Education and Jewish Culture in the Russian Empire, 1880–1914" (PhD thesis, Stanford University, 2000), 40–41, 195–99.

11. See Katz, *Tenu'at Ha-Musar,* 2:63; Hillel Lifshitz, "Gan Hashem," *Ha-Levanon,* July 7, 1875, 363; Shelomo Zalman Broida, "Kelm," *Ha-Levanon,* March 25, 1874, 254.

12. See Friedman, "Toledot Ba'alei Ha-Musar [Part 2]," 6; Friedman, *Sefer Ha-Zikhronot,* 81; Eliezer E. Friedman, *Le-Toledot Kittat Ha-Musaraim* (Jerusalem: Ha-Aḥim Rohald, 1926), 9; Mark, *Be-Meḥitzatam,* 220; Yehudah Aryeh Mondshein, "Warsaw," *Ha-Tzefirah,* February 10, 1885, 42; Katz, *Tenu'at Ha-Musar,* 2:66.

13. This model would follow Salanter's model of cultural change; see Etkes, *Rabbi Israel Salanter*, 111. For further discussion of Simḥah Zissel's model see Geoffrey Claussen, "Repairing Character Traits and Repairing the Jews: The Talmud Torahs of Kelm and Grobin in the Nineteenth Century," *Polin: Studies in Polish Jewry* 30 (forthcoming, 2017).

14. Regarding these numbers, see Claussen, "Rabbi Simḥah Zissel Ziv," 36.

15. Indeed, one might question whether the institution should be called a "yeshiva" at all if it neglected Talmud to such an extent. Shlomo Tikochinski raises this issue and suggests that the Talmud Torah is better conceived of as a school for the training of Musar teachers than as a "yeshiva in the full sense of the term." See Shlomo Tikochinski, "Yeshivot Ha-Musar Me-Lita Le-Eretz Yisra'el: Yeshivat Slobodka Ve-Shitatah Ha-Ḥinukhit, Aliyatah Ve-Hitbasesutah Be-Eretz Yisra'el Ha-Mandatorit" (PhD thesis, Hebrew University, 2009), 135.

16. Michel Eidelshtein, "Kelm," *Ha-Levanon*, September 30, 1873, 52.

17. Kaunus County Archives, documents from March 1878 to July 1879: Inventory No. 1, File No. B/26, Document No. 137–78. I am grateful to Regina Kopilevich for locating this material.

18. Katz, *Tenu'at Ha-Musar*, 2:65, dates this incident to "roughly" 1876; this probably happened, however, after the school had received its official license, and I imagine that it was probably in response to this official move. Though I have records of the licensing from the Kaunus archives, I have located no records regarding the accusations against the Talmud Torah.

19. Etkes, *Rabbi Israel Salanter*, 190, 353n64.

20. *Beit Kelm: Emunah U-Middot* (Benei Berak: Siftei Ḥakhamim, Va'ad Le-Hafatzat Torah U-Musar, 2010), 267; Tikochinski, "Yeshivot Ha-Musar," 140.

21. See Katz, *Tenu'at Ha-Musar*, 2:65–66; Moshe Shapira, "Grobin," *Ha-Tzefirah*, October 5, 1881; Mondshein, "Warsaw," 41; Yisrael ["Ba'al Makhshoves"] Elyashev, "Gerobin [Part 1]," *He-Avar* 2, no. 1 (1918): 107.

22. The Babylonian Talmud (BT), Rosh Hashanah 16b, teaches in the name of R. Yitzḥak that one's bad fortune can be canceled out by "charity, calling out [in prayer], changing one's name, and changing one's conduct. . . . And, some say, changing one's location." After his misfortunes in Kelm, Simḥah Zissel is likely to have engaged in all of these activities.

23. Shapira, "Grobin"; Ben Tzion Leib Tzizling, "Liboya," *Ha-Tzefirah*, September 12, 1882; Mondshein, "Warsaw," 41.

24. Tzizling, "Liboya." Similar formulations can be found at Katz, *Tenu'at Ha-Musar*, 2:193–94; Elyashev, "Gerobin [Part 1]," 109.

25. Elyashev, "Gerobin [Part 1]," 110; Katz, *Tenu'at Ha-Musar*, 2:201. See also Mondshein, "Warsaw," 42.

26. Mark, *Be-Meḥitzatam*, 220. See also Elyashev, "Gerobin [Part 1]," 110; Friedman, *Sefer Ha-Zikhronot*, 84–85.

27. Katz, *Tenu'at Ha-Musar*, 2:183. Katz notes his father's connection to Simḥah Zissel at 2:72. On Katz as a helpful source for historians, see Shaul

Stampfer, *Lithuanian Yeshivas of the Nineteenth Century: Creating a Tradition of Learning*, trans. Lindsey Taylor-Gutharz (Oxford, UK: Littman Library of Jewish Civilization, 2012), 256. While Katz's writings on Simḥah Zissel have not been translated into English, they are summarized in Eliezer Ebner, "Simha Zissel Broida (Ziff)," in *Guardians of Our Heritage: 1724–1953*, ed. Leo Jung (New York: Bloch, 1958), 317–36.

28. Katz, *Tenu'at Ha-Musar*, 2:175. The focus on students' moral failings is highlighted by Elyashev, "Gerobin [Part 1]," 114; and "Gerobin [Part 2]," *He-Avar* 2, no. 2 (1918): 103–4. On the sermon as the key event of the day at the Talmud Torah, see Mondshein, "Warsaw," 42; Mark, *Be-Meḥitzatam*, 220.

29. Katz, *Tenu'at Ha-Musar*, 2:174.

30. Mark, *Be-Meḥitzatam*, 220; Katz, *Tenu'at Ha-Musar*, 2:173–74; Elyashev, "Gerobin [Part 2]," 91. See Claussen, "Rabbi Simḥah Zissel Ziv," 44–45.

31. Katz, *Tenu'at Ha-Musar*, 2:176–77, 207; Elyashev, "Gerobin [Part 1]," 110, 114. Simḥah Zissel Ziv, *Sefer Ḥokhmah U-Musar (ḤuM)*, vol. 2 (Jerusalem, 1964), 340, speaks of the spiritual exercise of dedicating three hours to the central part of the prayer service, the silent Amidah.

32. Katz, *Tenu'at Ha-Musar*, 2:202–4; Elyashev, "Gerobin [Part 1]," 115; Elyashev, "Gerobin [Part 2]," 89; *Kitvei Ha-Sabba Mi-Kelm: Pinkas Ha-Kabbalot* (Benei Berak: Siftei Ḥakhamim, Va'ad Le-Hafatzat Torah U-Musar, 1984), 147ff; and see Simḥah Zissel's own words at *Sefer Ha-Zikaron: Beit Kelm* (Benei Berak: Siftei Ḥakhamim, Va'ad Le-Hafatzat Torah U-Musar, 2002), 151.

33. Katz, *Tenu'at Ha-Musar*, 2:183, 205; Elyashev, "Gerobin [Part 1]," 111.

34. Katz, *Tenu'at Ha-Musar*, 2:174; Elyashev, "Gerobin [Part 2]," 89, 91, 99.

35. Katz, *Tenu'at Ha-Musar*, 2:172.

36. Stampfer, *Families, Rabbis and Education*, 222–23.

37. Erving Goffman, *Asylums: Essays on the Social Situation of Mental Patients and Other Inmates* (Garden City, NY: Anchor Books, 1961), xiii, 4–7.

38. Stampfer, *Families, Rabbis and Education*, 157–58, 216–20.

39. Katz, *Tenu'at Ha-Musar*, 2:200. See Mark, *Be-Meḥitzatam*, 220; Stampfer, *Families, Rabbis and Education*, 222–23. Regarding the outside world's increasing heresy, see *ḤuM*, 1:106. Regarding self-indulgence, see *ḤuM*, 1:21. On a loss of sense of divine providence, see *ḤuM*, 2:23 (regarding modern newspapers); and *ḤuM*, 1:98 (regarding modern scientists). On decreased attention to those in need, see Katz, *Tenu'at Ha-Musar*, 2:171, and on the need to recover the past honor of musar, 2:210.

40. See Elyashev, "Gerobin [Part 1]," 112, 116; Elyashev, "Gerobin [Part 2]," 92–95; Katz, *Tenu'at Ha-Musar*, 2:200.

41. Elyashev, "Gerobin [Part 1]," 109. I discuss this vision at length in Geoffrey Claussen, "Repairing Character Traits and Repairing the Jews: The Talmud Torahs of Kelm and Grobin in the Nineteenth Century," *Polin: Studies in Polish Jewry* 30 (forthcoming, 2017).

42. See Friedman, *Sefer Ha-Zikhronot*, 85; Katz, *Tenu'at Ha-Musar*, 2:202; Lifshitz, "Gan Hashem"; Eidelshtein, "Kelm," 53; Broida, "Kelm"; Mondshein, "Warsaw." Rabbi Akiva's image is in Mishnah Avot 3:17.

43. See Harris Bor, "Moral Education in the Age of the Jewish Enlightenment" (PhD thesis, University of Cambridge, 1996), 52–53; Nancy Sinkoff, *Out of the Shtetl: Making Jews Modern in the Polish Borderlands* (Providence, RI: Brown Judaic Studies, 2004), 136. The absence of corporal punishment at the Talmud Torah is noted by Zevulun Leib Barit, "Kelm," *Ha-Levanon*, February 19, 1873; Lifshitz, "Gan Hashem."

44. Katz, *Tenu'at Ha-Musar*, 2:173.

45. Elyashev, "Gerobin [Part 2]," 103ff.

46. Katz, *Tenu'at Ha-Musar*, 2:31–43.

47. Ibid., 2:49.

48. Ibid., 2:48.

49. Ibid., 2:30–32, 38; Mark, *Be-Meḥitzatam*, 220.

50. Katz, *Tenu'at Ha-Musar*, 2:69; Friedman, "Toledot Ba'alei Ha-Musar [Part 2]," 7.

51. Katz, *Tenu'at Ha-Musar*, 2:44, 55–56, 183–84.

52. Ibid., 2:44–45, 58–59.

53. *Pinkas Ha-Kabbalot*, 170; Katz, *Tenu'at Ha-Musar*, 2:203–4.

54. Friedman, *Sefer Ha-Zikhronot*, 85.

55. Katz, *Tenu'at Ha-Musar*, 2:187–88, 202, 206.

56. Ibid., 2:190.

57. Elyashev, "Gerobin [Part 1]," 109–114. Elyashev notes that, despite Simḥah Zissel's interest in adopting general European notions of decorum, the students at the Talmud Torah did not do so well at keeping the Talmud Torah or themselves clean.

58. Friedman, *Sefer Ha-Zikhronot*, 81–82. Note also the focus on decorum in Eidelshtein, "Kelm," 53; Broida, "Kelm," 253; Shapira, "Grobin"; Mondshein, "Warsaw." On the broader cultural trend of those Jews who may have been more interested in superficial patterns of behavior than in engaging with Enlightenment ideas, see Steven J. Zipperstein, "Haskalah, Cultural Change, and Nineteenth-Century Russian Jewry: A Reassessment," *Journal of Jewish Studies* 34, no. 2 (1983): 193, 203.

59. Elyashev, "Gerobin [Part 1]," 111; Broida, "Kelm"; Lifshitz, "Gan Hashem." Friedman, *Sefer Ha-Zikhronot*, 81, however, recalls that only "an hour" was dedicated to such studies.

60. See Broida, "Kelm"; Lifshitz, "Gan Hashem"; Tzizling, "Liboya."

61. For various mentions of subjects taught at the Talmud Torah in its different eras, see Broida, "Kelm"; Lifshitz, "Gan Hashem"; Tzizling, "Liboya"; Aryeh Leib Frumkin, "Kovno," *Ha-Levanon*, March 31, 1875; Mark, *Be-Meḥitzatam*, 221; Shapira, "Grobin"; Mondshein, "Warsaw," 42; Katz, *Tenu'at Ha-Musar*, 2:208; Elyashev, "Gerobin [Part 1]," 111.

62. See Immanuel Etkes, "Haskalah," *YIVO Encyclopedia of Jews in Eastern Europe*, June 6, 2010, http://www.yivoencyclopedia.org/article.aspx/Haskalah.

63. See Benjamin Nathans, *Beyond the Pale: The Jewish Encounter with Late Imperial Russia* (Berkeley: University of California Press, 2002), 202, 206, 235.

64. See ibid., 216–17, 221; Rappaport, "Jewish Education and Jewish Culture," 15, 43–44; Stampfer, *Families, Rabbis and Education*, 166, 221–22; Michael Stanislawski, "Russian Jewry, the Russian State, and the Dynamics of Jewish Emancipation," in *Paths of Emancipation: Jews, States, and Citizenship*, ed. Pierre Birnbaum and Ira Katznelson (Princeton, NJ: Princeton University Press, 1995), 274–76.

65. See Nathans, *Beyond the Pale*, 235; Rappaport, "Jewish Education and Jewish Culture," 65.

66. Etkes, *Rabbi Israel Salanter*, 141–45.

67. Mordekhai Gimpel Yaffe, "Shalom Ve-Emet [part 2]," *Ha-Levanon*, December 31, 1872, 145–46.

68. See Barit, "Kelm," 207; Elyashev, "Gerobin [Part 1]," 108–9; Elyashev, "Gerobin [Part 2]," 101.

69. On this strategy of utilizing what Salanter called "worldly wisdom," and on Salanter's attitude toward general studies, see Israel Salanter, "Or Yisra'el," in *Or Yisra'el*, ed. Isaac Blazer (Vilna, 1900), 42–43, 45–46 (Letters Two and Four); Etkes, *Rabbi Israel Salanter*, 106–7, 246–47, 278–79, 283–86, 314–15; Goldberg, *Israel Salanter*, 39–44, 180; Claussen, "Rabbi Simḥah Zissel Ziv," 75–79, 85–89.

70. Katz, *Tenu'at Ha-Musar*, 2:193–94. (The text is reprinted without mention of the general studies subjects in *Sefer Ha-Zikaron*, 110.)

71. *Derekh eretz* is a highly ambiguous phrase. It was also the term used by another author (above, note 24) to describe the study of musar at the Talmud Torah.

72. Compare Hirsch's much more direct discussion in Samson Raphael Hirsch, "The Relevance of Secular Studies to Jewish Education," in *The Collected Writings of Rabbi Samson Raphael Hirsch*, ed. Elliott Bondi and David Bechhofer, trans. Gertrude Hirschler, corrected ed., vol. 7 (New York: Feldheim, 1997), 88.

73. Mordekhai Gimpel Yaffe, "Shalom Ve-Emet [part 1]," *Ha-Levanon*, December 25, 1872, 145; Elyashev, "Gerobin [Part 1]," 109; Mark, *Be-Meḥitzatam*, 219.

74. Midrash Yalkut Shimoni 1:34.

75. Simḥah Zissel (Broida) Ziv, *Or Rasaz: Al Ḥamishah Ḥumshei Torah*, ed. Ḥayyim Shraga Levin (Jerusalem; Benei Berak; Kefar Ḥabad, 1960), 1:51–52. My italics. See also *Sefer Ha-Zikaron*, 135–36.

76. Contrast Eliezer Schweid, *The Idea of Modern Jewish Culture*, ed. Leonard Levin, trans. Amnon Hadary (Boston: Academic Studies Press, 2008), 25.

77. See Shmuel Feiner, "Towards a Historical Definition of the Haskalah," in *New Perspectives on the Haskalah*, ed. Shmuel Feiner and David Sorkin (Oxford, UK: Littman Library of Jewish Civilization, 2001), 197, 199.

78. See Bor, "Enlightenment Values, Jewish Ethics," 52–53.

79. *Sefer Ha-Zikaron*, 151–52; Friedman, *Sefer Ha-Zikhronot*, 82; Friedman, "Toledot Ba'alei Ha-Musar [Part 2]," 7.

80. Katz, *Tenu'at Ha-Musar*, 2:68–69.

81. *Kitvei Ha-Sabba Ve-Talmidav Mi-Kelm*, vol. 1 (Benei Berak: Siftei Ḥakhamim, Va'ad Le-Hafatzat Torah U-Musar, 1997), 366. See Tikochinski, "Yeshivot Ha-Musar," 145.

82. See Tikochinski, "Yeshivot Ha-Musar," 144–52. See, for example, the discussion in *Sefer Ha-Zikaron*, 234.

83. Yeḥiel Ya'akov Weinberg, *Lifrakim* (Jerusalem: Va'ad Le-Hotsa'at Kitve Ha-Ga'on Ha-Rav Yeḥi'el Ya'akov Veinberg, 2002), 81–82. See Tikochinski, "Yeshivot Ha-Musar," 150.

84. Ibid.

85. Ibid., 146; on musar as a tactical defense, see also 148.

86. Nathan Kamenetsky, *Making of a Godol: A Study of Episodes in the Lives of Great Torah Personalities*, 2nd ed. (Jerusalem: PP Publishers, 2004), 508; Tikochinski, "Yeshivot Ha-Musar," 144n100. On Finkel's reticence to criticize Kelm, see Tikochinski, "Yeshivot Ha-Musar,"153–54.

87. Katz, *Tenu'at Ha-Musar*, 2:71–72; Stampfer, *Lithuanian Yeshivas*, 268. Strauss was a resident of Karlsruhe, Germany, which was also the home of Simḥah Zissel's brother Avraham Yosef. Avraham Yosef and Simḥah Zissel's close disciple Reuven Dov Dessler introduced Strauss to Simḥah Zissel's work. Stampfer suggests that donors such as Strauss and Baron Rothschild, "even though they themselves identified with German Orthodoxy . . . were anxious to prevent the crumbling of traditional society in eastern Europe and felt that the musar movement could help achieve this."

88. *ḤuM*, 1:57.

89. See Tikochinski, "Yeshivot Ha-Musar," 144.

90. *ḤuM*, 1:20–21; Katz, *Tenu'at Ha-Musar*, 2:69–71. This vision is discussed at length in chapter 5 of this book.

91. See Katz, *Tenu'at Ha-Musar*, 2:69, 72–73.

92. See ibid., 2:73.

93. Ibid., 2:69; Friedman, *Sefer Ha-Zikhronot*, 83, 107; "Meshiv Ke-Halakhah," *Ha-Melitz*, July 1, 1897, 2; *Edenu: Le-Zikhro Shel Rabenu Shelomoh Poliachek* (New York: Rabbi Isaac Elchanan Theological Seminary, 1929), 10.

94. See Katz, *Tenu'at Ha-Musar*, 2:74.

95. *Pinkas Ha-Kabbalot*, 135–38; Katz, *Tenu'at Ha-Musar*, 2:75–77.

96. Katz, *Tenu'at Ha-Musar*, 2:85. On the interest among Israel Salanter's students in emigrating to the land of Israel, see Hillel Goldberg, "Between Berlin and Slobodka: The Life and Writings of Yosef Zev Lipovitz," *Tradition* 22, no. 2 (1986): 65n18.

97. Shaul Stampfer, "Telz, Yeshiva of," *YIVO Encyclopedia of Jews in Eastern Europe*, February 17, 2011, http://www.yivoencyclopedia.org/article.aspx/Telz_Yeshiva_of.

98. See Dov Katz, *Pulmus Ha-Musar* (Jerusalem, 1972).

99. "Meshiv Ke-Halakhah," 2.

100. See Katz, *Tenu'at Ha-Musar,* 2:78, 210–12, 215; Katz, *Pulmus Ha-Musar,* 78–79, 158, 306, 316; Simḥah Zissel (Broida) Ziv, "Torah Ve-Yirah," *Moriah* 12, nos. 7–9 (1983): 111–14.

101. Katz, *Tenu'at Ha-Musar,* 2:87.

102. Ibid., 2:49.

103. Compare Mark, *Be-Meḥitzatam,* 221, and Katz, *Tenu'at Ha-Musar,* 2:211–12.

## Chapter Two

1. Julia Annas, *The Morality of Happiness* (New York: Oxford University Press, 1993), 142–58; Alasdair C. MacIntyre, *After Virtue: A Study in Moral Theory,* 2nd ed. (Notre Dame: University of Notre Dame Press, 1984), 52–53.

2. Jonathan Wyn Schofer, "Rabbinic Ethical Formation and the Formation of Rabbinic Ethical Compilations," in *The Cambridge Companion to the Talmud and Rabbinic Literature,* ed. Charlotte Elisheva Fonrobert and Martin S. Jaffee (Cambridge: Cambridge University Press, 2007), 314–15; Tirosh-Samuelson, *Happiness in Premodern Judaism,* 101–142, 192–245.

3. *ḤuM,* 1:422 (cf. 447).

4. Compare Moses Maimonides, "Eight Chapters," in *Ethical Writings of Maimonides,* trans. Raymond L. Weiss and Charles E. Butterworth (New York: New York University Press, 1975), 61 (Chapter One), 66 (Chapter Three). Simḥah Zissel attributes the medical analogy to Maimonides and "all of the philosophers" at *ḤuM,* 1:137; he invokes Aristotle in discussing the medical analogy at *ḤuM,* 2:56.

5. *ḤuM,* 2:8.

6. *ḤuM,* 1:60.

7. *ḤuM,* 2:8. Simḥah Zissel offers the Yiddish *fershmutzt* along with the Hebrew *mezuhemet.*

8. *ḤuM,* 1:9. See also 1:11, regarding "the person who shares his fellow's burden, who makes an effort to feel the nature of his fellow's pain, and who does not merely feel what is natural to feel."

9. *ḤuM,* 1:357.

10. Ibid., 1:91.

11. *ḤuM,* 2:91–92.

12. *ḤuM,* 1:456–58.

13. Ibid., 1:57.

14. Ibid.

15. Ibid., 1:80, 276.

16. On the "wisdom of the Torah," see ibid., 1:1, 2, 30, 57.

17. *ḤuM,* 2:273. For a parallel in Israel Salanter's writing, see "Or Yisra'el," 48 (Letter #6).

18. See *ḤuM,* 1:80; *ḤuM,* 2:29; *Pinkas Ha-Kabbalot,* 49–51.

19. On this theme in Maimonides, see *The Guide of the Perplexed,* trans. Shlomo Pines, vol. 1 (Chicago: University of Chicago Press, 1963), 22–23 (Part 1, Chapter 1). See also the references to Rashi at, e.g., *Ḥ͏uM,* 1:14, 77, 137, 444.

20. *Pinkas Ha-Kabbalot,* 50. Also see the discussion of reason and "sharing the burden" of God's creatures at *ḤuM,* 1:7, 14.

21. *ḤuM,* 2:171, in reference to Ibn Ezra's commentary on Exodus 31:18.

22. *ḤuM,* 1:14, 84, 140. See Maimonides's discussions at *The Guide of the Perplexed,* 1:22 (Part 1, Chapter 1), 1:33 (Part 1, Chapter 7); "Eight Chapters," 64 (end of Chapter One).

23. *ḤuM,* 1:191.

24. Ibid., 1:2; Katz, *Tenu'at Ha-Musar,* 2:149, 159.

25. *ḤuM,* 1:59.

26. Ibid., 1:14.

27. *Kitvei Ha-Sabba Ve-Talmidav Mi-Kelm,* 1:5.

28. See Jonathan Wyn Schofer, *The Making of a Sage: A Study in Rabbinic Ethics* (Madison, WI.: University of Wisconsin Press, 2004), 86–95.

29. *Kitvei Ha-Sabba Ve-Talmidav Mi-Kelm,* 1:97.

30. *ḤuM,* 1:456.

31. Ibid., 1:456, 464.

32. Ibid., 1:460.

33. See Annas, *The Morality of Happiness,* 48ff.

34. *ḤuM,* 2:21.

35. *ḤuM,* 1:87.

36. *Kitvei Ha-Sabba Ve-Talmidav Mi-Kelm,* 1:8. See also *ḤuM,* 1:162, 230.

37. *ḤuM,* 1:238.

38. Immanuel Kant, "The Metaphysics of Morals," in *Practical Philosophy,* ed. and trans. Mary J. Gregor, The Cambridge Edition of the Works of Immanuel Kant (Cambridge: Cambridge University Press, 1996), 515–16 (6:383–84).

39. See Annas, *The Morality of Happiness,* 49–52, 57–58.

40. *ḤuM,* 2:155. See also 2:132 and 2:3 (quoted below).

41. *ḤuM,* 2:226.

42. Ibid., 2:3.

43. Ibid., 2:10. I am grateful to Leonard Levin for his assistance with this passage. The comment by R. Hayyim is in *Ruaḥ Ha-Ḥayyim: Peirush Rabbi Ḥayyim Mi-Volozhin Le-Pirkei Avot* (Vilna, 1859), 21.

44. *ḤuM,* 1:148–49. See also 2:77.

45. *ḤuM,* 1:452. See *Sefer Ha-Zikaron,* 203–12; Katz, *Tenu'at Ha-Musar,* 2:149–50.

46. Compare Kant, "Groundwork of the Metaphysics of Morals," *Practical Philosophy,* 81, 96. On Simḥah Zissel's familiarity with Kant, see Kamenetsky, *Making,* 621.

47. *ḤuM,* 1:398. The reference is to Aristotle, *Nicomachean Ethics,* 2nd ed., trans. Terence Irwin (Indianapolis: Hackett, 1999), 93 (6.8.5–6; 1142a11–21).

48. See especially Immanuel Kant, "Critique of Practical Reason," *Practical Philosophy,* 199–211; Kant, "The Metaphysics of Morals," 513, 515, 536. As distinguished from this "Kantian" position, however, Kant himself did value moral emotions, such that his "Metaphysics of Morals" sometimes presents something of an "Aristotelian" approach; see Robert B. Louden, "Kant's Virtue Ethics," *Philosophy* 61, no. 238 (1986): 473–89.

49. Aristotle, *Nicomachean Ethics,* chap. 7; Maimonides, "Eight Chapters," 6.

50. See Salanter's discussion in "Or Yisra'el," 82–83 (Letter 30). I discuss this in Claussen, "Rabbi Simḥah Zissel Ziv," 136–38.

51. *ḤuM,* 1:148.

52. Ibid., 1:222.

53. Ibid. For the distinction between the virtuous person and this self-controlled person, see also *ḤuM,* 2:188.

54. *ḤuM,* 1:222.

55. *ḤuM,* 2:8.

56. *ḤuM,* 1:222–23. Here, Simḥah Zissel sees this sort of vice as characterizing most people, though at *ḤuM,* 2:8 he sees the masses as characterized by incontinence rather than by vice.

57. *Pinkas Ha-Kabbalot,* 125b, note 1.

58. *ḤuM,* 1:3.

59. Ibid., 1:58.

60. See, for example, ibid., 1:56.

61. Ibid., 1:2–10, 104, 136; *Kitvei Ha-Sabba Ve-Talmidav Mi-Kelm,* 1:150.

62. *ḤuM,* 1:65.

63. Martha C. Nussbaum, "Virtue Ethics: A Misleading Category?," *The Journal of Ethics* 3, no. 3 (1999): 187.

64. *ḤuM,* 2:221.

65. See Tamar Ross, "The Role of Intellect in Moral Education in the Discourses of Rabbi Simha Zissel of Kelm," *Proceedings of the 11th Annual Conference of the South African Association of Jewish Studies,* 1990, 234; Claussen, "Rabbi Simḥah Zissel Ziv," 146n145.

66. *ḤuM,* 1:452. See *Sefer Ha-Zikaron,* 203–12; Katz, *Tenu'at Ha-Musar,* 2:149–50.

67. *ḤuM,* 1:400. Simḥah Zissel cites Aristotle, *Sefer Ha-Middot* [Nicomachean Ethics], ed. Isaac Satanow, trans. Meir ben Solomon Alguadez into Hebrew from the Latin of Boethius (Lemberg: U.W. Salat, 1867), 6.6; the text in Irwin's English translation is in Aristotle, *Nicomachean Ethics,* 93 (6.8.5–6; 1142a11–21).

68. *ḤuM,* 2:188.

69. Ibid., 2:221–22.

70. *ḤuM,* 1:160.

71. Ibid., 1:161.

72. Ibid., 1:161; 2:276–77.

73. *ḤuM,* 2:221–22.

74. *ḤuM,* 1:102. Compare 1:311, 409.

75. *Ḥ uM*, 1:100. On the precedent in Maimonides, see Lawrence J. Kaplan, "An Introduction to Maimonides' 'Eight Chapters,'" *The Edah Journal* 2, no. 2 (2002): 10–11.

76. *ḤuM*, 2:223.

77. *ḤuM*, 1:81.

78. Raymond L. Weiss, *Maimonides' Ethics: The Encounter of Philosophic and Religious Morality* (Chicago: University of Chicago Press, 1991), 29–31, 188–90.

79. See Alexander Altmann, "Maimonides's 'Four Perfections,'" in *Essays in Jewish Intellectual History* (Hanover: Brandeis University Press/University Press of New England, 1981), 65–76.

80. The parallel is indicated at *ḤuM*, 1:66.

81. *ḤuM*, 2:19.

82. Ibid., 2:327.

83. *ḤuM*, 1:127, in reference to BT Berakhot 17a.

84. Ibid., 1:180, quoting BT Megillah 27a, Kiddushin 40b, Bava Kamma 17a (and see 1:95, 353–54).

85. See ibid., 1:6; *ḤuM*, 2:270–71.

86. *ḤuM*, 1:100.

87. *ḤuM*, 2:12.

88. *ḤuM*, 1:8.

89. Neil Gillman, *Doing Jewish Theology: God, Torah & Israel in Modern Judaism* (Woodstock, VT: Jewish Lights, 2008), 123–24, 151–63. Compare Gershom Gerhard Scholem, "Three Types of Jewish Piety," in *On the Possibility of Jewish Mysticism in Our Time & Other Essays*, ed. Avraham Shapira, trans. Jonathan Chipman (Philadelphia: Jewish Publication Society, 1997), 176–90.

90. Tirosh-Samuelson, *Happiness in Premodern Judaism*, 117.

91. See ibid., 192–245.

92. *ḤuM*, 1:19. The rabbinic praise of bad dreams is at BT Berakhot 55b.

93. *ḤuM*, 2:91.

94. Ibid., 2:246.

95. *Kitvei Ha-Sabba Ve-Talmidav Mi-Kelm*, 1:11–12.

96. Ibid., 1:84; *ḤuM*, 1:25, 60. Simḥah Zissel follows the interpretation of the verse in BT Eiruvin 54b, where words of Torah are compared to breasts.

97. *Kitvei Ha-Sabba Ve-Talmidav Mi-Kelm*, 1:15.

98. See, e.g., *ḤuM*, 1:51, 71, 149, 256, 347.

99. See *ḤuM*, 2:66.

100. *ḤuM*, 1:5.

101. Chaim Grade, *The Yeshiva*, trans. Curt Leviant (Indianapolis: Bobbs-Merrill, 1976), 1:33; the original Yiddish formulation is in Chaim Grade, *Tzemaḥ Atlas: Di Yeshive* (Los Angeles: Yidish-Natzionaln Arbeter-Farband, 1967), 1:40.

102. *Kitvei Ha-Sabba Mi-Kelm: Inyanei Elul Ve-Yamim Nora'im* (Benei Berak: Siftei Ḥakhamim, Va'ad Le-Hafatzat Torah U-Musar, 1997), 80.

103. *ḤuM*, 2:29.

104. Ibid., 2:24.

105. See *Ḥ uM*, 1:38, 60; *Ḥ uM*, 2:24, 26–27; Elyashev, "Gerobin [Part 2]," 91–92.

106. *Ḥ uM*, 1:49.

107. See Elyashev, "Gerobin [Part 1]," 114. On Salanter's view, see Etkes, *Rabbi Israel Salanter*, 94, 231. Compare Bor, "Enlightenment Values, Jewish Ethics," 52–53.

108. *Ḥ uM*, 1:78; *Ḥ uM*, 2:188.

109. *Ḥ uM*, 1:56. See *Kitvei Ha-Sabba Mi-Kelm: Inyanei Elul Ve-Yamim Nora'im*, 64–65.

110. Ross, "Ha-Maḥshavah Ha-Iyunit." The Talmudic dictum is cited on many pages of Talmud, e.g., BT Pesaḥim 50b.

111. Ibid., 66; Ross notes, for example, the business language at *Ḥ uM*, 1:184. See also *Kitvei Ha-Sabba Mi-Kelm: Inyanei Elul Ve-Yamim Nora'im*, 99.

112. *Ḥ uM*, 1:413–14.

113. Ibid., 1:380–81; *Ḥ uM*, 2:19, 276–77. See Walter S. Wurzburger, *Ethics of Responsibility: Pluralistic Approaches to Covenantal Ethics* (Philadelphia: Jewish Publication Society, 1994), 79–81.

114. *Ḥ uM*, 2:191–92. See also *Ḥ uM*, 1:13.

115. *Ḥ uM*, 2:304.

116. See Annas, *The Morality of Happiness*, 370ff.

117. Moses Maimonides, *The Guide of the Perplexed*, trans. Shlomo Pines, vol. 2 (Chicago: University of Chicago Press, 1963), 636–38 (Part 3, Chapter 54). Admittedly, most of Aristotle's virtues are other-regarding and do not aim at benefiting oneself; even Aristotle's emphasis on the importance of external goods may be, in part, because they facilitate other-regarding virtues. See Annas, *The Morality of Happiness*, 378–85.

118. Ross, "Ha-Maḥshavah Ha-Iyunit," 73, 80–109.

## Chapter Three

1. Jacob J. Schacter, "Rabbi Jacob Emden, Philosophy, and the Authority of Maimonides," *Tradition* 27, no. 4 (1993): 132–36.

2. On attitudes of Lithuanian traditionalists beyond and within the Musar movement, see Allan Nadler, *The Faith of the Mithnagdim: Rabbinic Responses to Hasidic Rapture* (Baltimore, MD: Johns Hopkins University Press, 1997), 143; Etkes, *Rabbi Israel Salanter*, 286; Goldberg, *Israel Salanter*, 170–76.

3. *Ḥ uM*, 1:398–99, 400.

4. Katz, *Tenu'at Ha-Musar*, 2:40.

5. Ibid., 2:37. Al-Ghazali might seem out of place on this bookshelf, as he was a harsh critic of philosophy, but Simḥah Zissel was probably reading from a Hebrew adaption of an ethical work by Al-Ghazali that depicts Al-Ghazali as a philosopher and has nothing negative to say about philosophy. See Claussen, "Rabbi Simḥah Zissel Ziv," 185n14.

6. Elyashev, "Gerobin [Part 1]," 114–15. Maimonides's dictum may be found in Maimonides, "Eight Chapters," 60 (Introduction).

7. *Ḥ uM*, 2:270. My emphasis.

8. *Ḥ uM*, 1:100. See ibid., 1:6.

9. *Ḥ uM*, 1:358.

10. *Kitvei Ha-Sabba Mi-Kelm: Inyanei Elul Ve-Yamim Nora'im*, 17.

11. Ibid., 122.

12. Moshe Isserles, *Torat Ha-Olah*, vol. 1 (Prague, 1854), 39a–b (11:4).

13. See Leonard Levin, *Seeing with Both Eyes: Ephraim Luntshitz and the Polish-Jewish Renaissance* (Leiden: Brill, 2008), 28–29.

14. *Ḥ uM*, 1:61, 312–13; *Ḥ uM*, 2:26–27; Katz, *Tenu'at Ha-Musar*, 2:151.

15. *Ḥ uM*, 1:61–62.

16. Eliyahu Lopian, *Sefer Lev Eliyahu*, ed. Shalom Mordekhai Shvadron (Jerusalem: Yefeh Nof, Y. Pozen, 2005), 263.

17. Katz, *Tenu'at Ha-Musar*, 2:215; *Ḥ uM*, 1:137, 398–400; *Ḥ uM*, 2:56, 91, 188.

18. See, for example, *Kitvei Ha-Sabba Ve-Talmidav Mi-Kelm*, 1:150; *Ḥ uM*, 1:78.

19. *Ḥ uM*, 1:51. Simḥah Zissel quotes the story from Natan ben Ḥayyim Amram, *Sefer No'am Ha-Middot* (Salonika, 1857), 71a.

20. *Kitvei Ha-Sabba Mi-Kelm: Inyanei Ḥanukkah U-Furim* (Benei Berak: Siftei Ḥakhamim, Va'ad Le-Hafatzat Torah U-Musar, 2001), 168; *Ḥ uM*, 1:239; *Ḥ uM*, 2:340. See Maimonides, *Mishneh Torah*, "Hilkhot Talmud Torah," 3:12; Mishnah *Pirkei Avot* 6:4, 6.

21. *Ḥ uM*, 1:280, 447. See also 1:456.

22. *Ḥ uM*, 1:280, 447, 456; Ziv, "Torah Ve-Yirah," 111.

23. *Ḥ uM*, 2:68.

24. Ibid.

25. Ziv, *Or Rasaz*, 1:51.

26. *Ḥ uM*, 1:12.

27. Ibid., 1:164.

28. Ibid.

29. Ibid., 1:344.

30. *Ḥ uM*, 2:95.

31. Ibid., 2:340.

32. For one example from the Haskalah, see the discussion of Menaḥem Mendel Lefin's concept of equanimity in Sinkoff, *Out of the Shtetl*, 153. Lefin used the language of both *menuḥat ha-nefesh* and *yishuv ha-da'at*. As Sinkoff writes, he stressed such virtues as "an antidote to the Hasidic emphasis on unbridled emotion and ecstatic worship." Hasidic concepts of equanimity are often in a somewhat different vein; see Joseph Dan, ed., *The Teachings of Hasidism* (New York: Behrman House, 1983), 138–140; Don Seeman, "Martyrdom, Emotion and the Work of Ritual in R. Mordecai Joseph Leiner's Mei Ha-Shiloah," *AJS Review* 27, no. 2 (November 2003): 253–79. On the history of the virtue of equanimity in Judaism, see Eitan P. Fishbane, *As Light*

*Before Dawn: The Inner World of a Medieval Kabbalist* (Stanford, CA: Stanford University Press, 2009).

33. See Salanter, "Or Yisra'el," 74; Etkes, *Rabbi Israel Salanter*, 217.

34. *ḤuM*, 1:282. See also Katz, *Tenu'at Ha-Musar*, 2:151.

35. *ḤuM*, 1:267, 282. Simḥah Zissel picks up on the Talmudic suggestion (BT Bava Batra 25b) that the lamp was a symbol of wisdom.

36. *ḤuM*, 2:10. The language of "stripping away materiality" echoes language commonly used by Hasidic sources, though Simḥah Zissel does not praise self-annihilation (*bittul ha-yesh*) and the rejection of the social domain as those sources often do. Compare Rachel Elior, *The Mystical Origins of Hasidism*, trans. Shalom Carmy (Oxford: Littman Library of Jewish Civilization, 2006), 117. I discuss Simḥah Zissel's rejection of Kabbalistic models of self-annihilation in chapter 5 of this book.

37. *ḤuM*, 2:10. See *ḤuM*, 1:222–24.

38. *ḤuM*, 1:100.

39. Ibid., 1:51.

40. Ibid., 1:134, 164; *ḤuM*, 2:10, 26–27; Katz, *Tenu'at Ha-Musar*, 2:151.

41. *ḤuM*, 1:26, 285.

42. Seeman, "Martyrdom, Emotion and the Work of Ritual," 266.

43. *ḤuM*, 1:1.

44. Ibid., 1:255.

45. Katz, *Tenu'at Ha-Musar*, 2:48, 53; Simḥah Zissel (Broida) Ziv, "Me-Igrotav Shel Ha-Ga'on Ha-Ḥasid Rav Simḥah Zissel Mi-Kelm," in *Kokhvei Or*, ed. Isaac Blazer (Jerusalem, 1974), 187. See also Etkes, *Rabbi Israel Salanter*, 232.

46. *ḤuM*, 1:255.

47. *ḤuM*, 2:340.

48. *ḤuM*, 2:221, building on BT Shabbat 88b.

49. Ibid., 1:49; see also 1:52.

50. *Pinkas Ha-Kabbalot*, 146.

51. *Kitvei Ha-Sabba Ve-Talmidav Mi-Kelm*, 1:100. This passage is introduced by words of praise for Maimonides's *Guide of the Perplexed*.

52. See Nadler, *The Faith of the Mithnagdim*, 139–41; Ross, "Ha-Maḥshavah Ha-Iyunit."

53. *ḤuM*, 2:7.

54. *ḤuM*, 1:93.

55. Ibid., 1:70, 92, 108. Animals are mentioned at 1:70; Simḥah Zissel sees the proof for their knowledge in Psalms 104:21 and Rashi's commentary on Genesis 8:11.

56. Ibid., 1:27.

57. Ibid., 1:104; *ḤuM*, 2:215. See also Simḥah Zissel's mention of Christians and Muslims building their religions on the Torah at *ḤuM*, 1:46.

58. *ḤuM*, 1:92.

59. BT Bava Metzia 59b; my translation generally follows Louis E. Newman, *An Introduction to Jewish Ethics* (Upper Saddle River, NJ: Pearson Prentice Hall, 2005), 48.

60. *Ḥ uM*, 1:106–7.

61. Ibid., 1:176. See Maimonides, "Eight Chapters," 80–83 (Chapter 7).

62. *ḤuM*, 1:18.

63. As we have seen, Simḥah Zissel sometimes does depict Jews as morally superior, whereas at other times, he depicts non-Jewish nations as superior to Israel.

64. *ḤuM*, 2:171.

65. Ibid., 2:171, 173.

66. Israel Salanter, *Even Yisra'el*, ed. Shneur Zalman Hirshowitz (Warsaw: Yitzḥak Goldman, 1883), 36 (Sermon 8). See Goldberg, *Israel Salanter*, 50–53.

67. *ḤuM*, 1:27.

68. Ibid.

69. See Lawrence J. Kaplan, "Daas Torah: A Modern Conception of Rabbinic Authority," in *Rabbinic Authority and Personal Autonomy*, ed. Moshe Sokol (Northvale, NJ: J. Aronson, 1992), 1–60. For the role of the Musar movement in developing this view, see Hillel Goldberg, "Israel Salanter and 'Orhot Zaddikim': Restructuring Musar Literature," *Tradition* 23, no. 4 (1988): 38n18; Kaplan, "Daas Torah: A Modern Conception of Rabbinic Authority," 4n6; Tamar Ross, "Tenu'at Ha-Musar Ve-Ha-Ba'ayah Ha-Hermeneutit Be-Talmud Torah" [The Musar Movement and the Hermeneutical Problem in Torah Study], *Tarbiz* 59 (1990): 191–214.

70. Elijah Eliezer Dessler, *Mikhtav Me-Eliyahu*, ed. Aryeh Carmel and Alter Halpern (London, 1955), 75–76. I am following the translation in Elijah Eliezer Dessler, *Strive for Truth*, trans. Aryeh Carmell (Jerusalem: Feldheim Publishers, 1978), 1:219. See also the discussion and translation by Lawrence Kaplan in Michael Walzer et al., eds., *The Jewish Political Tradition*, vol. 1 (New Haven: Yale University Press, 2000), 299–301, 304–6.

71. Dessler, *Mikhtav Me-Eliyahu*, 76–77; English translation in Dessler, *Strive for Truth*, 1:219–23; reprinted in *Kitvei Ha-Sabba Mi-Kelm: Inyanei Ḥanukkah U-Furim*, 119–21. Dessler heard this teaching in Simḥah Zissel's name from his father, Reuven Dov Dessler.

72. *ḤuM*, 1:145.

73. Ibid., 1:145–46.

74. *ḤuM*, 2:224.

75. Maimonides, *Mishneh Torah*, "Laws of Idolatry," 1:3.

76. *ḤuM*, 1:442–43. See also the similar discussion at 1:64–65.

77. *ḤuM*, 1:442–44. See 1:64–65, 2:3.

78. *ḤuM*, 1:65.

79. Ibid., 1:442.

80. *ḤuM*, 2:13.

81. Ibid., 2:16.

82. Ibid., 2:3.

83. *ḤuM*, 1:191; *Pinkas Ha-Kabbalot*, 46.

84. See, for example, his use of this text at *ḤuM*, 1:30.

85. Ibid., 1:179.

86. Ibid., 1:49.
87. Ibid., 1:46.
88. Ibid., 1:187; see also the admiration of the Maharal of Prague at 1:30.
89. *Ḥ*u*M*, 1:66.
90. Ibid., 1:66, 179, 293, 325; 2:97.
91. *ḤuM*, 1:187.
92. Ibid., 1:94.
93. Ibid., 1:96. See 1:112, 458.
94. *ḤuM*, 1:96.
95. Ibid., 1:112.
96. Ibid., 1:97.
97. Ibid., 1:98. See also 1:247.
98. *ḤuM*, 1:110.
99. *ḤuM*, 2:217.
100. Nadler, *The Faith of the Mithnagdim*, 228n17.
101. *ḤuM*, 1:97.
102. Ibid.
103. Ibid., 1:110, following Naḥmanides on Numbers 13:1.
104. Ibid., 1:103, 111–12, 114. See Geoffrey Claussen, "The Legacy of the Kelm School of Musar on Questions of Work, Wealth and Poverty," in *Wealth and Poverty in Jewish Tradition*, ed. Leonard J. Greenspoon (West Lafayette, IN: Purdue University Press, 2015).
105. Ibid., 1:109, a passage transcribed by Simḥah Zissel's son.

## Chapter Four

1. Simḥah Zissel takes what Louis Newman has described as a "covenantal" vision of the scope of Jewish morality, promoting "a kind of moral life that cannot be defined by adherence to rules alone." See Louis E. Newman, *Past Imperatives: Studies in the History and Theory of Jewish Ethics* (Albany: State University of New York Press, 1998), 76. Newman contrasts this "covenantal" approach with the "contractual" approach to Jewish ethics.
2. Rosalind Hursthouse, *On Virtue Ethics* (Oxford: Oxford University Press, 1999), 26 (with "if and only if" in place of "iff").
3. Ibid., 29; discussion of the perfectly virtuous agent is at 159–60.
4. See, for example, *ḤuM*, 2:194–95.
5. *ḤuM*, 1:180; *ḤuM*, 2:77, 177, 240. The phrase is from *Tanna De-vei Eliyahu*, 23 (25); for an English translation, see William G. Braude and Israel J. Kapstein, trans., *Tanna Dĕḇe Eliyyahu: The Lore of the School of Elijah* (Philadelphia: Jewish Publication Society of America, 1981), 316.
6. *ḤuM*, 1:11.
7. Ibid., 1:7–8, 255.
8. See, for example, ibid., 1:3–10, 13, 106, 145, 161.

9. For the Bible's view, see Michael Fishbane, "Biblical Prophecy as a Religious Phenomenon," in *Jewish Spirituality: From the Bible through the Middle Ages*, ed. Arthur Green (New York: Crossroad, 1986), 70.

10. *Ḥ uM*, 1:15, 16.

11. *Kitvei Ha-Sabba Ve-Talmidav Mi-Kelm*, 1:5. This ideal is found in Maimonides's thought as well; see Wurzburger, *Ethics of Responsibility*, 75.

12. See *Ḥ uM*, 2:328; 1:31, 32.

13. *Ḥ uM*, 2:113 (in reference to Ben Zoma's statement in Mishnah Avot 4:1: "Who is wise? The one who learns from every human being"), 194–95.

14. Ibid., 2:32.

15. Ibid., 2:25.

16. *Kitvei Ha-Sabba Ve-Talmidav Mi-Kelm*, 1:31–32.

17. *Ḥ uM*, 2:246.

18. *Ḥ uM*, 1:53.

19. Sifre Deuteronomy, Ekev, #49. Translation from Reuven Hammer, trans., *Sifre: A Tannaitic Commentary on the Book of Deuteronomy* (New Haven: Yale University Press, 1986), 105–6.

20. BT Sotah 14a.

21. *Ḥ uM*, 2:328.

22. Ibid., 2:11.

23. *Ḥ uM*, 1:31.

24. *Ḥ uM*, 2:11.

25. Ibid.

26. *Ḥ uM*, 1:12–13, 30, 174; *Ḥ uM*, 2:145, 328.

27. *Ḥ uM*, 1:30.

28. Ibid., 1:160.

29. Ibid., 1:87.

30. *Ḥ uM*, 2:10.

31. See *Ḥ uM*, 1:14, 86–87; 2:90–91.

32. *Ḥ uM*, 1:75.

33. Ibid., 1:75, 132.

34. *Ḥ uM*, 2:14–15. My italics.

35. *Kitvei Ha-Sabba Ve-Talmidav Mi-Kelm*, 1:17–18.

36. Ibid., 1:19.

37. *Ḥ uM*, 2:10. My italics.

38. Maimonides, *Mishneh Torah*, Hilkhot De'ot 1:6. See Claussen, "Rabbi Simḥah Zissel Ziv," 284.

39. *Ḥ uM*, 1:462.

40. Ibid., 1:167.

41. Ibid., 1:205.

42. Etkes, *Rabbi Israel Salanter*, 165–66.

43. *Ḥ uM*, 1:163. See Etkes, *Rabbi Israel Salanter*, 165; Katz, *Tenu'at Ha-Musar*, 2:52–53.

44. *Ḥ uM*, 1:114–15, following the commentary of Naḥmanides on Leviticus 19:1. On Maimonides's similar attitude toward going "beyond the

line of the law," see Robert Eisen, "*Lifnim Mi-Shurat Ha-Din* in Maimonides' *Mishneh Torah*," *The Jewish Quarterly Review* 89, no. 3/4 (1999): esp. 315–17. On the broader issue of supererogation in Judaism, see Newman, *Past Imperatives*, 17–44.

45. *Ḥ uM*, 1:422–23.

46. Ibid., 1:175.

47. Ibid.

48. Andrew Michael Flescher, *Heroes, Saints, and Ordinary Morality* (Washington, DC: Georgetown University Press, 2003).

49. *ḤuM*, 1:188, quoting BT Bava Kamma 50a, BT Yevamot 121b. See 1:73–4, 358; 2:280; *Kitvei Ha-Sabba Mi-Kelm: Inyanei Elul Ve-Yamim Nora'im*, 83–84.

50. *ḤuM*, 1:34.

51. *ḤuM*, 2:245.

52. *ḤuM*, 1:137.

53. Ibid., 1:286.

54. Ibid., 1:282. See also 1:51.

55. *ḤuM*, 2:257.

56. Goldberg, *Israel Salanter*, esp. 158–83.

57. *ḤuM*, 1:103.

58. Ibid., 1:91.

59. Ibid.

60. Ibid., 1:103–4, 105.

61. Ibid., 1:124. The original midrash is from Tanḥuma, "Va-yiggash," 5; in English translation, see Samuel A. Berman, trans., *Midrash Tanhuma-Yelammedenu: An English Translation of Genesis and Exodus* (Hoboken, NJ: Ktav, 1995), 273.

62. *ḤuM*, 2:6.

63. Ibid., 2:20.

64. See Ḥayyim ben Yitzḥak of Volozhin, *Nefesh Ha-Ḥayyim* (Benei Berak, 1989), 4:9 (220–21), translated below.

65. Nadler, *The Faith of the Mithnagdim*, 156–57.

66. Ḥayyim ben Yitzḥak of Volozhin, *Nefesh Ha-Ḥayyim*, 4:9 (220–21). The reference to the midrash on Proverbs refers to *Midrash Mishlei* on Proverbs 1:2.

67. Nadler, *The Faith of the Mithnagdim*, 164.

68. Etkes, *Rabbi Israel Salanter*, 123–34; Sinkoff, *Out of the Shtetl*, 151–52.

69. Salanter, "Or Yisra'el," 105, 107–8; Etkes, *Rabbi Israel Salanter*, 203; Goldberg, *Israel Salanter*, 87, 91, 166–67.

70. *ḤuM*, 1:109, 110; *Kitvei Ha-Sabba Ve-Talmidav Mi-Kelm*, 1:34.

71. See, e.g., *ḤuM*, 1:18.

72. Ibid., 1:64–65. My italics.

73. Ibid., 1:239.

74. Ibid., 1:78.

75. Ibid., 1:11. The emphasis is Simḥah Zissel's.

76. Ibid., 1:42.

77. *Ḥ uM*, 2:9.
78. Maimonides, *The Guide of the Perplexed*, 2:526 (Part 3, Chapter 32).
79. See *Ḥ uM*, 2:273.
80. Ibid., 2:10. My italics.
81. See Claussen, "Rabbi Simḥah Zissel Ziv," 316–17.
82. *Ḥ uM*, 2:98.
83. Ibid., 2:228.
84. Ibid., 2:240.
85. *Ḥ uM*, 1:21.
86. Ibid., 1:272. See also 1:204.
87. For a model of this sort of moral psychology, see Hursthouse, *On Virtue Ethics*, 157–59.
88. *Pinkas Ha-Kabbalot*, 8–9. My italics.
89. *Ḥ uM*, 1:78–79.
90. David E. Fishman, "Musar and Modernity: The Case of Novaredok," *Modern Judaism* 8, no. 1 (1988): 52.
91. This translation is from Ibid., 53. The original is at Yosef Yoizel Horowitz, *Madregat Ha-Adam* (New York: Keren Mefitsei Torah U-Musar, 1947), 130.
92. See William James, *The Varieties of Religious Experience* (New York: Barnes & Noble, 2004), 166, 171.
93. Joseph Dov Soloveitchik, *Halakhic Man*, trans. Lawrence Kaplan (Philadelphia: Jewish Publication Society of America, 1983), 75–76.
94. See Allan Nadler, "Soloveitchik's Halakhic Man: Not a 'Mithnagged,'" *Modern Judaism* 13, no. 2 (1993): 119–47.

## Chapter Five

1. *Ḥ uM*, 1:30. See Katz, *Tenu'at Ha-Musar*, 2:162–63.
2. Jerusalem Talmud, Nedarim 41c (9:4); Sifra, Kedoshim, 4:12; and Genesis Rabbah 24:7.
3. *Ḥ uM*, 1:1.
4. Ibid., 1:176. See also *Pinkas Ha-Kabbalot*, 153.
5. *Ḥ uM*, 1:6. See also 1:21.
6. *Ḥ uM*, 2:6.
7. Ibid., 2:7.
8. *Ḥ uM*, 1:191.
9. See Daniel Feldman, *The Right and the Good: Halakhah and Human Relations*, Expanded ed. (Brooklyn: Yashar Books, 2005), 169–77.
10. Of course, Ben Azzai might be offering a supplement and clarification rather than a dissent. See Lenn Evan Goodman, *Love Thy Neighbor as Thyself* (Oxford: Oxford University Press, 2008), 37.
11. See "Hilkhot Evel" [Laws of Mourning], chap. 14, article 1, in Moses Maimonides, *Mishneh Torah* (Jerusalem: Mossad Ha-Rav Kook, 1956), vol. 17.

12. *Ḥ*u*M*, 1:30–31.

13. *Pinkas Ha-Kabbalot*, 27.

14. Ibid., 193. My italics.

15. *ḤuM*, 2:6–7.

16. Ibid., 2:6–8. Thanks to Leonard Levin for aiding my understanding of this passage. Notably, Simḥah Zissel imagines Ben Zoma referring to "human beings, whether Jewish or not," whereas the Talmud here has traditionally been understood as referring only to Jews.

17. See also ibid., 2:95.

18. Ibid., 2:126–27; *Pinkas Ha-Kabbalot*, 9–10. For my translation of the passage, see "Notice Posted on the Door of the Kelm Talmud Torah Before the High Holidays," *Jewish Review of Books* 4, no. 3 (Fall 2013): 46. The image of Israel's unity can be found in standard prayer books, at the end of the "Shema and Its Blessings." On this theme, see Alan Mittleman, "Pluralism: Identity, Civility, and the Common Good," *Modern Judaism* 21, no. 2 (2001): 125–45.

19. See Louis Jacobs, *Religion and the Individual: A Jewish Perspective* (Cambridge: Cambridge University Press, 1992), 26; Ernst Simon, "The Neighbor (Re'a) Whom We Shall Love," in *Modern Jewish Ethics, Theory and Practice*, ed. Marvin Fox (Columbus: Ohio State University Press, 1975), chap. 5; Reinhard Neudecker, "And You Shall Love Your Neighbor as Yourself—I Am the Lord' (Lev 19:18) in Jewish Interpretation," *Biblica* 73, no. 4 (1992): 496–517; David Novak, *Covenantal Rights: A Study in Jewish Political Theory* (Princeton, NJ: Princeton University Press, 2000), chap. 5.

20. *ḤuM*, 2:8.

21. See Jacob Emden, *Pirkei Avot Im Peirush Leḥem Shamayim* (Berlin, 1834), 7b (on Mishnah Avot 1:12); *Collected Writings of Rabbi Samson Raphael Hirsch* (New York: Feldheim, 1997), 8:6.

22. *ḤuM*, 1:31. The prohibition of causing suffering to animals is found at BT Bava Metzia, 32b.

23. Ibid., 1:14. See mention of the "animal soul" at 1:60.

24. *ḤuM*, 1:140.

25. Ibid., 1:59.

26. *ḤuM*, 2:194–95.

27. *ḤuM*, 1:256–57. See Jeremiah 2:2, where God continues to remember Israel's own history of showing "lovingkindness" (*ḥesed*) and "love" (*ahavah*).

28. *ḤuM*, 2:20.

29. See Ibid., 2:276–77. In general, Simḥah Zissel views bringing public order and security to be an expression of lovingkindness, as at 2:187. Maimonides argues rather more clearly that punishing criminals is a form of kindness for the rest of the world at Maimonides, *The Guide of the Perplexed*, 2:536 (Part 3, chap. 35), 554 (Part 3, chap. 39).

30. *ḤuM*, 1:195.

31. *Pinkas Ha-Kabbalot*, 37.

32. *Pinkas Ha-Kabbalot*, 27.

33. *Pinkas Ha-Kabbalot,* 167, quoting Mishnah Avot 4:1. See also the comment of Simḥah Zissel's student Reuven Dov Dessler at *Pinkas Ha-Kabbalot,* 193.

34. *ḤuM,* 1:89, building on Jacob Emden, *Migdol Oz* (Zhitomir, 1874), 207.

35. *ḤuM,* 1:138–39.

36. Ibid., 1:173, following the approach of Solomon Luria.

37. *ḤuM,* 2:218.

38. See BT Arakhin 16b and the sources listed by Feldman, *The Right and the Good,* 182n99

39. *ḤuM,* 1:20, quoting BT Bava Batra 60b. Literally: "trim yourself."

40. Ibid., 1:23.

41. Ibid., 1:21, 23.

42. *ḤuM,* 1:21. Truth as the "seal of God" is a notion found at BT Shabbat 55a, BT Yoma 69b, BT Sanhedrin 64a, and throughout classical midrash.

43. *ḤuM,* 1:21. "There should not be an idol within you" is the interpretation of Psalms 81:10 given at BT Shabbat 105b. The student notes on this passage comment that "self-love is not like what many think, a minor flaw of "egoism" (*egoismus*)—but the grave sin of idolatry" (*ḤuM,* 1:23, #14).

44. *ḤuM,* 1:19, 20.

45. Ibid., 1:41.

46. *ḤuM,* 2:326.

47. *ḤuM,* 1:12–13. My italics. See also 1:6–8.

48. *ḤuM,* 1:20.

49. Ibid., 1:52.

50. Ibid., 1:316–17.

51. *ḤuM,* 2:304.

52. Ibid., 2:273.

53. Thanks to Jennifer Geddes for pointing out this parallel to me.

54. *Kitvei Ha-Sabba Mi-Kelm: Inyanei Elul Ve-Yamim Nora'im,* 147–48. The emphasis is mine.

55. The novelty of this interpretation is pointed out by Katz, *Tenu'at Ha-Musar,* 2:167–68. On the inadequacy of love that stems from a sense of duty, see Simḥah Zissel's student Reuven Dov Dessler in *Pinkas Ha-Kabbalot,* 193; and see Michael Stocker, "The Schizophrenia of Modern Ethical Theories," *The Journal of Philosophy* 73, no. 14 (1976): 453–66.

56. *ḤuM,* 2:326.

57. Moses Cordovero, *Tomer Devorah* (Königsberg, 1858), 22 (chap. 2). See Elliot R. Wolfson, *Venturing Beyond: Law and Morality in Kabbalistic Mysticism* (New York: Oxford University Press, 2006), 312; Eitan P. Fishbane, "A Chariot for the Shekhinah: Identity and the Ideal Life in Sixteenth-Century Kabbalah," *Journal of Religious Ethics* 37, no. 3 (September 2009): 400–401.

58. Menachem Mendel Levin [Lefin], *Cheshbon Ha-Nefesh,* ed. Dovid Landesman, trans. Shraga Silverstein (Jerusalem: Feldheim, 1995), paragraphs 87–88, 90. See Sinkoff, *Out of the Shtetl,* 137.

59. Naftali Herz Wessely, "Biur" (commentary) on Leviticus 19:18, in Moses Mendelssohn, ed., *Sefer Netibot Ha-Schalom (Netivot Ha-Shalom)* (Berlin: G. F. Starcke, 1783), 134a.

60. *Ḥ uM*, 1:21.

61. Mishnah Avot, 6:6. The more general virtue of "love of God's creatures" is also listed as one of the virtues necessary for the acquisition of Torah, but Simḥah Zissel understands "sharing the burden" as a particular manifestation of love.

62. *ḤuM*, 1:3.

63. Ibid., 1:6.

64. Ibid., 1:3. Cf. 1:58.

65. *ḤuM*, 1:9. Cf. 1:4.

66. Note that Moses is perceived as acting as judge in Ex. 2:14. The midrashic traditions are found in Exodus Rabbah 1:28–29.

67. *ḤuM*, 1:9–10.

68. *ḤuM*, 1:9–10.

69. Ibid., 1:6.

70. Ibid., 1:8.

71. *ḤuM*, 2:28. See the discussion in Geoffrey Claussen, "Jewish Virtue Ethics and Compassion for Animals: A Model from the Musar Movement," *CrossCurrents* 61, no. 2 (2011): 209, 215n9.

72. *ḤuM*, 1:8, quoting Exodus Rabbah 2:2. Simḥah Zissel also quotes the parallel story about David found in the same midrash.

73. Ibid., 1:8.

74. Ibid., 1:7.

75. Ibid., 1:4.

76. Ibid., 1:10, referring to Exodus Rabbah 2:5.

77. Note that "sharing the burden of one's fellow," the "essence of the way of God" (*ḤuM*, 2:95), "includes the entire Torah" (*ḤuM*, 1:12)

78. *ḤuM*, 1:3, with reference to Mekhilta Pisḥa 14.

79. Ibid., 1:2.

80. Ibid., 1:2–3.

81. *Kitvei Ha-Sabba Ve-Talmidav Mi-Kelm*, 1:148. My italics. The editors' footnote indicates uncertainty regarding authorship of the passage.

82. *ḤuM*, 1:56; the translation of "sense-experience" follows the suggestion of Goldberg, *Israel Salanter*, 29–30.

83. *ḤuM*, 1:14.

84. Ibid., 1:7, building on the tradition from BT Ta'anit 11a.

85. Ibid., 1:38. See also *Sefer Ha-Zikaron*, 29–30.

86. *ḤuM*, 1:69. See also 1:56.

87. BT Berakhot 18b.

88. *ḤuM*, 1:69; Isaac Blazer, "Kokhvei Or," in *Or Yisra'el*, ed. Isaac Blazer (Vilna, 1900), 71.

89. See, among many other passages, *ḤuM*, 1:2–3.

90. Ibid., 1:56.

91. See Katz, *Tenu'at Ha-Musar,* 2:30–32; Mark, *Be-Meḥitzatam,* 220.
92. *Ḥ uM,* 2:340.
93. Immanuel Etkes, *The Gaon of Vilna: The Man and His Image,* trans. Yaacov Jeffrey Green (Berkeley: University of California Press, 2002), 235; Etkes, *Rabbi Israel Salanter,* 19.
94. See Etkes, *Rabbi Israel Salanter,* 73–74.
95. *ḤuM,* 1:12–13.
96. See Etkes, *Rabbi Israel Salanter,* 59–60, 73, 158–59, 288.
97. *Kitvei Ha-Sabba Ve-Talmidav Mi-Kelm,* 1:95.
98. See the commentary of Rashi ad loc., BT Kiddushin 29a.
99. *ḤuM,* 1:112.
100. Compare Weiss, *Maimonides' Ethics,* 119. See my further discussion in Claussen, "The Legacy of the Kelm School."
101. *ḤuM,* 1:92.
102. Etkes, *Rabbi Israel Salanter,* 73–74, 288.
103. Friedman, "Toledot Ba'alei Ha-Musar [Part 2]," 7. See also Katz, *Tenu'at Ha-Musar,* 2:59–60.
104. *ḤuM,* 1:21. See Ibid., 1:23; Katz, *Tenu'at Ha-Musar,* 2:60.
105. *ḤuM,* 1:9, with reference to BT Gittin 62a.
106. Ibid., 1:8. Regarding the final sentence, see BT Shabbat 10a.
107. Ibid., 1:8.
108. *ḤuM,* 2:187.
109. *ḤuM,* 1:25. See also *ḤuM,* 2:126–27; *Pinkas Ha-Kabbalot,* 9.
110. *ḤuM,* 2:187.
111. For the alternative Musar movement view, found in Novaredok, see Fishman, "Musar and Modernity," 59.
112. As quoted in Etkes, *Rabbi Israel Salanter,* 18; Etkes, *The Gaon of Vilna,* 234; Etkes, "Marriage and Torah Study," 154.
113. Etkes, "Marriage and Torah Study," 171. For a Musar movement appreciation of this ideal by Yosef Yoizel Horowitz of Novaredok, see Fishman, "Musar and Modernity," 55.
114. See Katz, *Tenu'at Ha-Musar,* 2:42, 49, 64, 92; Shmuel Himelstein, *Wisdom and Wit: A Sparkling Treasury of Jewish Anecdotes and Advice* (Brooklyn: Mesorah Publications, 2003), 122. See also Katz, *Tenu'at Ha-Musar,* 2:30–32.
115. Levin [Lefin], *Cheshbon Ha-Nefesh,* 78–80 (#44). Note also the Haskalah writings that speak of obligations owed by men to their wives, as discussed by Tova Cohen, "Reality and Its Refraction in Descriptions of Women in Haskalah Fiction," in *New Perspectives on the Haskalah,* ed. Shmuel Feiner and David Sorkin (Oxford, UK: Littman Library of Jewish Civilization, 2001), 155–56.
116. Etkes, "Marriage and Torah Study," 172–73.
117. *ḤuM,* 1:11.
118. *ḤuM,* 2:26.
119. See Michael A. Slote, *The Ethics of Care and Empathy* (London; New York: Routledge, 2007), 56–59.
120. *Sefer Ha-Zikaron,* 181.

## Conclusion

1. This chronology and the teachings of Simḥah Zissel's successors can be found in *Kitvei Ha-Sabba Ve-Talmidav Mi-Kelm*; *Kitvei Ha-Sabba Ve-Talmidav Mi-Kelm*; *Sefer Ha-Zikaron*. On the reaction of Kelm's leaders to the Holocaust, see Shlomo Tikochinski, "Be-Ikvot Kayitz 1941: Askolet Kelm ve-Teguvtah La-Shoah" [Following the Summer of 1941: The Kelm School and the Theological Response to the Holocaust], in *Ha-Kayitz Ha-Nora Ha-Hu*, ed. Israel Rozenson (Jerusalem: Efrata College Publications, 2013).

2. See Ross, "Ha-Maḥshavah Ha-Iyunit."

3. See Dov Katz, *Tenu'at Ha-Musar*, 2nd ed., vol. 3 (Tel-Aviv: Avraham Tzioni, 1956), esp. 288–90; Fishman, "Musar and Modernity," 42; Stampfer, *Lithuanian Yeshivas*, 267–76.

4. Stampfer, *Lithuanian Yeshivas*, 267–68.

5. Ibid., 276. Cf. 267: "musar study was considered its central activity in terms of importance, though not in terms of the amount of time devoted to it."

6. As quoted in Tikochinski, "Yeshivot Ha-Musar," 150.

7. As quoted in ibid.

8. Ibid., 153–54.

9. Ibid., 150.

10. See ibid., chap. 4; Katz, *Tenu'at Ha-Musar*, 3:119–207.

11. Stampfer, *Lithuanian Yeshivas*, 274.

12. Ibid., 279–85, 311–23.

13. See, e.g., the standards of behavior from Kelm printed in the first issue of *Or Ha-Musar* (1922). For a discussion of the journal, see David E. Fishman, "The Musar Movement in Interwar Poland," in *The Jews of Poland Between Two World Wars*, ed. Yisrael Gutman et al. (Hanover, NH: Brandeis University Press/University Press of New England, 1989), 256.

14. Ḥayyim Efrayyim Zaitchik, *Sefer Ha-Me'orot Ha-Gedolim*, 3rd ed. (Jerusalem, 1966), 157; Tikochinski, "Yeshivot Ha-Musar," 148. The Novaredok attitude to non-Jewish philosophy is also discussed in literary sources such as Chaim Grade, "My Quarrel with Hersh Rasseyner," in *A Treasury of Yiddish Stories*, ed. Eliezer Greenberg and Irving Howe (New York: Schocken Books, 1973), 636.

15. Fishman, "Musar and Modernity"; see also Fishman, "Mussar Movement in Interwar Poland."

16. *Sefer Ha-Zikaron*, 119.

17. Ibid., 289; Yeruḥam HaLevi Levovitz, *Sefer Da'at Ḥokhmah U-Musar* (Jerusalem: Me'orai Oros Hamussar Publications, 2003), 1:5 (introduction).

18. Recent publications include *Pinkas Ha-Kabbalot*; *Kitvei Ha-Sabba Ve-Talmidav Mi-Kelm*; *Kitvei Ha-Sabba Mi-Kelm: Inyanei Elul Ve-Yamim Nora'im*; *Kitvei Ha-Sabba Mi-Kelm: Inyanei Ḥanukkah U-Furim*; *Sefer Ha-Zikaron*; *Beit Kelm: Emunah U-Middot*; Yisroel Levovitz, ed., *Masekhet Avot Im Peirushei Me'orei Orot Ha-Musar*, 2 vols. (Jerusalem: Me'orai Oros Hamussar & Daas Torah Publications, 2009).

19. Ross, "Ha-Maḥshavah Ha-Iyunit," chap. 7–10.

20. Jacob J. Schacter, "Facing the Truths of History," *The Torah U-Madda Journal* 8 (1998): 200–273.

21. Jacob B. Agus, *Guideposts in Modern Judaism: An Analysis of Current Trends in Jewish Thought* (New York: Bloch, 1954), 25–26.

22. Soloveitchik, *Halakhic Man,* 74–76.

23. See Geoffrey Claussen, "The Practice of Musar," *Conservative Judaism* 63, no. 2 (2011): 3–26.

24. Soloveitchik, *Halakhic Man,* 59. On the trend to "codify" musar, which began during Simḥah Zissel's lifetime, see Benjamin Brown, "'Soft Stringency' in the Mishnah Brurah: Jurisprudential, Social, and Ideological Aspects of a Halachic Formulation," *Contemporary Jewry* 27, no. 1 (2007): 11; Benjamin Brown, "From Principles to Rules and from Musar to Halakhah: The Hafetz Hayim's Rulings on Libel and Gossip [Heb.]," *Dinei Yisra'el* 25 (2008): 171–256.

25. Soloveitchik, *Halakhic Man,* 76.

26. This can easily be a problem for ethical systems along the lines of Aristotle's; see Nussbaum, "Virtue Ethics: A Misleading Category?," 187.

27. Elyashev, "Gerobin [Part 2]," 91; see *ḤuM,* 2:11.

28. "Meshiv Ke-Halakhah"; Katz, *Pulmus Ha-Musar,* 83–84; Elyashev, "Gerobin [Part 1]," 116. Cf. the critique of Novaredok by Grade, *The Yeshiva,* 1:350, 2:296.

29. Flescher, *Heroes, Saints, and Ordinary Morality,* 1.

30. See Geoffrey Claussen, "The American Jewish Revival of Musar," *The Hedgehog Review* 12, no. 2 (2010): 63–72.

31. Ira F. Stone, *A Responsible Life: The Spiritual Path of Mussar* (New York: Aviv Press, 2006), xxvi–xxix.

# Bibliography

Agus, Jacob B. *Guideposts in Modern Judaism: An Analysis of Current Trends in Jewish Thought.* New York: Bloch, 1954.

Altmann, Alexander. "Maimonides's 'Four Perfections.'" In *Essays in Jewish Intellectual History,* 65–76. Hanover, NH: Brandeis University Press/ University Press of New England, 1981.

Amram, Natan ben Ḥayyim. *Sefer No'am Ha-Middot.* Salonika, 1857.

Annas, Julia. *The Morality of Happiness.* New York: Oxford University Press, 1993.

Aristotle. *Nicomachean Ethics.* 2nd ed. Translated by Terence Irwin. Indianapolis: Hackett, 1999.

———. *Sefer Ha-Middot* [Nicomachean Ethics]. Edited by Isaac Satanow. Translated by Meir ben Solomon Alguadez into Hebrew from the Latin of Boethius. Lemberg: U.W. Salat, 1867.

Baḥya ben Joseph ibn Pakuda. *The Book of Direction to the Duties of the Heart.* Translated by Menahem Mansoor. Oxford, UK: Littman Library of Jewish Civilization, 2004.

Barit, Zevulun Leib. "Kelm." *Ha-Levanon,* February 19, 1873.

*Beit Kelm: Emunah U-Middot.* Benei Berak: Siftei Ḥakhamim, Va'ad Le-Hafatzat Torah U-Musar, 2010.

Berman, Samuel A., trans. *Midrash Tanhuma-Yelammedenu: An English Translation of Genesis and Exodus.* Hoboken, NJ: Ktav, 1995.

Blazer, Isaac. "Kokhvei Or." In *Or Yisra'el,* edited by Isaac Blazer. Vilna, 1900.

Bor, Harris. "Enlightenment Values, Jewish Ethics: The Haskalah's Transformation of the Traditional Musar Genre." In *New Perspectives on the Haskalah,* edited by Shmuel Feiner and David Sorkin, 48–63. Oxford, UK: Littman Library of Jewish Civilization, 2001.

———. "Moral Education in the Age of the Jewish Enlightenment." Ph.D. thesis, University of Cambridge, 1996.

Braude, William G., and Israel J. Kapstein, trans. *Tanna Dĕḇe Eliyyahu: The Lore of the School of Elijah.* Philadelphia: Jewish Publication Society of America, 1981.

Broida, Shelomo Zalman. "Kelm." *Ha-Levanon,* March 25, 1874.

Brown, Benjamin. "From Principles to Rules and from Musar to Halakhah: The Hafetz Hayim's Rulings on Libel and Gossip [Heb.]." *Dinei Yisra'el* 25 (2008): 171–256.

———. "'Soft Stringency' in the Mishnah Brurah: Jurisprudential, Social, and Ideological Aspects of a Halachic Formulation." *Contemporary Jewry* 27, no. 1 (2007): 1–41.

Claussen, Geoffrey. "Jewish Virtue Ethics and Compassion for Animals: A Model from the Musar Movement." *CrossCurrents* 61, no. 2 (2011): 208–16.

———. "Rabbi Simḥah Zissel Ziv: The Moral Vision of a 19th Century Musar Master." Ph.D. thesis, Jewish Theological Seminary of America, 2011.

———. "Repairing Character Traits and Repairing the Jews: The Talmud Torahs of Kelm and Grobin in the Nineteenth Century." In *Polin: Studies in Polish Jewry*. Vol. 30: *Jewish Education in Eastern Europe*, edited by Eliyana Adler and Antony Polonsky. Oxford, UK: Littman Library of Jewish Civilization, forthcoming.

———. "The American Jewish Revival of Musar." *The Hedgehog Review* 12, no. 2 (2010): 63–72.

———. "The Legacy of the Kelm School of Musar on Questions of Work, Wealth and Poverty." In *Wealth and Poverty in Jewish Tradition*, edited by Leonard J. Greenspoon. West Lafayette, IN: Purdue University Press, 2015.

———. "The Practice of Musar." *Conservative Judaism* 63, no. 2 (2011): 3–26.

Cohen, Seymour J., trans. *Orchot Tzaddikim: The Ways of the Righteous*. New York: Ktav, 1982.

Cohen, Tova. "Reality and Its Refraction in Descriptions of Women in Haskalah Fiction." In *New Perspectives on the Haskalah*, edited by Shmuel Feiner and David Sorkin, 144–65. Oxford, UK: Littman Library of Jewish Civilization, 2001.

Cordovero, Moses. *The Palm Tree of Deborah*. Translated by Louis Jacobs. London: Vallentine, 1960.

———. *Tomer Devorah*. Königsberg, 1858.

Dan, Joseph. *Sifrut Ha-Musar Ve-Ha-Derush* [Hebrew Ethical and Homiletical Literature]. Jerusalem: Keter, 1975.

———, ed. *The Teachings of Hasidism*. New York: Behrman House, 1983.

Dessler, Elijah Eliezer. *Mikhtav Me-Eliyahu*. Edited by Aryeh Carmel and Alter Halpern. London, 1955.

———. *Strive for Truth*. Translated by Aryeh Carmell. 3 vols. Jerusalem: Feldheim Publishers, 1978.

Ebner, Eliezer. "Simha Zissel Broida (Ziff)." In *Guardians of Our Heritage: 1724–1953*, edited by Leo Jung, 317–36. New York: Bloch, 1958.

*Edenu: Le-Zikhro Shel Rabenu Shelomoh Poliachek*. New York: Rabbi Isaac Elchanan Theological Seminary, 1929.

Eidelshtein, Michel. "Kelm." *Ha-Levanon*, September 30, 1873.

Eisen, Robert. "*Lifnim Mi-Shurat Ha-Din* in Maimonides' *Mishneh Torah.*" *The Jewish Quarterly Review* 89, no. 3/4 (1999): 291–317.

Elior, Rachel. *The Mystical Origins of Hasidism.* Translated by Shalom Carmy. Oxford: Littman Library of Jewish Civilization, 2006.

Elyashev, Yisrael ["Ba'al Makhshoves"]. "Gerobin [Part 1]." *He-Avar* 2, no. 1 (1918): 107–16.

———. "Gerobin [Part 2]." *He-Avar* 2, no. 2 (1918): 89–107.

Emden, Jacob. *Migdol Oz.* Zhitomir, 1874.

———. *Pirkei Avot Im Peirush Leḥem Shamayim.* Berlin, 1834.

Etkes, Immanuel. "Haskalah." *YIVO Encyclopedia of Jews in Eastern Europe,* June 6, 2010. http://www.yivoencyclopedia.org/article.aspx/Haskalah.

———. "Marriage and Torah Study among the Lomdim in Lithuania in the Nineteenth Century." In *The Jewish Family: Metaphor and Memory,* edited by David Charles Kraemer, 153–78. New York: Oxford University Press, 1989.

———. *Rabbi Israel Salanter and the Mussar Movement: Seeking the Torah of Truth.* Translated by Jonathan Chipman. Philadelphia: Jewish Publication Society, 1993.

———. *The Gaon of Vilna: The Man and His Image.* Translated by Yaacov Jeffrey Green. Berkeley: University of California Press, 2002.

Feiner, Shmuel. "Towards a Historical Definition of the Haskalah." In *New Perspectives on the Haskalah,* edited by Shmuel Feiner and David Sorkin, 184–219. Oxford, UK: Littman Library of Jewish Civilization, 2001.

Feldman, Daniel. *The Right and the Good: Halakhah and Human Relations.* Expanded ed. Brooklyn: Yashar Books, 2005.

Fishbane, Eitan P. *As Light Before Dawn: The Inner World of a Medieval Kabbalist.* Stanford, CA: Stanford University Press, 2009.

———. "A Chariot for the Shekhinah: Identity and the Ideal Life in Sixteenth-Century Kabbalah." *Journal of Religious Ethics* 37, no. 3 (September 2009): 385–418.

Fishbane, Michael. "Biblical Prophecy as a Religious Phenomenon." In *Jewish Spirituality: From the Bible through the Middle Ages,* edited by Arthur Green, 62–81. New York: Crossroad, 1986.

Fishman, David E. "Musar and Modernity: The Case of Novaredok." *Modern Judaism* 8, no. 1 (1988): 41–64.

———. "The Musar Movement in Interwar Poland." In *The Jews of Poland Between Two World Wars,* edited by Yisrael Gutman et al., 247–71. Hanover, NH: Brandeis University Press/University Press of New England, 1989.

Flescher, Andrew Michael. *Heroes, Saints, and Ordinary Morality.* Washington, DC: Georgetown University Press, 2003.

Friedman, Eliezer E. *Le-Toledot Kittat Ha-Musaraim.* Jerusalem: Ha-Aḥim Rohald, 1926.

———. *Sefer Ha-Zikhronot.* Tel Aviv: Aḥdut, 1925.

———. "Toledot Ba'alei Ha-Musar." *Ha-Melitz,* May 25, 1897.

———. "Toledot Ba'alei Ha-Musar [Part 2]." *Ha-Melitz,* May 29, 1897.

Frumkin, Aryeh Leib. "Kovno." *Ha-Levanon,* March 31, 1875.

Gillman, Neil. *Doing Jewish Theology: God, Torah & Israel in Modern Judaism.* Woodstock, VT: Jewish Lights, 2008.

Goffman, Erving. *Asylums: Essays on the Social Situation of Mental Patients and Other Inmates.* Garden City, NY: Anchor Books, 1961.

Goldberg, Hillel. "Between Berlin and Slobodka: The Life and Writings of Yosef Zev Lipovitz." *Tradition* 22, no. 2 (1986): 47–66.

———. "Israel Salanter and 'Orhot Zaddikim': Restructuring Musar Literature." *Tradition* 23, no. 4 (1988): 14–46.

———. *Israel Salanter: Text, Structure, Idea: The Ethics and Theology of an Early Psychologist of the Unconscious.* New York: Ktav, 1982.

Goodman, Lenn Evan. *Love Thy Neighbor as Thyself.* Oxford, UK: Oxford University Press, 2008.

Grade, Chaim. "My Quarrel with Hersh Rasseyner." In *A Treasury of Yiddish Stories,* edited by Eliezer Greenberg and Irving Howe. New York: Schocken Books, 1973.

———. *The Yeshiva.* Translated by Curt Leviant. 2 vols. Indianapolis: Bobbs-Merrill, 1976.

———. *Tzemaḥ Atlas: Di Yeshive.* 2 vols. Los Angeles: Yidish-Natzionaln Arbeter-Farband, 1967.

Hammer, Reuven, trans. *Sifre: A Tannaitic Commentary on the Book of Deuteronomy.* New Haven, CT: Yale University Press, 1986.

Ḥayyim ben Yitzḥak of Volozhin. *Nefesh Ha-Ḥayyim.* Benei Berak, 1989.

———. *Ruaḥ Ha-Ḥayyim: Peirush Rabbi Ḥayyim Mi-Volozhin Le-Pirkei Avot.* Vilna, 1859.

Himelstein, Shmuel. *Wisdom and Wit: A Sparkling Treasury of Jewish Anecdotes and Advice.* Brooklyn: Mesorah Publications, 2003.

Hirsch, Samson Raphael. *Collected Writings of Rabbi Samson Raphael Hirsch.* 8 vols. New York: Feldheim, 1997.

———. "The Relevance of Secular Studies to Jewish Education." In *The Collected Writings of Rabbi Samson Raphael Hirsch,* edited by Elliott Bondi and David Bechhofer, translated by Gertrude Hirschler, corrected ed., 7:81–100. New York: Feldheim, 1997.

Horowitz, Yosef Yoizel. *Madregat Ha-Adam.* New York: Keren Mefitsei Torah U-Musar, 1947.

Hursthouse, Rosalind. *On Virtue Ethics.* Oxford: Oxford University Press, 1999.

Ibn Gabirol, Shelomo. *The Improvement of the Moral Qualities.* Translated by Stephen Samuel Wise. New York: Columbia University Press, 1902.

Isserles, Moshe. *Torat Ha-Olah.* Vol. 1. Prague, 1854.

Jacobs, Louis. *Religion and the Individual: A Jewish Perspective.* Cambridge: Cambridge University Press, 1992.

James, William. *The Varieties of Religious Experience.* New York: Barnes & Noble, 2004.

Jonah ben Abraham Gerondi. *The Gates of Repentance.* Translated by Yaakov Feldman. Northvale, NJ: Jason Aronson, 1999.

Kamenetsky, Nathan. *Making of a Godol: A Study of Episodes in the Lives of Great Torah Personalities.* 2nd ed. Jerusalem: PP Publishers, 2004.

Kant, Immanuel. "Critique of Practical Reason." In *Practical Philosophy*, edited and translated by Mary J. Gregor. The Cambridge Edition of the Works of Immanuel Kant. Cambridge: Cambridge University Press, 1996.

———. "Groundwork of the Metaphysics of Morals." In *Practical Philosophy*, edited and translated by Mary J. Gregor. The Cambridge Edition of the Works of Immanuel Kant. Cambridge: Cambridge University Press, 1996.

———. "The Metaphysics of Morals." In *Practical Philosophy*, edited and translated by Mary J. Gregor. The Cambridge Edition of the Works of Immanuel Kant. Cambridge: Cambridge University Press, 1996.

Kaplan, Lawrence J. "An Introduction to Maimonides' 'Eight Chapters.'" *The Edah Journal* 2, no. 2 (2002): 1–23.

———. "Daas Torah: A Modern Conception of Rabbinic Authority." In *Rabbinic Authority and Personal Autonomy*, edited by Moshe Sokol, 1–60. Northvale, NJ: J. Aronson, 1992.

Katz, Dov. *Pulmus Ha-Musar.* Jerusalem, 1972.

———. *Tenu'at Ha-Musar.* 2nd ed. Vol. 1. Tel-Aviv: Beitan Ha-Sefer, 1952.

———. *Tenu'at Ha-Musar.* 2nd ed. Vol. 2. Tel-Aviv: Avraham Tzioni, 1954.

———. *Tenu'at Ha-Musar.* 2nd ed. Vol. 3. Tel-Aviv: Avraham Tzioni, 1956.

*Kitvei Ha-Sabba Mi-Kelm: Inyanei Elul Ve-Yamim Nora'im.* Benei Berak: Siftei Ḥakhamim, Va'ad Le-Hafatzat Torah U-Musar, 1997.

*Kitvei Ha-Sabba Mi-Kelm: Inyanei Ḥanukkah U-Furim.* Benei Berak: Siftei Ḥakhamim, Va'ad Le-Hafatzat Torah U-Musar, 2001.

*Kitvei Ha-Sabba Mi-Kelm: Pinkas Ha-Kabbalot.* Benei Berak: Siftei Ḥakhamim, Va'ad Le-Hafatzat Torah U-Musar, 1984.

*Kitvei Ha-Sabba Ve-Talmidav Mi-Kelm.* 2 vols. Benei Berak: Siftei Ḥakhamim, Va'ad Le-Hafatzat Torah U-Musar, 1997.

Levin [Lefin], Menachem Mendel. *Cheshbon Ha-Nefesh.* Edited by Dovid Landesman. Translated by Shraga Silverstein. Jerusalem: Feldheim, 1995.

Levin, Leonard. *Seeing with Both Eyes: Ephraim Luntshitz and the Polish-Jewish Renaissance.* Leiden: Brill, 2008.

Levovitz, Yeruḥam HaLevi. *Sefer Da'at Ḥokhmah U-Musar.* 3 vols. Jerusalem: Me'orai Oros Hamussar Publications, 2003.

Levovitz, Yisroel, ed. *Masekhet Avot Im Peirushei Me'orei Orot Ha-Musar.* 2 vols. Jerusalem: Me'orai Oros Hamussar & Daas Torah Publications, 2009.

Lifshitz, Hillel. "Gan Hashem." *Ha-Levanon*, July 7, 1875.

Lopian, Eliyahu. *Sefer Lev Eliyahu.* Edited by Shalom Mordekhai Shvadron. 3 vols. Jerusalem: Yefeh Nof, Y. Pozen, 2005.

Louden, Robert B. "Kant's Virtue Ethics." *Philosophy* 61, no. 238 (October 1986): 473–89.

Luzzatto, Moshe Hayyim. *Mesillat Yesharim: The Path of the Just.* 3rd ed. Translated by Shraga Silverstein. Jerusalem: Feldheim, 1990.

MacIntyre, Alasdair C. *After Virtue: A Study in Moral Theory*. 2nd ed. Notre Dame, IN: University of Notre Dame Press, 1984.

Maimonides, Moses. "Eight Chapters." In *Ethical Writings of Maimonides*, translated by Raymond L. Weiss and Charles E. Butterworth, 59–104. New York: New York University Press, 1975.

———. *Ethical Writings of Maimonides*. Translated by Raymond L. Weiss and Charles E. Butterworth. New York: New York University Press, 1975.

———. *Mishneh Torah*. 16 vols. Jerusalem: Mossad Ha-Rav Kook, 1956.

———. *The Guide of the Perplexed*. Translated by Shlomo Pines. 2 vols. Chicago: University of Chicago Press, 1963.

Mark, Ya'akov. *Be-Meḥitzatam Shel Gedolei Ha-Dor*. Translated by Shemu'el Ḥagai. Jerusalem: Gevil, 1958.

Mendelssohn, Moses, ed. *Sefer Netibot Ha-Schalom (Netivot Ha-Shalom)*. 5 vols. Berlin: G. F. Starcke, 1783.

"Meshiv Ke-Halakhah." *Ha-Melitz*, July 1, 1897.

Mittleman, Alan. *A Short History of Jewish Ethics: Conduct and Character in the Context of Covenant*. Chichester, UK: Wiley-Blackwell, 2012.

———. "Pluralism: Identity, Civility, and the Common Good." *Modern Judaism* 21, no. 2 (2001): 125–45.

Mondshein, Yehudah Aryeh. "Warsaw." *Ha-Tzefirah*, February 10, 1885.

Nadler, Allan. "Soloveitchik's Halakhic Man: Not a 'Mithnagged.'" *Modern Judaism* 13, no. 2 (1993): 119–47.

———. *The Faith of the Mithnagdim: Rabbinic Responses to Hasidic Rapture*. Baltimore, MD: Johns Hopkins University Press, 1997.

Nathans, Benjamin. *Beyond the Pale: The Jewish Encounter with Late Imperial Russia*. Berkeley: University of California Press, 2002.

Neudecker, Reinhard. "'And You Shall Love Your Neighbor as Yourself—I Am the Lord' (Lev 19:18) in Jewish Interpretation." *Biblica* 73, no. 4 (1992): 496–517.

Newman, Louis E. *An Introduction to Jewish Ethics*. Upper Saddle River, NJ: Pearson Prentice Hall, 2005.

———. *Past Imperatives: Studies in the History and Theory of Jewish Ethics*. Albany: State University of New York Press, 1998.

Novak, David. *Covenantal Rights: A Study in Jewish Political Theory*. Princeton, NJ: Princeton University Press, 2000.

Nussbaum, Martha C. "Virtue Ethics: A Misleading Category?" *The Journal of Ethics* 3, no. 3 (1999): 163–201.

Rappaport, Steven G. "Jewish Education and Jewish Culture in the Russian Empire, 1880–1914." Ph.D. thesis, Stanford University, 2000.

Ross, Tamar. "Ha-Maḥshavah Ha-Iyunit Be-Khitve Mamshikhav Shel Rav Yisra'el Salanter Bitnu'at Ha-Musar" [Moral Philosophy in the Writings of Rabbi Salanter's Disciples in the Musar Movement]. Ph.D. thesis, Hebrew University, 1986.

———. "Tenu'at Ha-Musar ve-Ha-Ba'ayah Ha-Hermeneutit Be-Talmud Torah" [The Musar Movement and the Hermeneutical Problem in Torah Study]. *Tarbiz* 59 (1990): 191–214.

———. "The Role of Intellect in Moral Education in the Discourses of Rabbi Simha Zissel of Kelm." *Proceedings of the 11th Annual Conference of the South African Association of Jewish Studies*, 1990, 230–42.

Salanter, Israel. *Even Yisra'el.* Edited by Shneur Zalman Hirshowitz. Warsaw: Yitzḥak Goldman, 1883.

———. "Or Yisra'el." In *Or Yisra'el*, edited by Isaac Blazer. Vilna, 1900.

Salmon, Joseph. "Enlightened Rabbis as Reformers in Russian Jewish Society." In *New Perspectives on the Haskalah*, edited by Shmuel Feiner and David Sorkin, 166–83. Oxford: Littman Library of Jewish Civilization, 2001.

Schacter, Jacob J. "Facing the Truths of History." *The Torah U-Madda Journal* 8 (1998): 200–273.

———. "Rabbi Jacob Emden, Philosophy, and the Authority of Maimonides." *Tradition* 27, no. 4 (1993): 131–39.

Schofer, Jonathan Wyn. "Rabbinic Ethical Formation and the Formation of Rabbinic Ethical Compilations." In *The Cambridge Companion to the Talmud and Rabbinic Literature*, edited by Charlotte Elisheva Fonrobert and Martin S. Jaffee, 313–35. Cambridge: Cambridge University Press, 2007.

———. *The Making of a Sage: A Study in Rabbinic Ethics.* Madison: University of Wisconsin Press, 2004.

Scholem, Gershom Gerhard. "Three Types of Jewish Piety." In *On the Possibility of Jewish Mysticism in Our Time & Other Essays*, edited by Avraham Shapira, translated by Jonathan Chipman, 176–90. Philadelphia: Jewish Publication Society, 1997.

Schweid, Eliezer. *The Idea of Modern Jewish Culture.* Edited by Leonard Levin. Translated by Amnon Hadary. Boston: Academic Studies Press, 2008.

Seeman, Don. "Martyrdom, Emotion and the Work of Ritual in R. Mordecai Joseph Leiner's Mei Ha-Shiloah." *AJS Review* 27, no. 2 (November 2003): 253–79.

*Sefer Ha-Zikaron: Beit Kelm.* Benei Berak: Siftei Ḥakhamim, Va'ad Le-Hafatzat Torah U-Musar, 2002.

Shapira, Moshe. "Grobin." *Ha-Tzefirah*, October 5, 1881.

Simon, Ernst. "The Neighbor (Re'a) Whom We Shall Love." In *Modern Jewish Ethics, Theory and Practice*, edited by Marvin Fox, 29–56. Columbus: Ohio State University Press, 1975.

Sinkoff, Nancy. *Out of the Shtetl: Making Jews Modern in the Polish Borderlands.* Providence, RI: Brown Judaic Studies, 2004.

Slote, Michael A. *The Ethics of Care and Empathy.* London: Routledge, 2007.

Soloveitchik, Joseph Dov. *Halakhic Man.* Translated by Lawrence Kaplan. Philadelphia: Jewish Publication Society of America, 1983.

Spinoza, Baruch. *Theological-Political Treatise.* Translated by Samuel Shirley. 2nd ed. Indianapolis, IN: Hackett, 2001.

Stampfer, Shaul. *Families, Rabbis and Education: Traditional Jewish Society in Eastern Europe.* Oxford: Littman Library of Jewish Civilization, 2010.

———. *Lithuanian Yeshivas of the Nineteenth Century: Creating a Tradition of Learning.* Translated by Lindsey Taylor-Gutharz. Oxford: Littman Library of Jewish Civilization, 2012.

———. "Telz, Yeshiva of." *YIVO Encyclopedia of Jews in Eastern Europe*, February 17, 2011. http://www.yivoencyclopedia.org/article.aspx/Telz_Yeshiva_of.

Stanislawski, Michael. "Russian Jewry, the Russian State, and the Dynamics of Jewish Emancipation." In *Paths of Emancipation: Jews, States, and Citizenship*, edited by Pierre Birnbaum and Ira Katznelson, 262–83. Princeton, NJ: Princeton University Press, 1995.

Stocker, Michael. "The Schizophrenia of Modern Ethical Theories." *The Journal of Philosophy* 73, no. 14 (1976): 453–66.

Stone, Ira F. *A Responsible Life: The Spiritual Path of Mussar.* New York: Aviv Press, 2006.

Tikochinski, Shlomo. "Be-Ikvot Kayitz 1941: Askolet Kelm ve-Teguvtah La-Shoah" [Following the Summer of 1941: The Kelm School and the Theological Response to the Holocaust]. In *Ha-Kayitz Ha-Nora Ha-Hu*, edited by Israel Rozenson. Jerusalem: Efrata College Publications, 2013.

———. "Yeshivot Ha-Musar Me-Lita Le-Eretz Yisra'el: Yeshivat Slobodka Ve-Shitatah Ha-Ḥinukhit, Aliyatah Ve-Hitbasesutah Be-Eretz Yisra'el Ha-Mandatorit." Ph.D. thesis, Hebrew University, 2009.

Tirosh-Samuelson, Hava. *Happiness in Premodern Judaism: Virtue, Knowledge, and Well-Being.* Cincinnati, OH: Hebrew Union College Press, 2003.

Tishby, Isaiah. *Mivḥar Sifrut Ha-Musar [Hebrew Ethical Literature: Selected Texts].* Tel Aviv: M. Newman, 1970.

Tzizling, Ben Tzion Leib. "Liboya." *Ha-Tzefirah*, September 12, 1882.

Walzer, Michael, Menachem Lorberbaum, Noam Zohar, and Yair Lorberbaum, eds. *The Jewish Political Tradition.* Vol. 1. New Haven, CT: Yale University Press, 2000.

Weinberg, Yeḥiel Ya'akov. *Lifrakim.* 2 vols. Jerusalem: Va'ad Le-Hotsa'at Kitve Ha-Ga'on Ha-Rav Yeḥi'el Ya'akov Veinberg, 2002.

Weiss, Raymond L. *Maimonides' Ethics: The Encounter of Philosophic and Religious Morality.* Chicago: University of Chicago Press, 1991.

Wolfson, Elliot R. *Venturing Beyond: Law and Morality in Kabbalistic Mysticism.* New York: Oxford University Press, 2006.

Wurzburger, Walter S. *Ethics of Responsibility: Pluralistic Approaches to Covenantal Ethics.* Philadelphia: Jewish Publication Society, 1994.

Yaffe, Mordekhai Gimpel. "Shalom Ve-Emet [part 1]." *Ha-Levanon*, December 25, 1872.

———. "Shalom Ve-Emet [part 2]." *Ha-Levanon*, December 31, 1872.

Zaitchik, Ḥayyim Efrayyim. *Sefer Ha-Me'orot Ha-Gedolim.* 3rd ed. Jerusalem, 1966.

Zaretsky, David. *Torat Ha-Musar.* Tel-Aviv: Moriah, 1959.

Zipperstein, Steven J. "Haskalah, Cultural Change, and Nineteenth-Century Russian Jewry: A Reassessment." *Journal of Jewish Studies* 34, no. 2 (1983): 191–207.

Ziv, Simḥah Zissel (Broida). "Me-Igrotav Shel Ha-Ga'on Ha-Ḥasid Rav Simḥah Zissel Mi-Kelm." In *Kokhvei Or*, edited by Isaac Blazer. Jerusalem, 1974.

———. "Notice Posted on the Door of the Kelm Talmud Torah Before the High Holidays," trans. Geoffrey Claussen, *Jewish Review of Books* 4, no. 3 (Fall 2013): 46.

———. *Or Rasaz: Al Ḥamishah Ḥumshei Torah.* Edited by Ḥayyim Shraga Levin. 5 vols. Jerusalem, 1960.

———. *Sefer Ḥokhmah U-Musar (ḤuM).* Vol. 1. New York, 1957.

———. *Sefer Ḥokhmah U-Musar (ḤuM).* Vol. 2. Jerusalem, 1964.

———. "Torah Ve-Yirah." *Moriah* 12, no. 7–9 (1983): 111–14.

# General Index

# Index of References to Biblical and Talmudic sources